IBERIAN AND LATIN AMERICAN STUDIES

Catalonia

IBERIAN AND LATIN AMERICAN STUDIES

Catalonia

National Identity and Cultural Policy, 1980–2003

KATHRYN CRAMERI

UNIVERSITY OF WALES PRESS
CARDIFF
2008

British Library Cataloguing-in-Publication Data
A catalogue record for this book is available from the British Library.

ISBN 978-0-7083-2013-6

This volume is supported by

 Arts & Humanities
Research Council

Typeset by Columns Design Ltd, RG4 7DH
Printed in Great Britain by CPI Antony Rowe, Wiltshire

Contents

Series Editors' Foreword

Over recent decades, the traditional 'languages and literatures' model in Spanish departments in universities in the United Kingdom has been superceded by a contextual, interdisciplinary and 'area studies' approach to the study of the culture, history, society and politics of the Hispanic and Lusophone worlds – categories which extend far beyond the confines of the Iberian Peninsula, not only to Latin America but also to Spanish-speaking and Lusophone Africa.

In response to these dynamic trends in research priorities and curriculum development, this series is designed to present both disciplinary and interdisciplinary research within the general field of Iberian and Latin American Studies, particularly studies which explore all aspects of **Cultural Production** (*inter alia* literature, film, music, dance, sport) in Spanish, Portuguese, Basque, Catalan, Galician and the indigenous languages of Latin America. The series also aims to publish research on the **History and Politics** of Hispanic and Lusophone worlds, both at the level of region and that of the nation-state, as well as on **Cultural Studies** which explore the shifting terrains of gender, sexual, racial and postcolonial identities in those same regions.

Acknowledgements

I am grateful to several institutions and individuals for their support while writing this book. Research in Barcelona was made possible by travel grants from Lancaster University and the British Academy. The first draft of the book was written during a period of research leave funded by the Arts and Humanities Research Council. Many people have generously offered advice on draft chapters or have corresponded with me on some of the issues I have been investigating. I would especially like to thank Chris Ealham, Frederic Barberà, John Urry, Ramón Ribera Fumaz, Lourdes Orozco and Andy Pratt.

Parts of chapters 5 and 6 appeared in an earlier form in 'Constructing a bridge between cultures: Catalan cultural policy and the new immigration', in *Mapping Identities in Modern Europe*, ed. Peter Wagstaff (Bern: Peter Lang, 2004; pp. 145–68), and 'Official, Artificial or (Arte)factual?: The Museu d'Història de Catalunya', *International Journal of Iberian Studies*, 19/2 (2006), 121–35.

All translations into English in this book are my own unless otherwise indicated.

Introduction

'In matters of culture, Catalonia should become the equivalent of a state, Catalan society fully nationalized.'[1] Joan Guitart made this pronouncement in 1990 while he was minister for culture within the Catalan government (Departament de Cultura, 1990: 17). By this stage, it had been ten years since his party had been elected as the first regional executive for Catalonia after the death of the dictator Francisco Franco in 1975. Spain was now a democracy, with a constitution that allowed substantial powers for its seventeen newly constituted autonomous communities, but Spain was, and still is, very much the dominant political force: the only state, and – as far as most Spaniards were concerned – the only nation. Under these circumstances, to aspire to become 'the equivalent of a state' (even in something as innocent-sounding as 'matters of culture') was no easy ambition. What would it really mean to build a Catalan nation through culture, and how could this be achieved through the normal democratic mechanisms of a regional cultural policy?

This explicit nation-building project makes Catalonia an interesting subject for a case study within the developing field of cultural policy studies, especially given the continuing regionalization of Europe and the much-debated phenomenon of 'glocalization'.[2] Cultural policy experts Adrienne Scullion and Beatriz García have already said that 'policy makers and researchers need to review their understanding of the "national" in a post-devolution context' (Scullion and García, 2005: 120). Catalonia, as a stateless nation that has become something of a model for other regional authorities, provides a litmus test of the kinds of issues they face. The case of Catalonia also demonstrates that questions relating to Spanish culture and identity cannot be properly answered without full reference to the diversity represented by Spain's Autonomous Communities, which in turn reminds us to be alert to such diversity in other nation states. However, cultural policy in Catalonia also responds to a set of very individual circumstances. As Tony Bennett warns, 'the "best practice" derived from one context may prove to be "worst practice" if simply translated to another context without due regard for its distinctive aspects' (Bennett, 2001: 24).

Cultural policy as an activity of government involves the marriage of some quite contradictory elements, as has been pointed out by Toby Miller and George Yúdice. According to their definition the term 'refers to the institutional supports that channel both aesthetic creativity and collective ways of life – a bridge between the two registers. Cultural policy is embodied in systematic, regulatory guides to action that are adopted by organizations to achieve their goals' (Miller and Yúdice, 2002: 1). In other words, institutions that engage in cultural policymaking are dealing with culture both in its specialized aesthetic meaning and in its broader, anthropological sense as 'ways of life'; these seemingly fluid and intangible things then have to be captured within specific projects and structures in order to produce the desired policy outcome, whatever that may be. In the process, a tension is generated between supporting culture for its own sake and using culture to support other things (the nation's image, the economy, the ruling party's popularity, etc.).

It is this tension that is the basic issue at the root of cultural policy research. Scullion and García have identified two main strands in academic approaches to cultural policy. One concentrates on 'an engagement with policy formulation, policy delivery and evaluation', and might involve academics having a direct or indirect input into policymaking (Scullion and García, 2005: 118). The other is what Justin Lewis and Toby Miller have called 'critical cultural policy studies', which 'necessitates both an understanding of the ways in which cultural policies have traditionally been deployed, and a disciplined imagining of alternatives' (Lewis and Miller, 2003: 2). Criticism, in this context, does not imply a negative or destructive intent but a form of independent thinking that can have constructive outcomes (McGuigan, 2004: 3–4). The main framework for my own study of Catalan cultural policy comes from this critical perspective, which has developed as a (contested) branch of cultural studies (Bennett, 1992; Cunningham, 1991; McGuigan, 2003; Osborne, 2006). However, the specific case studies included in this volume also engage with the way that particular policies were formulated and delivered, sometimes with the help of collaborative input from Catalan or foreign academics. This means that I am interested in 'what those in charge of [cultural policy] actually do and the consequences of their actions', as well as in broader matters of 'disputation over cultural issues' (McGuigan, 2004: 5).

Readers familiar with Catalan cultural life will recognize many of the debates that this volume explores. The arguments and critical stances that they generated have been rehearsed – sometimes ad nauseam – in the Catalan and Spanish media, in the political arena, and in private conversations. Some of them have attracted attention from foreign academics, especially those that relate to language policy or that overlap with issues of urban planning, tourism, and economic development. Other areas have received less interest from outside Catalonia, especially as far as developments since the end of the Franco regime are concerned. These include: the attempt to preserve distinctively Catalan forms of high culture, for reasons to do with national identity, at a time when the very notion of a national cultural canon is increasingly called into question; the challenges implied by Catalonia's increasing cultural diversity, thanks to immigration, the mobility of the population and the ease of access to 'global' culture; the possible role of traditional culture in maintaining a sense of collective identity in a diverse contemporary first-world society; the problem of formulating a cultural industries policy when culture has always had sacred values attached to it that seem incompatible with its new task of supporting the regional economy (as opposed to the national identity). This study seeks to fill some of these gaps in our understanding of the causes and effects of Catalan cultural policy, and therefore to contribute to the general debate about the potential roles and interactions of local, regional, national and transnational cultures in the new century. After a brief look at the factual context necessary to understand the relevance of the Catalan situation to these questions, the rest of this introduction will discuss some of the specific theoretical considerations that will underpin my approach.

Why Study Catalonia's Cultural Policy?

Having been granted autonomy under the terms of the Spanish constitution of 1978, Catalonia now has its own regional government – the *Generalitat de Catalunya* – which has control of substantial areas of policy and spending, especially in cultural matters. From the first elections to the *Generalitat* in 1980 until 2003, the same coalition and the same leader were in power: the centre-right, moderate nationalist *Convergència i Unió* (Convergence and Union – CiU), led by Jordi Pujol. This provided an extended and quite unique opportunity for a Catalanist party to develop an evolving cultural policy in order to defend and promote Catalan culture and the use of the Catalan language. Culture was always going to be an important area of political action for whichever party was elected to power in the *Generalitat*. It was cultural nationalism that had provided the most plausible means of resistance to the totalitarian Spanish nationalism of the Franco dictatorship, and culture that gave Catalanists one of their most important grounds for unity and consensus in the years leading up to the restoration of democracy. More specifically, Catalan culture held a special place in the particular nationalist ideology of CiU, since the party ideologues saw it as the primary defining factor of Catalan identity, legitimizing Catalonia's right to call itself a nation. The challenge, of course, was to marry the transcendental values attached to Catalan culture with the harsh realities of democratic policymaking.

As Jaume Lorés puts it, by the time of Spain's transition to democracy in the late 1970s the average Catalan had been drawn into 'a non-specific, but very heartfelt, Catalanism' (Lorés, 1985: 60).[3] CiU had to give this sentiment a particular political form, and was constrained in this by several factors, including the poor economic circumstances of the region (and the rest of Spain) after the recession of the 1970s, the democratic structures within which they had to work, the restrictions imposed on them by the Spanish state, the need to persuade voters to continue to support them, and their own ideological formation as a party. The policies of CiU have been criticized by some for going too far and by others for not going far enough, but there have been some measurable successes, such as a dramatic rise in the numbers of people able to speak, read and write Catalan, and the creation, largely from scratch, of a cultural infrastructure involving public buildings, administrative bodies, and facilities for disseminating cultural information to the public.

It is partly the cultural, economic and political achievements of CiU that have led to Catalonia, and Pujol himself, being regarded as something of a role model by the leaders of other regions and stateless nations in the West. For example, even before the Scottish Parliament was officially inaugurated, politicians such as Donald Dewar and Alex Salmond were making what journalist Peter Preston described as 'suspiciously regular pilgrimages to Catalonia'

(Preston, 1999). In 2002, Scotland's First Minister, Jack McConnell, signed an agreement of cooperation with the *Generalitat* to work together on policy issues. On that same occasion, a Member of the Scottish Parliament representing the Scottish National Party, Richard Lochhead, praised Catalonia as 'a prime example of not leaving a job half done'.[4] While this praise is mainly directed at Catalonia's insistence on capitalizing on, and increasing, its financial and political autonomy, other areas relating to cultural policy are also implicated. These include the regeneration of Barcelona as a city and tourist destination, the visible strengthening of the Catalan language, and determined attempts to show the world that Catalan culture is different from Spanish culture.

There are certain features of Catalan cultural policy that make it a particularly profitable area for investigation. In general, the mechanisms of cultural policy are quite transparent there, for several reasons. Firstly, after the Franco dictatorship and the beginning of autonomy there was a general consensus among Catalans that some kind of active cultural policy was necessary to restore the region's culture to its rightful place. This meant that people of all political persuasions backed direct regional and local government support for Catalan culture. Secondly, the constant attempts of nationalist policymakers to achieve a clear differentiation between Catalan identity and Spanish identity led to a high profile for cultural policy initiatives. Thirdly, the belief, firmly held by the majority of Catalans, that their culture is central to their identity means that cultural policy issues are often given prominent coverage in political and intellectual arenas, and, crucially, the media. As defined by Jordan and Weedon, 'cultural politics is the struggle to fix meanings in the interest of particular groups. This fixing at the same time defines, places and controls others.' (Jordan and Weedon, 1995: 543). In Catalonia, this struggle is an explicit part of daily life for politicians, intellectuals, writers, directors, educators, artists, journalists and others: this means that the mechanisms by which meanings are fixed are less covert and, importantly, more open to challenge from those who feel that they are being unjustly 'moved into contestatory positions' (Miller and Yúdice, 2002: 8).

This study does not set out to be comprehensive, as it could not possibly be so. It is therefore important to acknowledge its limitations before moving forward. Firstly, it is concerned almost exclusively with the policymaking of the *Generalitat de Catalunya* and not

with the other bodies that have significant cultural influence in
Catalonia, such as the Spanish state and Catalan local government.
Within local government, the cultural policy of Barcelona's
socialist-led city council has been crucial in shaping perceptions of
Barcelona's (and therefore Catalonia's) attractiveness as a place to
live, work and visit, but it will only be mentioned here when this is
necessary to shed light on a particular element of the work of the
Generalitat. It is nevertheless important to note that the policies of
the two bodies have been both complementary and contradictory,
mutually reinforcing and mutually undermining. I have also
elected largely to put aside questions of the relationship between
cultural policy and urban planning for the same reason, since it
would be impossible to tackle the subject properly without full
reference to the actions of Barcelona city council. The focus of this
study, then, is on the particular way in which the cultural nationalism of CiU was translated into cultural policy.

Secondly, in deliberately choosing to talk about the particular
cultural sectors that have already generated the most discussion
and the most direct intervention from the *Generalitat*, there is a
danger of reinforcing the already established exclusion of other
significant areas of culture that might have benefited from greater
exposure here. The choice of sectors was dictated by their prom-
inence in cultural policy debates over the period in question and,
in consequence, the amount and variety of relevant factual and
critical material available. However, they were also selected to
illustrate three very different areas of operation within cultural
policy: arts policy (chapter 3), cultural industries policy (chapter
4), and support for traditional culture and heritage (chapter 5).
These case studies are preceded by chapters on CiU's approach to
cultural nationalism and cultural policy (chapter 1), and their
linguistic policy, which was central to cultural policy as a whole
(chapter 2). The primary focus of the study revolves around the
remit of the *Generalitat*'s *Departament de Cultura* (Department of
Culture), although this should not be taken to mean that culture
was dealt with in isolation from other issues of governance. On the
contrary, the more the *Generalitat* got to grips with its role as a
cultural policy maker, the more it realized that culture could not be
pinned down to discrete areas of activity such as language, literature and the arts. This is why the last chapter of this book broadens
out the discussion to tackle the cultural implications of globalization and immigration (chapter 6).

Nation-Building and Culture

Catalonia's powers are fairly extensive compared with those that other non-federal states in Europe have granted to their regions. In some ways, the regional government functions as a kind of 'quasi-state', directly influencing the lives of residents and providing the primary political point of reference in certain key areas of their daily experience. On the other hand, the *Generalitat* is by no means a single authority and does not act on the state's behalf as the sole administrative body. This means that state institutions still have a strong presence and are not easily persuaded to make changes to their operations to suit the wishes of particular regions. Another drawback of Spain's 'State of the Autonomies' is that powers are often shared between the state and the autonomous communities, and the vagueness of the constitution makes the boundaries unclear, leading to legal disputes and bureaucratic duplication. Just as importantly, the public and private statewide media (mainly based in Madrid) have not adequately recognized the need to provide specific services tailored to communities with their own language, culture and concerns. They have therefore collaborated in the production of nationalizing messages for the state rather than giving a voice to the inherent plurality and diversity of Spain. This means that some Catalans see the Spanish media as a window onto a world that they do not recognize as their own.

On the other hand, other Catalans do recognize and inhabit this world, and are quite happy to do so. This fact represented a major preoccupation for CiU and the driving force behind its cultural policy, which it used first and foremost as a nation-building tool. For this reason, it is helpful to think of their actions in terms of the distinction Raymond Williams draws between cultural policy 'proper' and as 'display' (Williams, 1984; McGuigan, 2004: 61–91). Even though Williams's discussion of this distinction refers to the actions of states, and Catalonia is a nation without a state (Guibernau, 2004: 9–12), the level of autonomy enjoyed by the *Generalitat* means that it is legitimate to employ the same distinction here as long as it is not forgotten that Catalonia's nation-building powers are always conditioned by its ongoing struggles with the Spanish state. In Williams's definition, cultural policy 'proper' is 'primarily a policy *for the arts*, in relation to a whole and very diverse life' (Williams, 1984: 3). This would include elements such as 'public patronage of the arts', 'media regulation', and the 'negoti-ated construction of cultural identity' in a way that takes advantage of all the possibilities offered by cultural diversity (McGuigan, 2004: 64). In other words, the rationale behind cultural policy 'proper' is always explicitly related first and foremost to percep-tions of the intrinsic benefits of culture (however much we might disagree about what these are).

In contrast, cultural policy as 'display' involves the use of culture as a tool for other purposes. Williams reminds us that although we might be aware that the state uses pomp, ritual and performance in order to display its power, even in less obvious circumstances 'an arts policy of a certain kind turns out when examined to be not a policy for the arts but a policy for embellishing, representing, making more effective a particular social order or certain pre-ferred features in it' (Williams, 1984: 3). Jim McGuigan, in his elucidation of Williams's brief comments on the subject, labels this as 'national aggrandizement' (McGuigan, 2004: 62–3). Williams also identifies a second form of cultural policy as 'display', which refers to the tendency to think of culture in terms of its economic value, such as the opportunities it offers for growth and regenera-tion through business and tourism. McGuigan calls this 'economic reductionism'. Both these forms involve shows of power, even though one form is symbolic and the other material. Moreover, both forms are intrinsic to CiU's cultural policy, which raises the question of whether there is anything innovative about their approach, or whether this particular sector of the Catalan political elite simply borrowed the tactics of established nation states for use in a new setting.

Looking at the cultural policy of CiU in terms of its role as a nationalist elite with an overriding nation-building project also implies questions about motivation (Guibernau, 2004: 15–33). However, in a study entitled *Foundations of National Identity: From Catalonia to Europe,* Josep R. Llobera complains that explorations of Catalan nationalism have often been far too simplistic.

> Many authors have operated a double reductionism: they have tended to see nations in terms of class, and class wholly in terms of economic interests. The nationalist discourses must then be, by definition, a 'misleading' discourse, a discourse concealing the interests of a class. And what is the meaning of the word 'class'? Marxists and non-Marxists alike often take a purely economistic view of what class is. Hence, when the expression 'the hegemony of the

Catalan bourgeoisie' occurs, it is usually interpreted as meaning 'the material interests of the Catalan bourgeoisie'. In this way, the complexities of the nationalist discourse are completely lost, sacrificed to the gods of economic determinism. (Llobera, 2004: 73)

This criticism particularly applies to the 'modernist' view of nationalism, according to which nationalism is a product of the social, political and economic circumstances of modernity, linked to the need to consolidate industrially strong, sovereign nation states. In this reading, the ethnic heritage of the nation is important only because it provides elements that national elites can use to draw the other members of the nation into their project (Hutchinson, 2005: 10–13). In other words, this is a 'top down' theory of nationalism that concentrates its analysis on the nation-building actions of the most economically and politically powerful sectors of society. My aim in this book is to look specifically at regional government policy and the debates that it has generated, which means that the analysis is necessarily limited to a fairly narrow group of policymakers and the political, cultural, journalistic and intellectual elites who have the means to make their own opinions heard. However, I intend to avoid the reductionism Llobera criticizes by seeing their actions as part of a multilayered struggle for recognition, legitimacy and power that has far more complex concerns at its root than 'the material interests of the Catalan bourgeoisie'.

One helpful tool for this is offered by the work of Pierre Bourdieu, since it provides a broader way of thinking about concepts such as power, capital and class than the reductionist approach criticized by Llobera. For Bourdieu, power and capital are not reducible to the material, as they also have important symbolic dimensions. Individuals can benefit from 'tradable' advantages (such as a good education or a privileged position in society) that can win them power and respect even though no direct economic exchange is involved. This means that economic capital is just one aspect of capital and must be considered alongside other equally important forms, including social and cultural capital (Bourdieu, 1991: 230). In addition, Bourdieu's work proposes a more sophisticated idea of class than the 'purely economistic view' mentioned by Llobera. The dominant groups that Bourdieu identifies, on the basis of their elevated degree of possession of capital, may themselves be subordinate to other groups depending on which specific forms of capital are being taken into account. For example, a writer or artist may be rich in cultural capital but poor in economic capital, meaning that in the overall scheme of things s/he is 'dominated among the dominant' (Bourdieu, 1993: 164).

In *Distinction* (1984), *The Field of Cultural Production* (1993), and other writings, Bourdieu outlined a series of concepts for approaching the study of culture that are particularly useful in thinking about cultural policy. First of all, by considering the relationship between cultural capital and cultural policy, we can see that judgements about which forms of culture should receive official support respond to sophisticated forms of social conditioning that place particular kinds of cultural products in a hierarchy based not necessarily on their intrinsic artistic value, as we might like to think, but largely on their relationship to cultural and economic capital.

> Because the appropriation of cultural products presupposes dispositions and competences which are not distributed universally (although they have the appearance of innateness), these products are subject to exclusive appropriation, material or symbolic, and, functioning as cultural capital (objectified or internalized), they yield a profit in distinction, proportionate to the rarity of the means required to appropriate them, and a profit in legitimacy, the profit par excellence, which consists in the fact of feeling justified in being (what one is), being what it is right to be. (Bourdieu, 1984: 228)

In the Catalan case, judgements relating to the degree of distinction conferred by particular cultural products are complicated by the fact that the Catalan cultural field is not entirely autonomous from the Spanish cultural field.[5] Arguments about what actually constitutes Catalan culture have been raging for decades. Although CiU adopted its own definition, which tried to impose artificially strict boundaries between the two fields, there is still a very wide variety of possible positions on the issue, some of which have become associated with particular political discourses. For this reason, the question of legitimacy, or 'feeling justified in [. . .] being what it is right to be', is the main locus of struggle within debates on national identity and cultural policy: what, exactly, is it right for Catalans to be?

This complication necessarily extends to the habitus of the individuals who engage with the Catalan cultural field. The term 'habitus' refers to the way that individuals develop particular values and attitudes and translate these – often unconsciously – into

practice. Our environment conditions the forms of social knowledge that we are able to acquire and disposes us to think and
behave in particular ways. These 'dispositions' are generated over a
long period, beginning in childhood, and are dependent on such
things as our economic, family, class and educational background.
They then condition the way that we interact with any given field, so
that we feel most comfortable when we are operating within a field
for which our habitus has given us relevant knowledge and appropriate behaviours (Bourdieu, 1993: 63–73). Our tastes, lifestyles,
careers and material possessions therefore both reflect these dispositions and are generated by them (Bourdieu, 1984: 170–3).
Although it is too simplistic to speak of individual producers or
consumers of culture as having a 'Catalan cultural habitus' or a
'Spanish cultural habitus', it is important to note that in the
Catalan context the acquisition of cultural capital is made more
complex by the overlapping existence of the Spanish and Catalan
cultural fields. An individual's habitus might predispose him/her
to operate within the Catalan cultural field, or the Spanish cultural
field, in both, or in the fluid spaces between them. Furthermore,
s/he will most likely not be accorded the same status in one as in
the other.

Even if culture is viewed from the perspective of its broadest
anthropological definition, in which case 'Culture is *habitus*'
(Eagleton, 2000: 115), it is clear that an individual could be socially,
politically and economically disadvantaged if the elites and institutions governing a particular field lean towards defining principles
and structures which privilege a Spanish cultural background over
a Catalan one, or vice versa. In certain areas of politics or business it
might be more advantageous to have one background rather than
the other. In other words, cultural identity can become a factor in
an individual's status even in fields that are not primarily cultural.
According to Ernest Gellner, it is precisely this possibility of a
mismatch between, on the one hand, the expectations and defining practices of institutions and, on the other, the individual's own
cultural competences (in the broadest sense), that predisposes
some individuals to become nationalists:

> [T]he congruence between their own culture and that of the polit-
> ical, economic and educational bureaucracies which surround
> them, becomes the most important single fact of their lives. They
> must be concerned with that congruence, with its achievement or its

protection: and this turns them into nationalists. Their first political concern must be that they are members of a political unit which identifies with *their* idiom, ensures its perpetuation, employment, defence. That is what nationalism is. (Gellner, 1994: viii)

Following on from Gellner's assertion, once a group of nationalists achieve power over a 'political unit', whether this is a state, a region or a municipal institution, it is logical that they should shape it so that the 'idiom' they consider to be their own is dominant within that unit. This redefinition of the political field will cascade into redefinitions of related fields such as education, culture and economics through the application of policy and the development of new discourses, which in turn create new forms of inclusion and exclusion based on the fit between an individual's pre-existing habitus and the conventions of the reshaped field.

Bourdieu refers to these conventions as 'doxa', 'an adherence to relations of order which, because they structure inseparably both the real world and the thought world, are accepted as self-evident' (Bourdieu, 1984: 471). The uncritical acceptance of doxa by people who operate within a field is a form of 'misrecognition', which is what happens when we are so closely implicated in the field that we take its structures, and our place within them, for granted. These ideas are important because they stress that the structuring principles of both field and habitus predispose us to jettison anything that falls outside the core discourses of the field, automatically labelling it as irrelevant and even 'unthinkable'. National identities depend heavily on the operation of doxa, and the Catalan case is no exception. Moreover, we will see that CiU were influenced by, and perpetuated, a particularly clear cultural doxa based around the intimate identification of language with identity. The fact that this idea was shared by a large percentage of the population made it easy for CiU to construct a cultural policy whose legitimacy came from the 'common sense' association between the survival of the language and the continuation of the national identity.

Although this way of looking at cultural policy is more sophisticated than reducing everything to class (i.e. material) interests, some commentators feel that Bourdieu's framework still has a major flaw in that it gives no scope for recognizing that some actions are the result of neither 'deeply sedimented dispositions' nor 'semiconscious instrumental action' (Sayer, 1999: 60). Andrew

Sayer, for example, argues that decisions about taste and cultural value can have a moral dimension that involves conscious debate, reasoned judgement, and a sense that things or courses of action have an intrinsic worth (Sayer, 1999: 61–2). His point is that Bourdieu's approach itself is reductionist, since 'Social action is not wholly reducible to the effects of habitus and disguised battles for status over taste; it also involves judgements regarding the moral worth of particular actions or ways of life' (62). Sayer's point is rather like the arguments of those who criticize the modernist attitude to questions of national identity, since in both cases they refute the assumption that there cannot really be a selfless element to our actions, which means that they must instead represent class interests or a conditioned response based on the individual's acquired strategies for gaining power and influence. As John Hutchinson explains, those who see the modern nation not as a break from the past but in terms of 'a *novel* species of ethnic group', 'are critical of what they see as a top-down explanation of culture formation [. . .] that conflates nationalism with a political nationalism focused on the achievement of legal citizenship and the subversion of traditionalism. The terms "invention" and "construction" have strong connotations not only of novelty but also with intentionality and manipulation.' (Hutchinson, 2005: 13, 33). If we see modern nationalism only in these terms, the motivations of nationalists are oversimplified and instrumentalized in the same way that Bourdieu might be said to oversimplify the reasons for an individual's choices within the cultural field.

Despite the valid objections raised by Sayer and others, there are convincing reasons to look at Catalan cultural policy from the perspective outlined by Bourdieu. Firstly, cultural policy as 'display' is necessarily an activity that instrumentalizes culture and is, in itself, reductionist. It is therefore legitimate to enquire about the causes and effects of this element of cultural policy, without implying, by doing so, that Catalans cannot also hold other views of culture that are not reducible to the search for political or economic advantage. Secondly, Savage, Bagnall and Longhurst point out that Bourdieu's insistence on the physical embodiment of the dispositions that form the habitus (bodily hexis) means that these are 'necessarily territorially located' (Savage, Bagnall and Longhurst, 2005: 8; Bourdieu, 2000: 141). As a result, 'rather than see self-interest as the main mechanism for action, Bourdieu's embodied sociology leads him to focus more on feelings of "comfort" in place' (Savage, Bagnall and Longhurst, 2005: 8). This brings to the discussion a dimension not present in Gellner's comment about 'congruence', above, which refers only to the desire for comfort within the political and bureaucratic structures of the nation state. The territorial element that Savage, Bagnall and Longhurst identify is equally important as it explains the desire to inhabit familiar locations and, if possible, to mould problematic ones so that they start to become more conducive to producing feelings of comfort. These feelings might depend on a wide variety of factors, some of which are wholly or partly the domain of cultural policy, including language, customs and traditions, public art, the media, heritage and the built environment. CiU's cultural policy, then, could be said to be about achieving, as Bourdieu puts it, a 'quasi-perfect coincidence between habitus and habitat' (Bourdieu, 2000: 147). In other words, it is as much to do with creating a local environment that matches the habitus of those who are in a position to influence it as it is to do with generating any particular form of capital, whether symbolic or otherwise.

In the early 1980s, the idea of attempting to achieve a sense of 'comfort in place' through cultural policy may have looked like a realistic goal . The problems that Catalan culture faced seemed fairly obvious, even if there was disagreement over the potential solutions. The damage suffered under the Franco regime and the continued presence of large numbers of Castilian speakers were at least visible targets to aim at. There was also a great deal of consensus in both public and political spheres that direct government intervention was required, giving the *Generalitat* a mandate to orchestrate the recovery of Catalan culture from within its own institutions. However, as time went on the true complexity of managing culture became apparent, the number of dissenting voices multiplied, and the diversity of Catalan society began to assert itself. By the time CiU narrowly lost power to a left-wing coalition in 2003, the whole concept of cultural policy was necessarily seen in a broader light.

These changes, as Josep-Anton Fernàndez argues, were produced by 'a crisis of definition of cultural models that has typically postmodern roots', and so were not a specifically Catalan phenomenon (Fernàndez, 1997).[6] On the contrary, the crux of the crisis was that it became ever more difficult to describe anything as 'specifically Catalan' in a world that is increasingly characterized by connectivity and the mobility of people, information, culture and ideas, rather than by separate 'habitats'. In other words, it was globalization that further complicated CiU's already difficult task. As John Tomlinson has pointed out, 'globalization promotes much more physical mobility than ever before, but the key to its cultural impact is in the transformation of localities themselves. [. . .] This is in many ways a troubling phenomenon, involving the simultaneous penetration of local worlds by distant forces, and the dislodging of everyday meanings from their "anchors" in the local environment' (Tomlinson, 1999: 29). This book traces the process by which CiU came to recognize this problem and view cultural policy as one of the keys to tackling it.

NOTES

1   'En matèria de cultura, Catalunya hauria d'esdevenir homologable a un estat, la societat catalana plenament nacionalitzada'. ('Nationalized' here is used in the sense of 'made into a nation'.)

2   For a discussion of the term 'glocal', first coined by Roland Robertson (1992: 173–4), see Schirato and Webb, 2003: 156–9.

3   'un catalanisme inespecífic però molt sentit'.

4   Reported by BBC News Online, 'Scotland Seals Catalan Tie', 2 May 2002, *news.bbc.co.uk/1/low/scotland/1964574.stm*, accessed 5 February 2007.

5   'As I use the term, a field is a separate social universe having its own laws of functioning independent of those of politics and the economy' (Bourdieu, 1993: 162).

6   'una crisi de definició de models culturals que és d'arrel típicament postmoderna'.

Chapter One

Convergència i Unió: Nationalist Ideology and Cultural Policy

Cultural policy is necessarily grounded in practical issues such as budgets, staffing, information management and institutional structures. It is also dependent on compromise – balancing the desirable and the possible. As Miller and Yúdice put it, cultural policy is 'bureaucratic rather than creative or organic' (Miller and Yúdice, 2002: 1). This makes policymaking an essentially mundane activity, which does not seem to fit well with nationalist ideologies that explicitly make creativity a key part of the national character, and culture the main plank of a historic collective identity. This chapter will look at the way CiU tried to overcome this potential incompatibility by developing its cultural policy along lines that were as consistent as possible with the party's ideological heritage. This mainly meant sticking firmly to the belief that the Catalan language was the crux of Catalan culture, and that Catalan culture was, in turn, the key to the definition and legitimization of a Catalan national identity. This particular doxa conditioned policymaking from the outset and seemed to provide the best hope for producing a Catalan society that was conscious of itself as a nation, at least in the absence of a more substantial form of political autonomy.

Convergència i Unió was first a coalition, and is now a federation, of two parties: *Convergència Democràtica de Catalunya* (CDC) and *Unió Democràtica de Catalunya* (UDC). The first of these was created by Jordi Pujol in 1974, while the second was already in existence, having been founded in 1931, forced to operate clandestinely after the civil war, and then reconstituted as an official party during the transition to democracy. The two formed their coalition in 1978 and officially federated in 2001, although they retain slightly different ideological emphases as a result of their different histories. Of course, Pujol's own approach came to be dominant in Catalans' external perceptions of the partnership over the period of his presidency, but even so there remained a good degree of pluralism within the coalition that was sometimes a source of tension. In essence, though, CiU is a nationalist party with a liberal economic outlook, a commitment to social justice, and a strong Christian Democratic element (Etherington and Fernández, 2006: 75–82). As such, it has both centre-left and centre-right features that are partly responsible for its capacity to attract a wide spectrum of voters. As Montserrat Guibernau puts it, 'over the years it managed to develop a polyhedral image, allowing it, depending on the moment and the audience, to emphasize its character as nationalist, confessional, conservative in economics and progressive in some of its social policies' (Guibernau, 2004: 122).

One of the crucial elements of this image was the careful avoidance of any association with separatism: CiU chose to brand itself as a nationalist party that did not desire independence for Catalonia. The reasons for this stance are complex. The conservative ideological heritage of CDC and UDC is one element in this, since the more radical independentist agendas have tended to come from the Catalanist left, not the right. Specifically, the Catalan bourgeoisie has usually been hostile to any idea that would weaken their position within the Spanish state, and has preferred to concentrate on obtaining a stronger Catalan influence in Spanish decision making. The context of the transition to democracy is also a key factor, since the widespread fear and rejection of Basque separatism was evidence enough that any radical proposals were likely to lead to harsh reactions from the state, harming opportunities for realistic gains to be made. Equally, a separatist party was unlikely to win significant votes within Catalonia itself at that time.

However, it is not just these historical circumstances that influence CiU's thinking on the issue. The context of present-day Europe offers nations without states a chance to develop alternative discourses that concentrate on achieving recognition of their 'organic' status as nations and the devolution of powers appropriate to that status. As a result, according to Jennifer Todd:

nationalism in many of the historic regions has also taken a newly gradualist path, moderating its short-term aims and strategies and accepting a coexistence (at least temporary) with the state. [. . .] This new gradualism is most marked where institutions are put in place which allow nationalist and regionalist aims to dovetail, so that a range of constituencies – from the non-nationalist, through the liberal nationalist to the classic nationalist – can see benefits in the prospects of relatively limited (but indefinitely expandable) regional autonomy and internal reform. (Todd, 2003: 233)

CiU is a nationalist party because its members believe Catalonia is a nation, and not because they think it should be an independent nation state. However, in the European context, they present themselves very much as regionalists, supporting efforts to devolve power to the regions and implement the principle of subsidiarity that was enshrined in the Maastricht Treaty. They are even happy to use the language of regionalism in this context, as Pujol himself has admitted: 'On a European level we have been, and are, promoters of the idea of regionalism. This is an idea which doesn't fit very well with our nationalism, but it has been useful as a way of having a presence in European politics with a proposition which we think is good for the peoples of Europe' (Generalitat de Catalunya, 2001: 33).[1] As well as showing CiU's talent for 'gradualist' pragmatism, this quotation also reveals the party's ambitions to shape, rather than follow, the EU's regional agenda. Although Catalonia is denied any significant input into EU decision making, it has taken every available route to wield some kind of influence. This includes forming interregional partnerships, having a strong voice in the Committee of the Regions, active lobbying in Brussels, and tireless personal involvement in European affairs by Pujol himself.

In general, then, CiU's form of Catalan nationalism has been what we might call a combination of progressive nationalism and 'bourgeois regionalism', with the nationalist elements being more visible in the context of Spain and Catalonia, and the regionalist elements more visible in dealings with the rest of the world, although of course there are elements of both present in each case (Keating, 1998: 104–9; Keating, Loughlin and Deschower, 2003: 55–6). One of the cornerstones of both approaches is the portrayal of Catalan nationalism (or regionalism) as a modern, inclusive form of identity – a civic rather than ethnic form of nationalism. Elements that might be considered exclusive are shunned in CiU's discourse as indeed they are by the majority of the population. This means that questions of birth or ancestry are not central in saying who can define themselves as a Catalan. However, as we will see in chapter 6, the Catalan language has come to substitute for ancestry as a marker of group belonging or common descent, in the sense that by learning Catalan, new residents are not only acquiring new communicative capabilities but also buying into a linguistic identity whose historic territorial roots confer a form of ethnic identity 'by association' on the speaker.

Despite the clear and generally consistent nationalist message given out by CiU, it seems that it was not identity, culture, language or even questions related to autonomy that gave them power in the *Generalitat* in 1980 and kept them there – however precariously at times – for 23 years. Using survey data collected in 1996, Kenneth McRoberts demonstrates that, 'only a minority of respondents agree with the fundamental premise of all Catalan nationalist discourse, that Catalonia is a "nation"',[2] and that 'the moderate nationalist objective of an autonomous community with additional powers is the preferred objective of only a minority of Catalans' (McRoberts, 2001: 164, 168). This suggests that at that time many people voting for CiU were doing so not because they agreed with their particular form of nationalism or their stance on Catalonia's relationship with Spain, but were more interested in their economic and social policy, or supported them by default having ruled out the other alternatives (McRoberts, 2001: 170; Lorés, 1985). CiU were aware of this and saw the solution of people's everyday needs as one way to strengthen their sense of national affiliation to Catalonia. However, as Albert Balcells points out, the high rate of abstention in elections to the *Generalitat* is another indication that CiU actually represented a minority of Catalans even in the years when it governed with a clear majority of the votes cast. Moreover, he sees this as a worrying side effect of CiU's own strategy of trying to appeal pragmatically to a broad spectrum of voters.

> It is not normal in a country like Catalonia for 45 per cent of its citizens to be so indifferent to self-government that they do not even bother to vote, either because they think the government is incapable of sorting out the problems that worry them or because they are disillusioned with it. Pragmatism as a main line of policy can produce apathy (Balcells, 1996: 196).

Summing up the twenty years of CiU government from 1980 to 2000, Pujol himself admitted that 'putting more emphasis on roads than on identity' in order to gather support for CiU's nationalizing project had meant that some Catalans had lost touch with the broader questions of identity (Bou, 2000).[3]

On the other hand, language, history and culture were the clear winners when respondents in the survey cited by McRoberts were asked to rank the main characteristics that make Catalonia a nation, so these were still vital as markers of collective identity (McRoberts, 2001: 166). The difference here is that loyalty to these elements was not so dependent on party allegiances and had much more to do with the history of Catalonia prior to the granting of autonomy. Cultural Catalanism translates into a wide range of political options and can involve either an active interest in the culture or just broad support for the idea that Catalonia is 'different' because of its culture. Before turning to look at the general lines of development of CiU's cultural policy, then, it is necessary to review briefly some of the factors that had produced this particular understanding of Catalan identity by the time the *Generalitat* was properly re-established in 1980.

The Context in 1980

The deliberate damage done to Catalan culture by the Spanish state's treatment of it since the 1920s needs to be strongly stated. The dictatorship of Primo de Rivera from 1923 to 1930 was a small taste of the brutal denial of Catalan identity that was to come with Franco. Primo de Rivera imposed censorship, banned the public use of Catalan, and abolished the *Mancomunitat*, a Catalan authority that had brought together the region's four provinces, in a strictly limited fashion, from 1914 to 1925. Franco – incensed by Catalonia's actions during the Second Republic (1931–6) when it was granted autonomy, and by the support of the majority of the population for the republicans during the civil war – abolished all Catalan institutions, reimposed the ban on public use of the Catalan language, and set out to purge the region of Catalanist influences by deporting, imprisoning or executing anyone with even the slightest link to political Catalanism of whatever shade. This was enough to paralyse Catalanist activity for the first few years after the civil war, but it is perhaps more important to recognize the long-term effects of the ideological battle against Catalanism that continued throughout the regime. Education, censorship and the

Church were all used to convince Spaniards that Spain was a single nation with one national culture and language, and that proper adherence to the Catholic faith required recognition of this fact. Military and police powers ensured that anyone fighting the imposition of this ideology did so in fear of the consequences. Even so, the repression bred resistance that would turn out to be crucial in putting autonomy for Catalonia high on the agenda for democratic Spain after 1975.[4]

By the time the *Generalitat* was fully re-established in 1980, Catalan culture was down but definitely not out. The following list shows the main items on the agenda for the recuperation of the culture that developed in the later years of the regime and during the transition to democracy.

1. Language

Very few Catalans born after 1936 had had any formal teaching in the language. The few that could write Catalan had often learnt it from older family members or through self-teaching. The rhetoric of the regime had convinced many people, inside and outside the region, that Catalan was a worthless dialect and an 'unchristian' way of speaking. This led some to abandon Catalan because this was the easy option, or because not to do so might harm their personal prospects. However, many others still had Catalan as their first spoken language despite these obstacles, simply because their parents had passed it to them as their maternal tongue. In some of the rural areas of Catalonia people's command of Spanish was so poor they had no choice but to continue operating in Catalan on a day-to-day basis. Some middle-class Castilian speakers also made a deliberate choice to learn Catalan as a form of resistance to the regime, and some immigrants learnt it to facilitate their integration into Catalan society. By 1981, around half of Catalans could speak the language – which is a testament to their determination not to give it up – but only 15 per cent could write it (Siguan, 1992: 161).

The challenge, then, was to find a way of reversing the damage that had been done and restoring the rights of Catalan speakers. This would have been less complicated if Catalonia still had the same demographic characteristics it had in the 1930s, but this was not the case. Mass immigration by Castilian speakers, encouraged by the regime, had introduced significant social changes which would make it impossible simply to restore the language by giving people the right and opportunity to speak it and expecting them to take advantage of this. For around one-third of residents, Catalan was not in any sense part of their heritage as they had been born outside the region in purely Castilian-speaking areas such as Andalucía (Conversi, 1997: 191). These people would need to be persuaded to use it, as would those native Catalans who had lost interest in the language.

2. Literature and the Arts

Despite censorship and persecution, literary activity in Catalan had by no means ceased, thanks to the efforts of dedicated individuals who were either writers themselves or helped to disseminate the work of others. Nevertheless, interest in Catalan literature had become confined to a small intellectual elite, partly of course because of the decline in reading skills enforced on younger generations by the dictatorship, although also because most of the works themselves were directed at this particular audience (Molas, 1990). When authors such as Manuel de Pedrolo championed more popular genres such as crime fiction they had to endure criticisms of the quality of their writing. This meant that literature in Catalan had a very small potential audience, and one of the main challenges in the 1980s was therefore to broaden the market in terms of both supply and demand. Nevertheless, as will be discussed in chapter 3, Catalan literature has always played an important symbolic role in legitimizing Catalan culture and identity, which was very much enhanced by the achievements of writers during the dictatorship.

Other forms of high culture were secondary to literature as far as their symbolic role was concerned, but still important markers of Catalonia's cultural creativity. Catalan theatre had been banished from publicly run venues and largely existed in a marginal world of private initiatives and one-off performances that once again limited its audience. However, new performance groups developed in the slightly more open climate of the 1960s, introducing experimental forms and paving the way for the successful development of Catalan theatre once democracy came. Art and classical music were more problematic areas because of the difficulty of demonstrating the 'Catalan-ness' of any particular style or work in a climate in which everything was Spanish or it was nothing. In the end, particular artists and musicians came to perform symbolic roles as representatives of Catalan culture: the cellist Pau Casals, for example – famous for his playing of the *Cant dels Ocells*, exiled, and willing to do all he could to bring Catalonia's plight to the world's attention even if that meant sacrificing his music. In practical terms, though, the Franco regime's physical neglect of Catalonia's museums and cultural facilities, and its lack of support for all but the most patriotic and traditional forms of art, needed to be urgently addressed once the *Generalitat* had the power to do so.

3. Traditional and Popular Culture

Traditional festivals (*festes*) were able to survive during the regime if they were protected by a religious context that made them seem like a local manifestation of the Catholic traditions of Spain. This reduced the importance of some traditions so that they appeared to have no connection to a wider local community outside a particular town or village, or to a history different from that of the rest of Spain. It also meant that some of the younger people who turned away from the Church towards the end of the regime had turned away from Catalan traditions at the same time, because they associated them only with the church (Roma, 1999: 21). On one hand, the church as an institution played its part in this by discouraging participation in anything other than religious festivals for moral and religious reasons (Carnival had already been banned by the regime on these grounds). On the other hand, some individual priests who sympathized with Catalanist aims were able to shelter groups with more radical agendas behind innocent-sounding traditional activities. Other traditions that were seen to have a political or Catalanist element were banned or restricted, and even non-political but non-religious traditions were viewed with suspicion unless they could be seen as harmless folklore.

As far as modern popular culture was concerned, Catalans were forced to consume the same forms as other Spaniards: football, television, cinema – all framed within a Spanish nationalist discourse. One exception here was the *Nova Cançó* (New Song), a form of popular music that grew out of the mood of protest against the regime of the 1960s. Sung in Catalan by singer-songwriters such as Raimon and Joan Manuel Serrat, this form of music was directly inspired by the desire for democracy in Spain and recognition of Catalonia's identity. Appealing to young people, especially students, it helped to create a sense of a distinctive Catalan culture that had largely been missing in this age group, as well as bringing the Catalan language to a mass audience. However, Toni Strubell argues that even here Catalonia showed a glimpse of cultural elitism: lyrics were often 'intellectual', and contained obscure literary and historical allusions, which meant that they were not easily understood by working-class audiences (Strubell, 1997: 102, 105). He also comments that few songs contained explicitly nationalist lyrics, although other political issues were directly addressed (102–3). Nevertheless, the *Nova Cançó* was an important part of Catalonia's cultural and political resistance to the regime, and of the revival of interest in the Catalan language that would prepare the ground for linguistic demands during the transition to democracy.

4. The Missing Elements

Some forms of culture were almost entirely missing from the Catalan repertoire from 1939 to 1975. For example, the mass media was a virtual no-go area for Catalan-language products because of the heavy censorship involved. Television had started in Spain in the 1950s and was under the strict control of the regime, but Catalan was accorded minimal airtime even after Franco's death, until the *Generalitat* started its own channels in the 1980s. Even today the private Spain-wide channels are unwilling to put any effort into regional programming. There was no daily press in Catalan until the dictatorship ended, although there were a few periodicals. The most important of these was *Serra d'or*, which was partially protected by its religious connections as one of the publications of the Abbey of Montserrat but was still subject to censorship like everything else. It began in the mid 1950s and was a general cultural review that became an obligatory point of reference for anyone interested in Catalan language and culture. As such, it was a limited but vital substitute for the kind of journalistic, historical, educational and critical information that would normally be found in a vast range of published materials. One of the main preoccupations by 1980, then, was to make sure that these kinds of gaps were filled, giving Catalan culture back the range and dynamism that it had enjoyed before the dictatorship.

5. The New Context

The main challenge that the *Generalitat* faced in 1980 was one which had been clear for some time, not just to those newly elected to political office but to the many people who had been involved in discussions about Catalonia's future in the decade or so before that. Catalonia had changed significantly since 1939, Spain had changed and the world had changed. As Kenneth McRoberts puts it, 'the end of the Franco regime opened up great opportunities [. . .] But the tasks to be faced were little short of staggering' (McRoberts, 2001: 47). Any attempt to take political Catalanism forward would need to deal with the new make-up of Catalan society, the new framework for democracy and autonomy set by the Spanish state, and new relationships with Europe and the rest of the world. Crucially, this would have to be achieved without any active support – and indeed with plenty of active opposition – from successive Spanish governments, which thought that the state had done quite enough by writing provisions for autonomy into the constitution. The one stable factor in all this was the general agreement that Catalonia's language and culture still remained at the heart of its collective individuality. Cultural resistance had become a substitute for political resistance in the first two decades after the civil war, and the effort that committed individuals put into this throughout the dictatorship was recognized and appreciated. It was therefore no surprise that the intellectual and political elites were absolutely convinced of the central role that culture must play in the reconstruction of Catalonia.

What about those who were not actively involved in Catalanist politics – were they, too, convinced of the importance of language and culture? Groups who were certainly not convinced included the Castilian-speaking Francoist elite, at the top of the social hierarchy, and those working-class migrants who lived a ghettoized life with little contact with Catalan speakers, at the bottom. But aside from these groups, support for the restoration of the language and culture came from a very broad spectrum of Catalans. Some of the middle classes had been brought up speaking Catalan in the family and were strong supporters of action to restore the language even if they were not particularly politicized in other ways. Some migrants had come into contact with Catalan speakers through work and had become interested in the language as a potential asset as they looked for a better position in life, or simply because they were fascinated by this identity that they had known nothing about before they arrived. Others had been drawn into illegal labour movements in which Catalan provided a symbolic means of resistance against the regime; it then became so firmly associated with the idea of democracy that to ask for political freedom in Spain was unthinkable if it did not include at least cultural autonomy for Catalonia. In rural areas, people had not easily forgotten their heritage and were still living a basically Catalanized everyday life. It was this kind of continuity, despite the difficulties involved, that made culture and language stand out as the primary markers of collective identity.

To sum up, then, by the time the transition to democracy began, the majority of Catalans had a general sense that language and culture were the main markers of Catalan identity. This also meant that there was a general consensus that something would need to be done to recognize and support Catalan culture. However, culture could not therefore be the deciding factor in the first democratic elections, either to the state government or the *Generalitat*. All but the most right-wing of parties agreed that culture, language and autonomy were important issues, which meant that 'On the right, centre and left, everyone can find their own Catalan option' (Avui, 1977).[5] CiU's conservative heritage was an advantage here, though, because it stressed precisely the elements of historical continuity that people had come to value during the difficult times. Just as crucially, its more left-of-centre social and economic elements also allowed it to give out a progressive and inclusive message about the groups that could benefit from that continuity.

Historical Precedent

Despite this progressive component, it is the conservative heritage of CiU that is most apparent in its approach to cultural policy, in which language, high culture and popular traditions dominate over other elements and have the key function of proving and perpetuating the existence of a distinct Catalan national identity.

Xavier Bru de Sala has commented that Pujol had a very abstract idea of culture, and was not interested in the actual existence of orchestras, publishers, writers, performers and artists, who were supposed to just look out for themselves (Bru de Sala, 2003). In other words, Pujol saw Catalan culture as a symbol and legitimizing factor for Catalan identity, but did not think it important in its own right. Equally, the role of cultural policy in promoting social inclusion in a broad sense was not a priority for CiU. Rather, the issue was seen in terms of *national* inclusion, that is, the invitation to participate in Catalonia's national culture – as they themselves defined it.

Their definition was of course coloured by the history of Catalan nationalism and the ideological basis of the party's formation. One of the key influences for CDC – and Pujol – was Enric Prat de la Riba, who was largely responsible for consolidating conservative political Catalanism in the early twentieth century. In 1906, Prat de la Riba published *La nacionalitat catalana* (The Catalan Nationality), which was designed as a doctrinal text. In it, he stressed the widely held (and romantically inspired) view that culture and language were the cornerstone of Catalan nationality, and that these legitimized the desire for political recognition of the nation (Prat de la Riba, 1993: 48–9, 61–2). His pronouncements on culture and language find continuity in Pujol's own thinking on the topic (see chapter 2). For UDC, these sentiments are also combined with a spiritual element drawn from the influence of Bishop Josep Torras i Bages (1846–1916) and the poet Joan Maragall (Guibernau, 2004: 134). The identifying elements of language and culture are therefore framed within a context of Christian belief, which brings a different perspective to questions of the relationship between personal and collective identity.

These conservative elements of CiU's thinking on culture raise the question of class, as I have already indicated in the introduction. Although in politico-economic terms CiU's relationship with the financial and industrial bourgeoisie was far from straightforward (Guibernau, 2004: 143; Lorés, 1985: 56–7), when it came to culture CiU had a largely bourgeois conception of the function and hierarchy of cultural forms. According to Bourdieu's study of France in *Distinction*, there are several defining features of bourgeois taste, which include a preference for 'older, more consecrated works' that allow the world to be viewed through 'rose-coloured spectacles' (Bourdieu, 1984: 292). Petit-bourgeois attitudes to culture differ slightly because the members of this group do not enjoy the same level of cultural knowledge, but they nevertheless recognize the inherent legitimacy of bourgeois culture and attempt to reflect this in their own 'middle-brow' tastes (Bourdieu, 1984: 318–28). They therefore revere culture, partly because of their own 'sense of unworthiness' (321), and partly because of the symbolic and material advantages that can be attained by increasing one's stock of cultural capital.

The same kind of attitude to culture can be found in the mechanisms of the nineteenth-century revival of interest in Catalan identity, which Joan-Lluís Marfany explores in depth in his book entitled *La cultura del Catalanisme* (The Culture of Catalanism). Nineteenth-century Catalanism was the domain of the educated middle classes: professionals, students, factory owners, landowners. Not only this, but it appealed particularly to the young and 'upwardly mobile' as an ideal which could transform them not only politically but also culturally and spiritually (Marfany, 1995: 280–1). The genteel meetings of Catalanist groups, at which poems were read, music was played and the history and characteristics of the nation were debated, functioned much like acts of worship, in which these cultural forms acted as hymns to the nation. 'Catalanism and "art" were inseparable' (Marfany, 1995: 273).[6] It was no surprise, then, that the artistic movements of the early twentieth century also sprang from this association, producing the distinctive Catalan *Modernisme* that is typified by the work of the architect Antoni Gaudí, and the conservative *Noucentisme* that had a very restricted view of what constituted culture worthy enough to represent the Catalan nation.

The Franco regime cut off the flowering of Catalan culture that had come to be so intimately linked to political Catalanism. Under these circumstances, many of those who had been the producers of that culture felt a desire and duty to continue in this role, despite the obstacle of censorship and the fear of persecution. By ensuring that Catalan culture kept its high standards, something could be saved and passed on to future generations. As Toni Strubell says:

> this generation's response to the annihilation the country had suffered was self-affirmation through perfection in their cultivation of the language and literary aesthetics. Maybe Catalonia had lost the war. But its writers would make sure that at least the linguistic and literary excellences of the country would not be lost. In the words of Fuster, now 'perfection is their protest'. (Strubell, 1997: 79)[7]

The strategy worked, in the sense that new generations who were too young to remember Catalonia before the war were at least able to connect with it through literature under the guidance of intellectual and political mentors. However, the retreat into high culture and perfectionism limited the audience for these works so that cultural Catalanism once again became the preserve of the educated middle classes. The gains that had been made in the early twentieth century, when the range of culture available in Catalan was larger than it had been for centuries, were reversed. Coupled with the demographic changes outlined above, this meant that the bourgeois conception of culture that had come to CiU through its conservative heritage was reinforced by the general perception, especially in the cities, that Catalan culture was middle class.

Under these conditions, an individual's cultural capital became more explicitly linked to his or her degree of loyalty to the nation than would be the case in a nation state, because it involved the visible exercise of ideologically marked choices. If the cultural goods with which an individual dealt were marked as Catalan, then this said something about his/her level of cultural capital – because Catalan culture was perceived to be middle class – but also about the way in which s/he prioritized the identity-giving elements available in the surrounding context. Even though, as has already been discussed, these 'choices' might be the result of 'unconscious dispositions' rather than strategic calculation, observers will tend to make inferences about the motivations behind these actions. Although the political and social context has changed, the set of possible inferences remains much the same in the present day because the identification of language and culture with Catalan identity still predominates. This means that as we turn now to look at the general evolution of CiU's cultural policy, it is important to bear in mind that in the Catalan context, cultural choices are more visibly politicized than in the established European nation states that would seem to provide logical points of comparison.

Developing a Cultural Policy

According to Lluís Bonet, the approaches to cultural policy taken by previous Catalan bodies were a key influence in the direction taken by the Pujol-era *Generalitat* (Bonet, 2001: 304–5). The work of Enric Prat de la Riba, before and during his leadership of the

Mancomunitat, was particularly important since many of the institutions he created still form part of the cultural infrastructure supporting the policies of the *Generalitat*. The limitations on the political and administrative remit of the *Mancomunitat* meant that culture and language were part of its core activities and one of the few areas in which it could make a significant mark. For example, great progress was made towards the standardization of the Catalan language during this time as a direct result of the *Mancomunitat*'s support for this work. Bonet reports Emiliano Fernández Prado as saying that this was the first real example of a concerted cultural policy anywhere in Spain (304). The *Generalitat* of the 1930s built on this work and appointed a *Conseller de cultura* (Minister for Culture) at a time when it was highly unusual for any government in Europe to do so (305).

Another vital element in the evolution of CiU's cultural policy was the *Congrés de Cultura Catalana* that took place from 1975 to 1977. Experts from around the *Països Catalans*[8] took charge of conducting discussions in their areas of expertise, which included language, literature, music and the visual arts, but also law, industry, tourism and agriculture. In this sense, the remit of the *Congrés* was very broad – and speculative, given that there was no way of knowing what kinds of democratic political structures would eventually be put in place – but it did come up with specific recommended lines of action for each of the separate sectors it tackled. The *Congrés* highlighted the importance of cultural and political autonomy in the democracy that was to come, and ensured that the debate on cultural policy had already acquired some focus even before there was a *Generalitat* in place to implement it. In this respect, it is worth noting that few people in Catalonia at this point would have advocated an 'arm's length' approach to culture. For anti-Francoist groups of all persuasions, the damage done to Catalan identity by the dictatorship was a shared concern that required action. This meant that there was clear backing for direct regional and local government involvement in culture, even by those from political traditions that in other circumstances would have been against political interference in culture as a matter of principle. This means that Catalan politicians have been able to – or even required to – engage in overt policymaking and direct administration.

It probably goes without saying that Catalonia has not looked very much to Spain as a model for its cultural policy – partly because the Catalans have often been ahead of the Spanish state in their thinking – although they do keep a close eye on any indices that might reveal areas in which other regions of Spain have a competitive edge. This means that the traditional rivalry with Madrid for the title of 'cultural capital of Spain' continues, although the odds are stacked against Barcelona because of the state's tendency to concentrate its funds and activities in the political capital.[9] Spain retains a *Ministerio de Cultura* and certain powers in the area of culture and heritage, in accordance with article 149.2 of the Spanish constitution of 1978, which describes culture as a responsibility always to be shared by the autonomous communities and the state. This means that any competencies accorded to the autonomous communities in the area of culture run concurrently with the state's own cultural institutions (Real Instituto Elcano, 2004: 9–11, 20–1). Some of the major cultural projects undertaken in Catalonia have therefore involved collaboration and co-funding by the *Ministerio de Cultura*. These include the running of the Liceu opera house (since 1990), and the ongoing project to provide a provincial library for Barcelona (described in chapter 5 of this volume). Nevertheless, some Catalans argue that the *Ministerio de Cultura* should be abolished and all of Spain's powers in culture devolved to the autonomous communities and local government.

Partnerships, and rivalries, have also been forged with the other local authorities of Catalonia, which have their own budgets and responsibility for the local cultural services in their area (e.g. libraries, museums and cultural centres). Most importantly, the tensions between the *Generalitat* and the socialist-led city council of Barcelona (the *Ajuntament de Barcelona*) have both stimulated and hindered creativity. The *Ajuntament* supports its own cultural infrastructure, including theatres, museums, libraries and festivals. This increases the variety of culture on offer in Barcelona but can also lead to the duplication of provision and administrative structures, and to the fragmentation and politicization of support for cultural ventures. In other areas of Catalonia, the *Ajuntaments* provide basic cultural services which are supplemented by the less extensive work of the *Generalitat* outside Barcelona. The four provincial *Diputacions* of Barcelona, Lleida, Tarragona and Girona, which are a legacy of the system of local government in place during the Franco regime, form an intermediate layer between the municipalities and the *Generalitat*. They were robbed of many of their powers by the

Generalitat's reforms of local government but still have a coordinating role, encouraging the towns and cities to participate in what the *Diputació de Barcelona* has called 'networked culture', 'by setting up joint networks to manage services and investment in facilities' (Diputació de Barcelona, 2000: 3). In the non-governmental sector there are private or charitable cultural foundations, and companies with a philanthropic arm, that support publications, exhibitions, performances or festivals either on their own or in partnership with public bodies. Finally, of course, there are amateur associations, which are particularly important in the area of traditional and popular culture but also manifest themselves as theatre groups, book clubs, choirs and so on.

As far as international influences are concerned, the dominant model during the early stages of the establishment of the *Departament de Cultura* was that of France. This is not surprising given that France was the main democratic reference point for Catalans during the dictatorship. Summing up the *Generalitat*'s cultural policy at the end of Pujol's presidency, Agustí Fancelli goes as far as to say that 'Pujol devised, 40 years on, a cultural model à la De Gaulle, but without the benefit of an André Malraux to direct it' (Fancelli, 2003).[10] Elements of the French approach can be found in the way that legislation and the management of cultural institutions have been designed and implemented, as well as in specific borrowings such as the creation of a Catalan national theatre along French lines with a Catalan artistic director who had worked in the *Comédie Française* (see chapter 3). However, the 1990s saw an increased interest in British and Canadian cultural policy, especially towards the end of Pujol's presidency when issues to do with the economic potential of the cultural industries and the threat of global cultural homogenization were high on the agenda. The gradual strengthening of interregional links within Europe and with Quebec also provided new ideas, and there was a similar willingness to learn from 'smaller' European cultures that were under some of the same pressures as Catalonia despite enjoying recognition as nation states. As a result, CiU's thinking moved more towards concerns with the stimulation of creativity, and therefore with the cultural industries as motors of economic growth, tourism and social wellbeing.

Even so, the French influence is still present in this later period in the shape of CiU's agreement with the idea of cultural exceptionalism. For example, CiU's take on cultural diversity, in which

each culture is seen as having a uniqueness that must be preserved
(see chapter 6), has much in common with the way the French
Ministre de Culture from 2002 to 2004, Jean-Jacques Aillagon, linked
the two concepts of cultural exception and cultural diversity:
'Cultural exception is [. . .] not a "typically French" notion, it
corresponds to the will to defend all cultures. From this perspective, it is the very foundation of cultural diversity' (quoted in
Escande and Delvainquière, 2002: 14). Also, the practical application of 'l'exception culturelle' to policy on the audiovisual sector,
as a strategy to guard national production against the Hollywood
steamroller, continues to attract advocates of all political persuasions in Catalonia and has been part of CiU's recent electoral
programme (Convergència, 2005: 35).

It will be clear from this discussion of the ideas on which the
Catalans drew that it is possible to identify a number of different
stages in CiU's cultural policy, which in broad terms could be said
to be the following: deciding how to respond to the freedoms
offered by the new democracy and the challenges of recovering
suppressed aspects of Catalan culture; the drive for cultural
normalization; the consolidation of a cultural infrastructure; and
an attempt to enhance Catalonia's visibility and competitiveness
within the Spanish and global markets for cultural products. These
stages are not mutually exclusive and therefore overlap – which is
why I have not attempted to allocate dates to each stage – but a
broad evolution in these terms is perceptible. Furthermore, there
have been different *Consellers de Cultura* over the period in question, and these have tended to steer cultural policy in particular
directions. They were Max Cahner (1980–4), Joan Rigol (1984–6),
Joaquim Ferrer (1986–8), Joan Guitart (1988–96), Joan Maria
Pujals (1996–9) and Jordi Vilajoana (1999–2003).

In a volume of conference papers given in 1982 entitled
Reflexions crítiques sobre la cultura catalana (Critical Reflections on
Catalan Culture), a number of Catalan intellectuals set out their
own particular ideas of the direction cultural policy should take in
those early stages (Vilar et al., 1990). The fact that the preface to
the volume was written by *Conseller de Cultura* Max Cahner suggests
that they could expect their opinions to be given a fair hearing in
political circles. Indeed, Cahner 'was a clear exponent of a concept
that made Catalan culture "the central axis of nationalist politics in
Catalonia"' (Giner, Flaquer, Busquet and Bultà, 1996: 134).[11]
Although each contributor to the volume had his own axe to grind,

the main ideas being put forward can be summarized as follows (the author of the main contribution(s) on each theme is given in brackets):

- Catalan culture has become disconnected from the Catalan language through the repression they have suffered. A successful cultural policy would reconnect the two. (Joan Triadú)
- Similarly, the public has lost touch with Catalan culture and a cultural policy is needed to combat this and encourage participation. (Josep M. Castellet, Joaquim Molas)
- Catalan culture has become concentrated in 'high' or 'elite' forms: an effort must be made to democratize the culture and make sure that forms of mass or popular culture are available too. (Molas, Xavier Rubert de Ventós)
- It is important to consolidate forms of culture which are already in existence as well as branching into new directions. (Molas)
- Special attention must be given to the effects of immigration on Catalan culture. (Josep Termes)
- The cultural relationships between Catalonia and the other Catalan-speaking areas must be fully acknowledged. (Joan Fuster)

Clearly, there were a number of important issues to be tackled, but the budget for culture at this time was pretty meagre because the process of transferring funds and responsibilities from central government was slow and the *Departament de Cultura* itself was only just beginning to function. The main progress in this period was in establishing the department's own internal structures and producing the first legislation, including the vital Linguistic Normalization Act of 1983 (see chapter 2). Even so, Cahner is mainly remembered for setting out a restrictive approach which turned Pujol's abstract idea of 'culture as identity' into a cultural policy that only supported those elements of culture that best fitted this ideology.

The reaction against this approach led to one of the most painful episodes in Catalan cultural policy: the *Pacte Cultural*. The idea was first mooted by writer and literary critic Josep M. Castellet and was supposed to be a cross-party agreement that would involve all the cultural institutions in Catalonia in a policy of cooperation. The intention was to stop party political disagreements from interfering with the successful rejuvenation of Catalan culture, providing a truly supportive and coordinated environment in which it could flourish. The idea was taken up by Joan Rigol, who became *Conseller de Cultura* after Cahner in 1984. After much debate, the agreement was ratified by all the relevant institutions except the *Diputació de Tarragona*, only to be quietly dropped by the *Generalitat*, ostensibly because of unforeseen budgetary constraints, but more probably because most members of the government had never been convinced by the idea. It has even been suggested that it was Pujol's growing mistrust of the Catalan and Spanish Socialists, as a result of their attempts to investigate his business dealings, that sunk the *Pacte* (Bru de Sala, 2003). According to Jordi Font, the failure of the *Pacte Cultural* was a disaster because it meant continuing administrative chaos and overlap between institutions (Font, 1991: 176). Rigol resigned and was replaced by Joaquim Ferrer.

> After his nomination there begins a process of a certain political normalization: the dramatic tone is left behind and the *Conselleria de Cultura* becomes a department like any other. It is worth saying that from that moment on the government of *Convergència* is not willing to relinquish its sovereignty in the management of cultural policy, and even less willing to renounce a certain monopoly on political and cultural Catalanism. (Giner, Flaquer, Busquet and Bultà 1996: 135).[12]

In other words, cultural policy moved down the political agenda but there was no further attempt to remove it from the domain of party politics. Instead, Ferrer, and Joan Guitart after him, paid more attention to the task of 'administering' culture.

This drive for a more practical approach is apparent from a second volume of *Reflexions crítiques*, published in 1987 once again as proceedings from a conference, which concentrates much more on specific recommendations regarding different cultural forms, including literature, art, cinema and television (Gifreu et al., 1987). Two main preoccupations were guiding Catalan cultural policy at the time the second volume was published: cultural normalization, and the provision of a solid cultural infrastructure. Cultural normalization, intimately related to linguistic normalization, involves a number of different tactics to try to restore Catalan culture to 'normality', that is, to give it back its place as the predominant culture of Catalonia and the one in which citizens would 'normally' choose to participate. Considerations regarding infrastructure were a fundamental part of this, since it was obvious that Catalan culture would not reach the people it was intended to reach if they did not have access to libraries, theatres, sports facilities, concert halls, museums and so on. A great deal of money was spent on providing or modernizing such facilities and both the *Generalitat* and other local government bodies, such as the *Ajuntaments*, were involved in the process. This phase of cultural policy reached a peak during the 1990s with the inauguration of facilities such as the *Teatre Nacional de Catalunya* (National Theatre of Catalonia) and the *Museu d'Història de Catalunya* (Museum of the History of Catalonia) in Barcelona, as well as libraries, museums and cultural amenities for local communities throughout Catalonia (Cubeles and Fina 1999: 31). Parallel to this was the enactment of legislation that was supposed to regulate the administration of these facilities and ensure that they completed the mission for which they had been designed. Thus, further laws were passed regarding heritage, archives, museums, and popular traditions (see chapter 5). Unfortunately, many of these laws were slowly or only partially implemented, which severely hindered their effectiveness.

Aside from these internal matters, the question of the international projection of Catalan culture steadily gathered pace throughout Pujol's six terms as president. Joan Guitart oversaw the creation of COPEC, the Catalan Consortium for the External Promotion of Culture, which was designed to act as a link between Catalan culture and its European neighbours. The subject really came to the fore, though, under Joan Maria Pujals and his successor Jordi Vilajoana, who began to devote more thought to the economic potential of culture, as encapsulated within the term 'cultural industries' (see chapters 4 and 6). Pujals was unable to make any very significant moves in this area as he was tied up with the political wrangles over the Linguistic Policy Act of 1998, and the *Teatre Nacional* (see chapters 2 and 3, and Bonet, 2001: 311). It was therefore Vilajoana who oversaw the most significant steps to improve Catalonia's international profile, with the creation of the *Institut Ramon Llull* (a cultural institute designed to coordinate the projection of language, literature and 'high culture' outside Spain) and the *Institut Català de les Indústries Culturals* (Catalan Institute for the Cultural Industries (ICIC); see chapter 4).

As far as the budget for these activities was concerned, this was naturally seen as completely insufficient by all practitioners and opposition politicians. The main problem in the 1980s was that the resources were simply not available, because of the slow transfer of funds from central government. The situation stabilized in the 1990s, with the budget for cultural activities fluctuating between 120 and 170 million euros per year and showing a clear upward trend in the last few years up to 2003. Even so, one of the first things the new *Consellera de Cultura* for the left-wing tripartite government (elected in 2003) did when appointed was to promise to radically increase the budget for culture during their first legislature. Caterina Mieras committed herself to spending, within four years, 51 euros per inhabitant on culture rather than the 29 finally reached by CiU (Moix and Massot, 2004). This would mean spending 2 per cent of the *Generalitat*'s total budget on culture rather than the 1 per cent spent by CiU.

The scarcity of funds, and the determination of CiU to keep tight control of spending decisions after the failure of the *Pacte Cultural*, led to the development of a heavily clientelistic style of budget management. This was apparent both from the way the *Generalitat*'s own institutions were staffed and from the way in which subsidies were distributed to particular projects and practitioners. Many members of the Catalan cultural elite who were in some way sympathetic to CiU's political aims were drafted in to posts either within the *Departament de Cultura* or in other areas, often as *assessors* (advisers) who received salaries and perks that seemed out of proportion with the task they were asked to perform (Martínez and Oliveres, 2005: 394–7). Subsidies and prizes were also sometimes given by public bodies to individuals whose personal links with CiU made others suspicious of the motivation behind the award. The writer Baltasar Porcel was one of the most talked-about of these favoured few, as he was the first director of the *Institut Català de la Mediterrània* (The Catalan Institute of the Mediterranean), and then chaired the jury of the *Premi Internacional Catalunya*.[13] There was much speculation about both the financial and the more intangible rewards he received for this work. He later commented that his political closeness to Pujol had been a mistake, in the sense that it coloured the reception of his literary works and therefore prejudiced his career as a writer (Bonada, 2005: 79). Nevertheless, Porcel was not the only cultural practitioner who had a direct involvement with the CiU *Generalitat*, and others with different political sympathies often had formal or informal links with the socialist-led Barcelona city council. This led to a polarization of the cultural elite along political lines, making it difficult to keep politics out of culture even for individual writers or artists, let alone for the companies or cultural institutions with which they were associated.

As far as the distribution of financial support for culture was concerned, this too increasingly clustered around particular projects, institutions or individuals. The stress on providing Catalonia with a cultural infrastructure worthy of its status as a nation absorbed a large percentage of the budget for cultural works, which meant that the *Generalitat* was primarily funding its own projects. The *Museu d'Història de Catalunya*, the *Teatre Nacional* and other major drains on capital expenditure left little money for other areas such as traditional culture and heritage, or for supporting private sector or amateur initiatives (Bonet, 2001: 313–4). When these were supported, it was often felt that they were chosen more because they fitted in with CiU's vision of Catalan culture and identity than because of their artistic or social value. In other words, cultural policy under Pujol was nationalist even in the finer details. The *Generalitat* did not even pretend to be culturally neutral when deciding which forms of culture to support, although there were vain attempts to deny that party political criteria were involved.

Catalan Intellectuals and Cultural Policy

There is little wonder, then, that critics considered Pujol as having very little interest in culture per se. He was also said to mistrust intellectuals as a group, finding their constant critique of just about everything tedious and hypocritical, which also explains his lack of willingness to engage with them except when they were directly useful to him (Antich, 1994: 97).[14] The most visible opposition to CiU's cultural policy certainly came from intellectuals writing in the press – perhaps more so than from the other parties in the *Parlament*, since much of the actual legislation on culture was the result of consensus, and it was the everyday administration of culture, in which the *Parlament* had little say, that drew dissent. The pages of Catalan-language newspapers and magazines, or Spanish-language publications and supplements designed for a Catalan audience, were constantly filled with comment on cultural policy from different points of view. There have also been a wide variety of books and pamphlets published on the subject, often by people directly involved in either the administration or production of culture, or by policymakers. For example, Jordi Font and Xavier Bru de Sala offered critical commentaries on the cultural policy of local and regional government (e.g. Font, 1991; Bru de Sala, 1987, 1999, 2003; Bru de Sala et al. 1997); Joan Guitart's published speeches provided summaries of the progress made during his time in the *Departament de Cultura;* and Joan Maria Pujals tried to think through, in print, the ways of responding to the challenges faced by Catalan culture and identity at the end of the 1990s (Pujals, 1998). However, academic studies of cultural policy within Catalonia are much thinner on the ground. In fact, what should have been the most rigorous 'neutral' analysis of Catalan culture during the early Pujol years, on which future cultural policy could have been based, actually became another of the casualties of the *Pacte Cultural.* This was the *Llibre blanc de la cultura* (Handbook of Culture[15]) commissioned from the Fundació Jaume Bofill as a direct result of the *Pacte,* a mammoth task that was well underway when the *Pacte Cultural* was dropped. It now exists only as a series of unpublished typescripts, available in the *Biblioteca de Catalunya.* It consists of a detailed inventory of the state of Catalonia's cultural infrastructure in the early 1980s, an analysis of how this was financed in the year 1985, and a final volume exploring ways in which the project could be taken forward – including a suggestion that Bourdieu's *Distinction* should form the model for any analysis of cultural practices (Cardús, 1988: 96). Nothing official ever came of it.

The last volume of the *Llibre blanc* was written by the sociologist Salvador Cardús, who is one of the most important contributors to both the debate and the academic literature on cultural policy in Catalonia. Having written on issues in Catalan culture as diverse as traditions, multiculturalism, the media, nationalism, and the economic potential of culture – as well as on other aspects of sociology – over the last twenty-five years, Cardús's work probably provides the most extensive critique of Catalan cultural policy from inside Catalonia itself. A decade after the *Llibre blanc,* Salvador Giner, Lluís Flaquer, Jordi Busquet, and Núria Bultà published *La cultura catalana: el sagrat i el profà* (Catalan Culture: The Sacred and the Profane), in which they apply their own analytical framework to the role of culture in defining Catalonia's identity. This is based on the idea that the administration of culture revolves around two axes – communion/domination and innovation/tradition. 'Communion' indicates the aspects of culture that involve participation, shared belief and group loyalty, whereas 'domination' relates to inter and intra-group conflict, hierarchies and power structures; however, the terms do not indicate mutually exclusive processes as elements of both will be present in a particular culture. The authors explore different debates within Catalan culture in the light of these concepts, including the failure of the *Pacte Cultural*, which in a sense reappears in their own conclusion when they advocate a cultural policy for Catalonia based on consensus, plurality and dialogue.

Moving to the end of the Pujol era, we find a different kind of approach to cultural policy being taken by another Catalan academic, this time with a background in economics. Lluís Bonet was the director of the project to map the state of Catalonia's cultural industries at the beginning of the twenty-first century which was commissioned by the fledgling *Institut Català de les Indústries Culturals* (see chapter 4). His work on the cultural industries, especially the audiovisual sector, has a clear empirical foundation and tackles the mechanisms of policymaking more directly than Cardús or Giner et al. have done. The same can be said of media and communications expert Josep Gifreu, whose publications include a strategy document on audiovisual media in Catalonia commissioned by the *Generalitat de Catalunya* (Gifreu, 2003). He also edits the journal of the Audiovisual Council of Catalonia (*Consell de l'Audiovisual de Catalunya*), whose remit is to oversee the *Generalitat*'s involvement in the audiovisual sector. The contributions of Bonet and Gifreu – and Cardús's input into the *Llibre blanc de la cultura* – show that academics can have an important role to play in ensuring that government policy is based on sound research and informed thinking.

One more *Llibre blanc* requires a mention here, and that is the *Llibre blanc de la cultura a Catalunya* published by the *Partit dels Socialistes de Catalunya* (Socialist Party of Catalonia – PSC) in 1999 (edited by Ferran Mascarell, who was himself to become *Conseller de Cultura* in 2006). The title was no doubt carefully chosen, as it refers to 'Culture in Catalonia', rather than 'Catalan culture'. In fact, the debate about what constitutes Catalan culture provides the main thread of the book's argument, since one of the PSC's most ardent criticisms of CiU policy was its failure to support any form of culture produced by Catalans using Spanish. In the opinion of the contributors to this *Llibre blanc*, CiU's cultural policy was blind to the dynamism inherent in contemporary culture, artificially constrained by the stress on language, obsessed with the rhetoric of normalization, and orientated towards short-term party political gains. Instead, they propose a cultural policy based on social inclusion and the recognition of diversity. This would mean greater development of the cultural infrastructure outside Barcelona, more support for local amateur associations, the inclusion of Spanish-language writers in literary institutions and events, and a real effort to reach out to the public and interest them in what is on offer. In his prologue to the book, Pasqual Maragall says that he wants Catalan culture to be understood as the sum of all the layers and points of view of all the citizens who want to contribute to it (Mascarell, 1999: 12).

The publication of the PSC's *Llibre blanc* did reinvigorate the debate on culture, especially since it came at the time that the *Generalitat* was planning the creation of the ICIC. Barcelona's successes in the cultural industries, which had been stimulated in part by the PSC-led Barcelona city council, meant that CiU could not afford to ignore their proposals in that area. Some commentators have also indicated that there was a slight relaxation of the emphasis on language during Pujol's last term in office. This is partly because of the same stress on the cultural industries, which prompted a downgrading of concerns about language in favour of economic success and international competitiveness. It has also been suggested that the decision of the *Institut Ramon Llull* to co-sponsor a tour of Australia and New Zealand by a Catalan writer best known for writing in Spanish, Manuel Vázquez Montalbán, was symbolic of a general will to broaden the parameters of institutional support for culture. Nevertheless, CiU's official rhetoric is still based on the premise that Catalan culture and the Catalan language are essential elements in preserving the distinctive identity of the Catalan people.

Briefly, then, the *Generalitat*'s cultural policy under CiU basically started as a language policy coupled with an arts policy and a limited concern with traditional culture. As time went on, this broadened to include more elements related to media policy, heritage, and then a specific cultural industries policy. These were all developed in a climate of broad consensus on the general lines of policy – as reflected in parliamentary support for most of the items of legislation on cultural matters – but of criticism and dissent regarding its implementation and administration. Most importantly, this was a cultural policy thoroughly marked by its primary function as a nation-building tool. As such, it was largely a policy of 'display' based around 'national aggrandizement', (Williams, 1984;

McGuigan, 2004: 61–4) although in this case with the added responsibility of legitimizing Catalonia's contested claims to national status within a larger nation state. The rest of this book will illustrate some of the specific ways in which what McGuigan (2004: 62) calls the 'ritual symbolization of nationhood' was achieved.

NOTES

1   'A escala europea hem estat, i som, impulsors de la idea regionalista. Idea que no encaixa ben bé amb el nostre nacionalisme, però que ens ha servit per ser presents en la política europea amb una oferta que creiem que és bona per als pobles d'Europa'.

2   In the survey cited by McRoberts only 34.1% of respondents described Catalonia as a nation. Data collected almost ten years later suggested that the position had reversed and a slim majority of Catalans (51.1%) now thought of Catalonia as a nation (*El Periódico*, 9 October 2005, p. 2; survey conducted by GESOP). It may be the case that the debate over whether Catalonia could and should call itself a nation in the articles of its new statute of autonomy had raised public awareness of the issue. Similarly, the cumulative effect of many years of having Catalan politicians describe Catalonia as a nation could also be a factor.

3   'posar més l'accent en les carreteres que en la identitat'.

4   See Guibernau, 2004: 34–69 for a detailed account of the ideologies of the Franco regime and Catalan resistance to them.

5   'A dreta, centre i esquerra, tothom pot trobar la seva opció catalana'.

6   'Catalanisme i «art» eren inseparables'.

7   'la resposta d'aquesta generació a l'anorreament que havia patit el país era l'autoafirmació a través de la perfecció en el conreu de la llengua i de l'estètica literària. Potser Catalunya havia perdut la guerra. Però els seus escriptors s'encarregarien que almenys no es perdessin les excel·lències lingüístiques i literàries del país. En paraules de Fuster, ara *«la perfecció és la seva protesta»*.'

8   This term ('The Catalan Countries') refers to the areas that had a historic relationship with Catalonia, where Catalan is still spoken to some extent. It is mainly used to denote Catalonia, Valencia, the Balearic Islands, and the area around Perpignan in the south of France.

9   See Real Instituto Elcano 2004 for a summary of Spanish cultural policy.

10   'Pujol perfilaba, 40 años más tarde, un modelo *à la De Gaulle* para la cultura, pero sin contar con un André Malraux para dirigirlo.'

11   'era un clar exponent d'una concepció que feia de la cultura catalana «l'eix central de la política nacionalista a Catalunya»'

12   'Amb el seu nomenament s'entra en un procés d'una certa normalitza-ció política: se supera el to dramàtic i la Conselleria de Cultura passa a

ser un departament com els altres. Val a dir que a partir d'aquest moment el Govern de Convergència no està dispost a cedir sobirania en la gestió de les polítiques culturals, ni molt menys a renunciar a un cert monopoli del catalanisme polític i cultural.'

13 A prize awarded annually to a single outstanding individual from any country and in any field.

14 According to Bourdieu, anti-intellectualism is another 'determinant characteristic of some fractions of the bourgeoisie and petite bourgeoisie' (Bourdieu, 1984: 293).

15 *Llibre blanc* literally means 'White Book': a comprehensive survey or report on an area or issue. The *Generalitat* uses 'Handbook' as the preferred English translation.

Chapter Two

Language Policy

It is not possible to understand the causes and effects of CiU's cultural policy without first considering linguistic policy as a separate category. Much has already been written in English about Catalan language policy and planning, including a very clear summary of the issues and legislative process by Kenneth McRoberts (2001: 139–60). In Catalan and Spanish, of course, there are reams on the subject, in the press, in books and on the internet, some of it written by those involved in policymaking or language planning, and some of it by interested bystanders with their own particular criticisms or suggestions for doing it better. It is not my intention to give a comprehensive survey of this material. Instead, this chapter will give some background information on key aspects of Catalan language policy from 1980–2003, before highlighting the factors that explain CiU's (almost) unshakable insistence on language policy as the fundamental basis of their cultural policy. Chapters 3 and 4 will develop and exemplify the issues introduced here.

As Ronald Wardhaugh (2002: 353) defines it, 'Language planning is an attempt to interfere deliberately with a language or one of its varieties', which means that there must be some kind of perceived need or justification for this interference. For this reason, Clare Mar-Molinero (2000: 73–7) draws a distinction between language policy and language planning which I intend to follow in this chapter. She equates language policy with 'decision-making' and language planning with 'implementation', and warns that the two should not be confused when trying to form a picture of a particular situation (74). For the purposes of this chapter, I will be concentrating more on policy than planning, and therefore looking at 'decisions and choices which to be understood must be set in the ideological and political context in which they are taken' (74).

Of course when we talk about the results that CiU has achieved it goes without saying that these are dependent on practical implementation as much as on policymaking, and that important benefits can come from initiatives that were not stimulated by *Generalitat* policy.

Unfortunately, evidence from a wide variety of settings suggests that language planning for minority languages is likely to fail because of factors beyond the planners' control. Wardhaugh (2002: 376) comments that there is no hard evidence that intervention can even slow down processes of language change, which means that the decision to intervene (or not) is always based on ideological factors rather than anything else. It therefore seems as though no matter how committed the Catalans might be to the task, they may be attempting to achieve the impossible in trying to reverse what is known as 'language shift'. This process has been responsible for the deaths of many thousands of languages through the ages and has accelerated in recent decades. David Crystal (2000: 19) estimates that over the next hundred years we may lose half of the current total of world languages, which means approximately two languages per month. Language shift occurs when the circumstances of a linguistic group change and they come into contact with another culture which is dominant over theirs. In this situation, there is pressure to adopt the language of the dominant culture, either through force or because it is seen as advantageous. This results in a period of bilingualism in which the majority of the population are able to use both languages, although not necessarily to an equal standard. Although collective bilingualism might seem like an ideal solution, in reality bilingual situations tend to be unstable. Younger generations who do not feel as attached to their autochthonous language as their grandparents start to abandon it in favour of exclusive use of the dominant language, which is the only one they need for practical purposes. The minority language then goes into decline, and is condemned to die with the last generation of remaining speakers unless something dramatic happens to save it. This is the situation the *Generalitat* has been desperately trying to avoid.

Under CiU, responsibility for language planning and policy came under the remit of the *Departament de Cultura*. It is interesting to note that one of the first things the new left-wing government did when it came to power in 2003 was to transfer this responsibility to the *Departament de la Presidència*, as a direct response to what they saw as the unhealthy link between language and culture that had become institutionalized during the previous twenty-three years. However, even though policy and planning had been managed by the *Departament de Cultura*, activity on language had not solely been confined to their sphere of action and other departments had also been heavily involved. When policy was made which touched on areas outside the direct control of the *Departament de Cultura*, other departments needed to implement and oversee that policy and dedicate part of their own budget to it. This meant that a substantial total sum was devoted to language planning – more than five billion euros in 2002 (Departament de Cultura, 2003d: 22). Nevertheless, the main engine for language policy and planning was the Directorate General for Linguistic Policy (*Direcció General de Política Lingüística*) which was part of the *Departament de Cultura*. The Directorate oversaw bodies such as the Institute for Catalan Sociolinguistics (*Institut de Sociolingüística Catalana*), the Linguistic Normalization Service (*Servei de Normalització Lingüística*) and the Linguistic Advice Service (*Servei d'Assessorament Lingüístic*).

The remit of the Directorate was to address two basic concerns. Firstly, whole generations of Catalans had missed out on the opportunity to learn their language in a formal setting since 1939. Acquisition planning was therefore going to be essential: whether through school, adult education or exposure to Catalan in the media and the workplace, it was important that all residents should acquire the ability to speak, read and write Catalan. Secondly, those who already knew Catalan or were in a position to learn it needed to be persuaded to use it in every possible circumstance, which meant that status planning would be necessary to ensure that Catalan regained its reputation as a language fit for any setting. When teachers, police officers, politicians, actors and newsreaders spoke Catalan, it would be clear that it was an advantageous language to know and use. Underlying both of these goals was the need for corpus planning to make sure the language had an agreed vocabulary and grammar (a standard form). This task was made easier by the fact that standardization had already been attempted in the early twentieth century thanks to the work of Pompeu Fabra, whose dictionaries and grammar books became the obligatory reference point for all subsequent users of the language. This gave Catalonia an advantage over the Basque Country and, particularly, Galicia, which were not able to standardize their languages until decades later and so faced more of a problem when it came to corpus planning. Even so, Catalan still had to overcome some ongoing issues regarding the definition of 'correct' and 'incorrect' Catalan, and needed to catch up with modern terminology. The latter task was delegated to TERMCAT, a Centre for Terminology which set about producing vocabulary lists for everything from engineering to Chinese food.

At the moment, Catalonia seems to be having some success in at least slowing the shift towards Spanish. As will become evident, numbers of speakers are increasing and Catalan now has at least a presence in all domains and is dominant in some of them. However, there are clear signs that long-term language shift is still underway, and a greater degree of interventionism will probably be required to have any chance of halting it. This then raises the thorny issue of how far a language policy can legitimately target the behaviour of individuals if it constrains their freedom of choice. Complicated ethical dilemmas arise when trying to reconcile the need to protect a minority language with the fact that this might only be achievable through linguistic and educational policies that may seem illiberal (Kymlicka, 2001: 76–7, 79). If in order to protect the national language and allow its speakers to use it twenty-four hours a day, others must also be persuaded to become speakers, to what extent can this persuasion include obligations and sanctions as well as rewards?

The problem of reconciling collective and individual rights has been at the heart of CiU's struggles with linguistic policy. Unable to impose the sole use of Catalan on the whole territory because of restrictions generated by the Spanish state, it has instead had to take a series of cumulative steps towards the linguistic Catalanization of the community. This aim is legitimized in several ways: by the argument that Spanish has been artificially imposed and would never have become the language of Catalonia if it was not for acts of aggression and oppression; by the historic association of Catalonia's language with its national identity; by the popular support for the rights of Catalan speakers expressed before, during and after the transition to democracy; and by the general claim that Spain is a 'nation of nations' that would be enriched by recognizing its multi-lingual make-up in a way similar to countries such as Belgium or Switzerland. In other words, most Catalans feel that there is a collective right for the Catalan nation to express itself in its own language. However, the process of mass migration from southern

Spain to Catalonia that took place during the Franco regime introduced a substantial community whose first language was Spanish, not by imposition or choice but by origin (Woolard, 1989). By 1970, over a third of the population of Catalonia had been born outside the region (Balcells, 1996: 152). Catalanist claims that the restoration of their language is a legitimate goal therefore conflict with the claims of another community who, under current law, are also quite legitimate in feeling that they only moved to another part of the same state and are therefore at liberty to use the official state language rather than that of the autonomous community. As we examine the development of language policy in Catalonia it will be clear that this conflict of rights has not been resolved.

The 1970s and 1980s

Despite these complications, it is important to stress that the policies on the Catalan language that were put in place in the years immediately following the restoration of the *Generalitat* were the result of a consensus and a momentum that had been gathering pace throughout the 1970s. The persecution of Catalan following the civil war had driven it behind closed doors, where it was largely confined to private everyday use, although it also acted as a symbolic vehicle of protest among small groups of people who were trying to keep alive at least some kind of cultural and ideological resistance to the regime. There was also some significant, although necessarily limited, support for these attempts from Catalans in exile. This meant that as the regime started to lose its grip a little in the 1960s, there was still enough support for Catalan for it to become a key factor in the more open protests of that decade. Importantly, the right to speak Catalan was an issue on which many different opposition groups and factions agreed. For them, Catalan was the language of freedom, whereas Castilian was the language of repression (Triadú, 1978: 16). This made it a fundamental element in the Catalans' emerging vision for a democratic Spain.

Even though many alliances and agreements broke down in the late 1970s when the brutal realities of party politics became apparent, the consensus surrounding the importance of the Catalan language remained. This show of strength was important during the drafting of the Spanish constitution, as pressure from the Catalans was especially vital in persuading the 'Fathers of the

Constitution' to make legal provision for languages other than Spanish in the new state. The – now infamous – article on language reads as follows:

> 1. Castilian is the official Spanish language of the State. All Spaniards have the duty to know it and the right to use it.
>
> 2. The other Spanish languages will also be official in their respective Autonomous Communities in accordance with their Statutes.
>
> 3. The richness of the different linguistic varieties of Spain is a cultural heritage that will be accorded special respect and protection.[1]

This is the third article in the document – a position which seems to underline the importance of linguistic issues. However, various crucial ambiguities or limitations in the article mean that its impact is not as radical as its positioning would suggest. The ambiguities have been meticulously examined by authors such as Mar-Molinero (2000: 86–92), and I do not intend to go into detail about them here. However, the main elements of the law that have been crucial for the subsequent development of language policy in Catalonia are the following:

- Castilian (Spanish) is official throughout the state, whereas the other languages are only official in the autonomous communities which have declared them to be so in their statutes of autonomy. Spanish therefore remains dominant over the other languages.
- Even where another language has official status, it is always co-official with Spanish. All citizens of Spain have the duty to know Spanish (but, according to the constitution, no duty to know the other co-official language of their place of residence). Even though prescribing the duty to know a language would be hard to police in any practical form, this is not the issue, as the importance of this statement is not really to do with its legal implications for the citizen, but the fact that it gives the state the right to assume that all Spaniards speak Spanish, exempting it from having to engage with them in any other language.
- The promise of 'special respect and protection' for the other autochthonous linguistic varieties of Spain is vague enough to

be meaningless. Crucially, it could be argued that the provisions established in points 1 and 2 of the article are in themselves a sufficient guarantee of 'protection' to fulfil the promise in point 3, leaving the matter entirely to the autonomous communities and once again exempting the Spanish state from the need to take direct action itself.

The first Catalan statute of autonomy was forced to follow the model set out by the constitution, although there was some attempt to push against the boundaries it imposed. Article 3 of the Statute of 1979 read:

1. Catalonia's own language [*llengua pròpia*] is Catalan.
2. Catalan is Catalonia's official language, as is Castilian, which is official in the whole of the Spanish State.
3. The Generalitat will guarantee the normal and official use of both languages, take the necessary measures to ensure that they are known, and create the right conditions for them to become fully equal in terms of the rights and duties of the citizens of Catalonia.
4. The Aranese tongue will be taught and accorded special respect and protection.[2]

The way the article was written stressed the symbolic importance of Catalan as Catalonia's *llengua pròpia* (the language that 'belongs to' Catalonia) thus appearing to give it precedence over Castilian. However, its legal outcome was actually a guarantee of equality for Catalan and Castilian. While this might seem like a major advance compared with the situation just a few years earlier, many Catalanists were already aware that equality on these terms would not be enough to ensure the future of Catalan, and more people have come to realize this since. As Pujol has said (1995: 23), 'we need to warn against the fallacy of total freedom when two languages – one stronger, one weaker – coexist'.[3]

Nevertheless, the first of Catalonia's new language laws, the Linguistic Normalization Act (*Llei de Normalització Lingüística*) of 1983, had to be constructed on the basis of official bilingualism established by the constitution and confirmed by the statute. However, as with article three of the statute, the wording of the law stressed the importance of Catalan as the *llengua pròpia* of the autonomous community, which appeared to be opposed to the mere 'duty to know' Spanish imposed by the state on Catalan citizens. This distinction was more than an exercise in rhetoric because it lead to an assumption designed to tip the balance in favour of Catalan at least in internal institutional settings: 'Catalan, as Catalonia's own language, is also the language of the *Generalitat*, territorial administration in Catalonia, local administration and the other public corporations that depend on the *Generalitat*' (article 5.1).[4] If it is the language of Catalonia and the *Generalitat*, then it is also the language of education (article 14.1) and of any publicly owned local media (article 21) – areas in which the *Generalitat* has substantial autonomy. The main thrust of the 1983 law, therefore, apart from guaranteeing all citizens the right to use either language, was to establish a basis upon which Catalan could come to be the dominant language in certain institutional settings. These were seen as key elements in the drive for what had come to be known as 'linguistic normalization', a shorthand term coined specifically in the Spanish context and enshrined in the name of this first law. It refers to the use of language planning in order to place a disadvantaged language at 'a "normal" level of equality vis-à-vis other (majority) languages' (Mar-Molinero, 2000: 80).

Although there was of course much debate during the painstaking process of drafting the law, it was eventually passed by the Catalan parliament without a single vote cast against it. This consensus was partly a result of Pujol's own insistence that the process should not be allowed to generate conflict (Delclós, 2003). He also described the way the law was passed as 'one of the best examples of patriotism and sense of responsibility that has been seen in Catalonia for years' (Pujol, 1995: 32).[5] It is sometimes remarked that Catalans forget that the initial moves towards re-establishing the place of the Catalan language in official settings should really be attributed to the Catalan parliament as a whole, and not just to CiU. This solidarity held throughout the difficult period in which the law was challenged in Spain's Constitutional Court, two articles eventually having to be withdrawn. Furthermore, despite some high-profile protests by Spanish-speakers who feared for their job security if they were forced to learn Catalan (McRoberts, 2001: 142), the vast majority of Catalans backed both the law and the principle of promoting Catalan in education and public administration. However, by the beginning of the 1990s, cracks had begun to appear in this unity as policymakers and language planners began to extend their activities further into areas that affected the everyday lives of all Catalans.

The 1990s to 2003

Elisa Roller (2002: 285) points out that the consensus about language policy began to break down because although there was a general agreement that Catalan should be vigorously promoted, there was a much greater divergence regarding the degree to which the *Generalitat* should be permitted to interfere in its actual use. The most important debates on this question have been played out in the field of education, which of course was one of the key areas covered by the 1983 law. As the years went by, policy on the use of Catalan was gradually strengthened in order to comply with the premise that Catalan should be the preferred language in educational settings (Mar-Molinero, 2000: 158–65; McRoberts, 2001: 147–8). This led to a gradual extension of immersion policies, and the establishment of a general principle (based on a decree passed in 1992)[6] that in all but the very early years of schooling (if necessary), the language of instruction will be Catalan, while Spanish is taught as a separate subject. Once again, this was not just attributable to CiU but to the *Parlament* as a whole. However, public opposition to the idea was more noticeable, and came especially from parents concerned about their right to choose how their children were to be educated, some non-Catalan 'observers' such as the conservative Spanish newspaper *ABC*, and, later, the Spanish government under the PP. The latter, exercising its right to make framework legislation on education, included in the Organic Law on the Quality of Education (LOCE)[7] of 2002 a provision that the number of hours dedicated to Spanish should be increased. This was a direct result of concerns over the marginalization of Spanish in communities with their own languages. Since the increase in Spanish teaching could only have been achieved within the constraints of the curriculum by reducing the time given to the autochthonous variety, the stipulation was seen as a direct attack on communities with their own co-official language.

On the other hand, there was a growing feeling among some sectors of Catalan society that the provisions of the 1983 law and its subsequent implementation had not gone far enough. Many people complained that while it was perfectly possible to get through the tasks of an average day speaking nothing but Spanish, the same was not possible in Catalan. Areas that the use of Catalan had been slow to penetrate included private-sector businesses and the Catalan offices of statewide institutions. The reasons for these

lacunae ranged from genuine worries about costs, technical problems and international communications, to overt hostility towards
Catalan from a small number of managers and employees. The
predominance of the Spanish-language mass media was also a
major concern, since even advances such as the successful launch
of Catalan television could not compete with the visibility, range,
influence and availability of Spanish media. Most importantly,
despite encouraging figures showing that the education system and
other forms of acquisition planning were succeeding in raising
competence in Catalan to respectable levels, this did not seem to be
accompanied by a radically increased desire in individual speakers
to elect to use Catalan rather than Spanish. It was for these reasons
that in the mid 1990s CiU proposed to review the legislation on
language in order to extend its scope and influence.

On this occasion, there was no consensus that a new law was even
necessary, let alone on what it should include. The very idea
worried some people so much that it led to the publication of a
'manifesto' against it by the *Foro Babel*, an organization supported
mainly by intellectuals who argued that the 1983 law went far
enough and anything else would infringe the rights of Spanish
speakers. The signatories to the 1997 manifesto included some
high-profile names: the theatre director Albert Boadella, and the
writers Juan Marsé, Terenci Moix and Eduardo Mendoza, for
example. In their opinion, the Linguistic Normalization Act had
succeeded in providing the conditions for Catalan to achieve
'normality' and all that was left was for the *Generalitat* to ensure that
every Catalan was competent in both languages. It was not up to the
government to interfere in language use, and they should remain
strictly neutral in such matters, 'as should be the case in a socially
bilingual country' (Santamaría, 1999: 79).[8] This attitude dismayed
those on the other side of the argument who saw the 1983 law as
ineffective and were hoping that the new legislation would provide
a radical response to the dangers to Catalan they perceived as
inherent in the form of bilingualism currently in operation. The
result of these differences was a battle, fought mainly in the press,
that provided a rather heated context for the debates taking place
in the *Parlament* itself.

Nevertheless, the Linguistic Policy Act (*Llei de Política
Lingüística*) was approved in December 1997 and came into effect
in 1998, after a series of bitter disputes and forced compromises
which meant that the eventual law bore little relation to the

ambitious plans for it at the outset. A survey reported in *La Vanguardia* on 22 March 1998 revealed that 51.8 per cent of the public supported the law, with 31.5 per cent against. In the *Parlament*, the PP voted against it because they considered that it went too far in establishing priority for Catalan over Spanish; *Esquerra Republicana de Catalunya* (Republican Left of Catalonia – ERC) voted against because they considered that it did not go far enough. The other parties, including the PSC, voted in favour as a result of the compromises that had been made, which included a watering-down of the provisions for sanctions against those who were found not to comply with the law. In essence, the new law incorporates the basic elements of the 1983 legislation and subsequent decrees on education, public administration and media, adding certain nuances to them to further strengthen the position of Catalan in these areas, while also including a section on the use of Catalan by public and private companies. Private companies are only covered by the law in areas relating to their interaction with the public. For example, utilities companies must provide bills in Catalan unless a customer asks for them in Spanish, and all companies must make arrangements to be able to deal with enquiries in Catalan if a customer approaches them in this language. In addition, any product which is marketed on the strength of its Catalan origins (e.g. speciality foods and wine) must be labelled in Catalan, alongside any other languages they wish to use. These very limited stipulations would have no effect on the main language of communication used internally by companies.

The weaknesses of the 1998 law are a direct reflection of the limitations faced by CiU in trying to construct a language policy that would go any further than the basic line of 'official bilingualism plus promotion of Catalan' that had been enshrined in the 1983 law. As we have already seen, many of these constraints are related to the way in which the Spanish constitution, and subsequently Catalonia's first statute of autonomy, were drafted. This is why CiU's outline for a new statute of autonomy, which was presented before the 2003 elections, contained substantial amendments to the 1979 document that would have removed many of the obstacles to a more radical linguistic policy. Their aim was that citizens would have a 'duty to know' both Catalan and Spanish, and ignorance of one of the languages would not constitute a reasonable excuse in law. This would mean that Catalan could then be used as the sole language in many contexts, whether oral or written, without having to be accompanied by Spanish, even though citizens would retain the right to be attended in the language of their choice in situations where the communication was individual to them. (This provision was indeed included in the new statute that was finally approved by referendum in 2006, although it had been steered through by the PSC and not CiU.) The other important element in the draft statute was a demand that the Spanish state recognize its own obligation towards Catalan. The draft included the requirement that the state should use Catalan in all documents pertaining to Catalan citizens (including passports), allow the use of Catalan when dealing with state institutions, include provisions regarding quotas for Catalan programming in the conditions for state-licensed media, and persuade the EU to adopt Catalan as one of its official languages. This emphasis on the role of Spain in promoting the use of Catalan raises important questions that will be addressed later in the chapter.

It could be argued that CiU should not have attempted to reopen the question of linguistic legislation in the 1990s since the gains have been small and the damage, in terms of revealing deep divisions on the question in political and intellectual circles, greater. However, public opinion on CiU's language policies was generally favourable and remained so after the controversial law was put in place. A survey conducted in 2000 showed that the public, when asked to give marks out of ten for different aspects of CiU's performance, rated its actions on language at 6.62 – the highest score of any area (Forcadell Lluís, 2001). Even the study which revealed that nearly one third of Catalans were against the 1998 law also showed that more than 70 per cent thought that language issues presented no problem for social cohesion (*La Vanguardia*, 1998). Another survey in 1999 showed that over half of Catalans had a positive opinion of CiU's linguistic policy in general, with only around 15 per cent having an actively negative opinion (Fernández, 1999). The same year, the *Departament de Cultura* found that half to three-quarters of Catalans thought that the presence of Catalan should be increased in certain specific areas such as product labelling (71.4 per cent), cinema (62.9 per cent) or in court (50.6 per cent) (*Avui*, 2000). In other words, the public was mainly in favour of the kind of positive discrimination towards Catalan that the *Generalitat* had attempted to put into practice and might possibly have supported more radical proposals than CiU were actually able to present. On the other hand, the statistics also suggest that the majority of the public were less exercised by the whole issue of language than the heated debates among politicians and intellectuals would suggest.

The results of the *Generalitat*'s attempts at linguistic normalization have been measured in countless surveys and censuses, although of course they cannot show what has been achieved as a direct result of CiU policy and what should be attributed to other individual or collective efforts. In broad terms, there has been a clear and positive evolution of the numbers of people able to understand, speak, read and write Catalan since normalization planning began. Figure 1 shows rough statistics which, although taken from different sources and therefore not entirely comparable, nevertheless show a clear improvement over the two decades they represent. However, a more detailed look at the late 1990s (Figure 2) using directly comparable figures reveals that progress had halted by this stage in the areas of understanding and speaking. The *Institut d'Estadística de Catalunya* (2003b: 2) attributes this to the phenomenon of immigration, which had a particular impact in this later period and meant that there were new residents who had not yet had enough time to pick up the language. On the other hand, progress continued to be made in the areas of reading and writing, largely because of the increase in the percentage of the population for whom Catalan has now been either a compulsory subject at school or a part of adult learning linked to professional requirements. There is no reason why these figures, along with the figure for speaking Catalan, should not continue to rise steadily as this percentage naturally increases. Logically, there should come a point in a few decades' time where all residents born and educated in Catalonia can understand, speak, read and write the language.

Figure 1. General evolution of competence in Catalan, 1981–2001

Catalans who . . .	1981	1991	2001
Understand Catalan	74%	89%	95%
Speak Catalan	53%	71%	75%
Write Catalan	15%	41%	50%

Statistics taken from Siguan, 1992: 161; *The Economist*, 1997: 55; Institut d'Estadística de Catalunya, 2003b: 2.

Figure 2. Detailed figures for the period 1996–2001

Catalans who . . .	1996	2001
Understand Catalan	94.96%	94.49%
Speak Catalan	75.3 %	74.5 %
Read Catalan	72.35%	74.35%
Write Catalan	45.84%	49.76%

Statistics taken from Institut d'Estadística de Catalunya, 2003b: 2.

However, the mid 1990s saw a different concern gather momentum: the suspicion that even though more people than ever before were competent in Catalan, its actual use had not risen in parallel. In other words, it seemed to be the case that even when people were able to speak to their neighbour or order a beer in Catalan, many were still choosing to use Spanish. This was related to a similar phenomenon which meant that even people who actually preferred to use Catalan were switching to Spanish in certain circumstances, especially when they made the judgement that the person they were speaking to was more likely to be a Spanish speaker (Woolard, 1989). So, for example, automatic assumptions are made about people who do not 'look' Catalan or who have certain jobs which have traditionally been taken by Spanish-speakers. It is often the case that Catalans will switch to Spanish even if they have begun a conversation in Catalan if the person they are speaking to seems not to have a perfect command of the language. Jordi Pujol used a speech he gave in 1995 to berate Catalans for these behaviours, and especially criticized the idea that it was more 'polite' to use Spanish in such circumstances, since this means that people who are trying to learn Catalan never get the opportunity to actually speak it (Pujol, 1995: 30, 37). In other words, by being 'polite' the Catalan-speaker is actually denying others the chance of full linguistic and cultural integration into the society in which they live.

A study of linguistic habits published by the *Institut d'Estadística de Catalunya* (2003b: 7), containing data from 2003, shows that slightly more residents of Catalonia consider Catalan to be their 'own language' (48.8 per cent) or 'habitual language' (50.1 per cent) than Spanish (for which the figures were 44.3 per cent and 44.1 per cent respectively). Only around 5 per cent described themselves as entirely bilingual. On the other hand, when asked which language they had first spoken at home, the majority (53.5 per cent) said Spanish. This clearly shows that linguistic policies are having an effect, even if it is not as great as some would hope or expect. However, the survey reveals worrying differences between different parts of Catalonia, with the Metropolitan Area of Barcelona having by far the largest percentage of both Spanish speakers and true bilinguals (*Institut d'Estadística de Catalunya*, 2003b: 9). Around two-thirds of the population is concentrated in this area, which makes it the key battleground for linguistic normalization. Although the report's analysis of the use of Catalan in various public and private domains reveals a finely balanced situation in which Catalan has a very slight edge, there is once again a disturbing geographical imbalance (*Institut d'Estadística de Catalunya*, 2003b: 10). Only around 20 per cent of those surveyed in Barcelona would use nothing but Catalan with their friends, neighbours or work-mates, whereas figures for other areas tend to be around 40–60 per cent (*Institut d'Estadística de Catalunya*, 2003b: 11). A ranked list for exclusive use of Catalan puts Barcelona bottom in every category – seventh out of the seven areas used in the study (*Institut d'Estadística de Catalunya*, 2003b: 12).

This general survey of use is complemented by a few questions about key cultural products, and here the answers are even more revealing. When asked about the language of the press they read and their default homepage on the internet, Catalan came out the clear loser in almost every one of the seven geographical areas (13, 14). In contrast, when asked about the radio stations they listened to, Catalan was the clear winner even in Barcelona. It is statistics like these that illustrate the complexity of the linguistic situation in Catalonia and the importance of cultural products in the normal-ization process. The relationship between cultural products and language planning can be reduced to three simple problems (with complex solutions!). First of all, the more closely the range of products in Catalan mirrors the range available in Spanish, the more useful the Catalan language will seem. This is especially the case when it comes to questions of status and legitimacy, since only languages which can be used for any purpose from rap to nuclear physics seem to have a claim for continued existence in the modern world. These questions aside, individuals also make choices about linguistic usefulness in even the simplest of everyday situations, and these can be based on very pragmatic criteria. Secondly, policies promoting the use of Catalan in education would never be effective unless they were backed up by examples of 'language in use', including textbooks and works of high culture that are direct objects of study, but also a general cultural context that reinforces learning through constant contact with the language in all its guises. Thirdly, there is the problem of availability: if there is no Catalan version or equivalent of the kind of book, DVD, newspaper or computer game the consumer wants to buy, they are unable to make a choice solely based on their linguistic preferences, and also less likely to develop a preference for Catalan in the long term because it becomes easier just to stick to Spanish. For example, availability is one of the keys to explaining the above statistics for choices regarding the language of the press, internet pages and radio, although it is not the only factor.

Saving Catalan

The issue of choice, then, is the nub of the problem as far as linguistic policy in Catalonia is concerned. The primary aim of language planning is to change the linguistic behaviour of individuals within a community. In a democratic society, this can only be achieved by persuading people that it is in their best interests to choose one language rather than another in any given situation. This persuasion might include some elements of 'stick' as well as 'carrot', but as we have seen it cannot be pushed so far as to infringe individual rights without risking a backlash. If forms of persuasion are necessarily limited, then public backing for the task is an important ally. In the Catalan case, one of the major worries has been that the initial enthusiasm for Catalan during the early years of autonomy seems to have died down. Like the members of the *Foro Babel*, many Catalans now feel that the situation is now, if not 'normal', then 'normal enough'. Certainly, some observers have seen this attitude in younger generations, in the sense that, as Kenneth McRoberts (2001: 150) puts it:

> young people, it seems, are simply indifferent to language. Clearly, this does not reflect a lack of solidarity with their linguistic group; in fact Catalan-speaking youth have a strong sense of Catalan identity and are more receptive to nationalist messages than their elders. But they seem unaware of what is at stake [. . .]

Perhaps, then, we are seeing a new form of Catalanism emerging among the younger generations in which language is no longer a primary focus of nationalist demands and actions.

Lluís-Anton Baulenas considers this prospect when he asks whether it is possible to imagine a future consisting of an independent Catalonia in which the majority language is actually Spanish (Baulenas, 2004: 144). His own feeling is that this could be possible, as could a future Catalonia that is happy to be an integral part of the Spanish state, but where the majority language is Catalan. He cites a survey conducted by M. Àngels Viladot among a group of students between the ages of sixteen and nineteen, in which 84.4 per cent of Catalan speakers and 83.3 per cent of Spanish speakers affirmed that to *be* Catalan it was enough to *feel* Catalan, regardless of place of birth, family history, or preferred language.[9] Baulenas draws the conclusion that this means that this age group attaches little importance to traditional forms of self-identification. Clearly, this could be related to the growing influence of cultural globalization and other trends in modern Western living such as increased personal mobility, a declining emphasis on origins and family ties, and the growing acceptance of cultural and ethnic pluralism and hybridity. Whatever the reasons behind it, if the majority of Catalans in future prefer to fight their battles on other grounds, with only a minority remaining convinced of the importance of language and a distinctive cultural identity, then the type of nationalist message transmitted by parties such as CiU will cease to have widespread appeal. But to what extent is CiU itself responsible for these trends?

Albert Pla, in an article in *Avui*, described linguistic normalization as 'a fiction we want to believe in' (Pla, 2003).[10] If this description is accurate, then much of the stimulus for believing it has come from the *Generalitat* as a direct result of its policies and promotional rhetoric. The institutionalization of Catalan has improved its status and visibility, but has also given it a false veneer of dominance in certain key areas. Now that Catalan is part of the school curriculum it is in danger of being regarded as just another academic subject to love or hate; furthermore, whatever the reality of its subordinate status vis-à-vis Spanish, Catalan is the language of authority in educational situations and local government, and the medium for promotional messages about Catalan identity emanating from the *Generalitat*. It might therefore be more attractive to some bilinguals to use Spanish, because this is perceived as the most communicatively useful language in everyday situations, or even because they see it as a form of resistance to the attempts of Catalan institutions to promote Catalan to the dominant position (Flaquer, 1996: 354–5). It could be argued that by putting the emphasis on institutional settings, the symbolic value attached to the language has been substantially altered, at least for those people who were born after about 1975. No longer the language of freedom, it is instead the language of bureaucracy, election campaigns, the gas bill and the university entrance exam.

This is not to say that the *Parlament* should not have insisted on this kind of institutionalization of Catalan – it would have been very odd if it had not done so. But critics of the way CiU went about it tend to coincide in seeing the normalization of Catalan as something that has only been half tackled and therefore half accomplished. This is not only because of the constraints that we have already identified. It seems that CiU were unable to complement the institutionalization of Catalan with something else that would balance the equation on the 'unofficial' side. Since language has both communicative and symbolic functions, this could potentially have been achieved in two ways: by ensuring that Catalan was the most useful language in every possible domain, and not just in certain settings; and/or by devising a more modern slant on its symbolic and affective connotations that would appeal to a broader range of people and convince them that their language matters. The importance of an affective attachment to Catalan will become evident when we start to look at how cultural products in Catalan have fared: even when citizens are well equipped to read the language and have a decent range of quality products to choose from, this is no guarantee that they will choose a book, newspaper or film in Catalan rather than Spanish. Since it would have been very difficult to extend the communicative function of the language without the support of the state, the symbolic function was the main area in which CiU could act outside institutional settings.

Pujol's own words on the importance of language for Catalan identity show that the symbolic function he attributes to it is the 'traditional' one:

So, the identity of Catalonia is mainly linguistic and cultural. [. . .] There are many components in our identity, a whole bunch of them, but language and culture are its backbone. This means that if the

language and culture were badly affected the personality of
Catalonia would be too. (Pujol, 1995: 6)[11]

We can compare this with the words of Enric Prat de la Riba ninety
years earlier: 'Anyone who attacks the language of a people attacks
its soul, and wounds the very sources of its life' (1993 [1906]: 48).[12]
The vocabulary may be different ('personality'/'soul'; 'backbone'/
'sources of its life') but the main message is the same. In choosing to
continue this kind of rhetoric about the nation, for example by
attributing a specific personality to 'Catalonia' rather than to 'the
Catalans', Pujol risked alienating younger citizens who might
instinctively reject the idea that the nation can be anthropomor-
phized, and who are less sentimental about matters of identity.
Despite this, some sense of group solidarity is clearly necessary if the
Catalan language is to overcome the communicative shortcomings
that are currently beyond its control.

Sociolinguist Albert Branchadell certainly blames CiU's rhetoric
and policies for this failure to convince some Catalans of the
importance of active loyalty to the Catalan language. In an essay
published in 1999, he criticizes CiU's dogmatic insistence on the
idea of the *llengua pròpia*, a term which he sees as too vague to be
useful, and on the relationship between language and Catalan
identity, which he sees as outdated and therefore in crisis
(Branchadell, 1999). He characterizes CiU's position on language
as 'nationalist' and compares it with that of the *Foro Babel* and
certain other groups, whose position is 'liberal' because they stress
the rights of the individual and expect governments to remain
neutral in matters of culture. This leads him to point out that the
two actually have something in common: 'their claim that linguistic
policy logically derives from a higher principle' (62).[13] In the case
of CiU, this higher principle is the nation, whereas in the case of
the *Foro Babel* it is a strict application of liberalism. In asking
Catalans to accept these a priori arguments, they are therefore
asking for adherence to a particular doctrine. For Branchadell,
there is a more practical and reasonable way of looking at linguistic
issues that does not require this: '*while it remains the wish of the
Catalans*, Catalan will be the predominant language in public life'
(63).[14] In other words, while Catalans continue to vote for parties
with strong language-planning agendas, and while surveys continue to show backing for their actions, this democratic endorse-
ment is all that is needed to justify the promotion of Catalan in

whatever form it appears. Group solidarity would then come from a purely civic form of collective consciousness, having completely removed the 'last vestiges of ethnic nationalism' (53)[15] that correspond to the stress on language and culture as the core values of the nation.

Branchadell's formulation still leaves the way open for elites to engage the public's support using particular ideological tools. It does not, therefore, remove the conflict between 'nationalists' and 'liberals', but does reduce its importance and, especially, provide a different way of conceptualizing the basic legitimacy of language planning. Civil society is asked to decide what it wants and then mandate its representatives to carry it out. As John MacInness (1999) points out, the very survival of Catalan during periods of repression such as the Franco regime indicates the strength of feeling and determination of ordinary Catalans regarding their language. MacInness goes on to suggest that, given the changing circumstances of nation states, cultures and societies in today's world, the survival of Catalan will once again be orchestrated by the general public and not by political institutions: 'it is civil society, rather than the state, that has hitherto been responsible for the strength of Catalan and will also determine its future' (MacInness, 1999: n.p.). However, the very nature of language planning means that it can only be directed and implemented by political and academic elites who will then control the terms in which the issues can be debated by the public. Even with a purely liberal-democratic legitimating framework, elites would still engage in 'strategies of symbolic manipulation' which would give them the power to 'establish meaning and a consensus about meaning' as far as the Catalan language is concerned (Bourdieu, 1991: 220, 221).

The Spanish State

Do the Spanish state and people also have a role to play in deciding the future of Catalan? As we have seen, it is possible to interpret the Spanish constitution as implying that by creating autonomous communities and giving them broad control over language, culture and education, the state has discharged its responsibilities towards 'the other Spanish languages'. This certainly seems to have been the attitude of Spanish governments up until 2004. (The backing of the socialist Zapatero government for some limited use of the other languages in the Senate, in private statewide television broadcasting, and in certain types of communication with the EU suggests at least a minor shift from this position after 2004. Up until this point, requests for such recognition in contexts pertaining to the Spanish state were normally met with flat refusals.) This meant that the *Generalitat* under CiU was acting largely in isolation in its language policies. It could not even count on the support of the autonomous governments of Valencia and the Balearic Islands, since their views and agendas were often radically different. The only real support for linguistic normalization from outside Catalonia came from Catalans living abroad or from academic institutions and international cultural organizations. It has often been said that it is easier to find Catalan being taught in a British, German or North American university than in a Spanish one.

This lack of interest from other Spaniards cannot solely be attributed to state government policy. Sympathy amongst Spanish left-wing intellectuals for the position of Catalonia during the 1970s, which derived from its treatment under the Franco regime, was sorely tested in the 1980s by the bitter political and legal struggles over the details of the framework for autonomy and the extent of Catalonia's new rights (Baulenas, 2004: 216–17, 220). This led to negative treatment of Catalonia even in the left-wing media, which was consolidated by high-profile moral panics about the immersion programme and the new Linguistic Policy Act in the 1990s. The expression of these attitudes in the media has clearly had an influence on the general public. In a survey published in *Avui* in 2001 that generally showed a fairly tolerant attitude from other Spaniards towards manifestations of Catalanism, language issues came out as one of the few negative points (Grau, 2001: 13). Ironically, whereas it seems that Catalans do not think language issues are a major source of social conflict, Spaniards not resident in Catalonia think they are. For 68 per cent of respondents, Catalan was a barrier to going to work in Catalonia and nearly 54 per cent said that the presence of the language made them feel like foreigners when they visited Catalonia (although it is not clear from the report whether this question was only asked of those who had actually visited Catalonia!). Two-thirds thought that Catalan should have a secondary place behind Spanish. Furthermore, nearly 60 per cent saw the use of Catalan primarily as a way for Catalans to differentiate themselves from other Spaniards.

In other words, it seems that many Spaniards have come to believe that Catalan is used as a deliberate way of accentuating the difference between Catalans and Spaniards and creating barriers between them, rather than simply because it is the language with which a given individual feels the most natural affinity. This could be partly a result of CiU's insistence on the *fet diferencial* ('the fact of being different') in their rhetoric on Catalan identity and the rights of the 'historic nations'. Since language is one of the main factors in Catalonia's difference, and Catalans obviously value that difference because their leaders keep going on about it, it is not hard for the average Spaniard to come to the conclusion that Catalans speak Catalan mainly to perpetuate difference. In fact, this idea has been explored in a British academic journal by Juan Lodares, who describes the promotion of the minority languages of Spain as a form of 'linguistic border control' (Lodares, 2005: 13).[16] His thesis is that language provides a mechanism to enforce a socio-cultural and economic buffer zone between the elites of the 'historic nations' and others who might reside or wish to reside in the areas they control. By offering social and professional opportunities only to those who speak the language of the elite, they create a grateful clientele that are happy to return the favour through their political support. In other words, 'The demand for linguistic protectionism actually reveals the formation of systems of social, political, employment or economic protectionism that are guaranteed by the particular language rather than the common language, and opinions or measures that put this in jeopardy would not prove popular'.[17]

This theory might seem attractive to an outsider for whom the use of Catalan is hard to understand, but it certainly falls into the kind of reductionism criticized by Josep R. Llobera (2004: 73; see introduction), in which 'the complexities of the nationalist discourse are completely lost, sacrificed to the gods of economic determinism'. Nevertheless, Lodares's opinion demonstrates the general difficulty of asking the Spanish government, and therefore other Spaniards, to back proposals for further state support for Catalan. If they cannot understand the reasons for the request except in terms of creating economic and social advantages for Catalan-speakers over Spanish-speakers, then they are unlikely to want to get involved in the promotion of Catalan. To solve this problem would require not only a more open-minded attitude from non-Catalans but a careful effort by the Catalan elites to foster a more sophisticated understanding of the reasons for their demands. This would probably involve toning down the rhetoric of 'difference' which seems to have done nothing to dispel the idea that Catalans might be out for what they can get at the expense of other Spaniards. One possibility might be to adopt Branchadell's 'democratic' model and suggest that it does not matter why the Catalans want their language to be protected and recognized but their democratic right to do so should be respected. The problem with this is that their democratic right as Catalans conflicts with the democratic right of all Spaniards because the territorial autonomy of Catalonia is subordinate to the rule of the state, and therefore its democratic rights in this context are those of a regional (and not even national) minority. Only Catalan independence or possibly the rearrangement of Spain into a federal state (along the lines of Belgium, for example) would reduce to a manageable level this conflict of interests which operates in many areas of Catalan life and not just in relation to language. This is one reason why Catalanist parties continue to push for a rethink of the constitutional make-up of the state.

This discussion of the context and development of Catalan linguistic policy has demonstrated numerous reasons why sticking to the belief that language and culture were the backbone of Catalan identity was the logical option for CiU. It was part of their ideological heritage, it corresponded with the feelings of most native Catalans, and it allowed the development of a strong nationalist rhetoric based around the *fet diferencial*. To separate language from culture – that is, to treat the Catalan language separately from the culture that could be produced using it – was unthinkable within this framework. However, also unthinkable, or at least unsayable, was the proposition that Catalan language and culture would entirely displace Spanish language and culture within Catalonia. CiU needed the votes of Spanish-speakers and largely operated on the basis of achieving social and political consensus when devising linguistic policy. Its hands were also tied by the weak legal position of Catalan established in the Spanish constitution and the original Catalan statute of autonomy, which in turn gave the *Generalitat* a legal obligation towards the Spanish language. This led CiU to opt for what Albert Branchadell (1996: 9, 105–21) calls 'weak normalization', the objective of which was that anyone who wanted to live entirely in Catalan should be able to do so. He comments that they were unable to commit in practice to 'strong normalization' – the expectation that everyone in Catalonia *will* eventually live entirely in Catalan – even though some of their rhetoric strayed in this direction.

The conflict between the doxa that language and culture were at the heart of Catalan identity and the limited room for manoeuvre imposed both by the state and the need for consensus led CiU to adopt an entrenched position on the link between language and culture which informed virtually all cultural policy decisions. On one hand, this link allowed the creation of a discourse that tapped into the symbolic and affective potential of language and culture in order to persuade Catalans to care about their national identity. On a more practical level, there is of course a necessary relationship between language planning and cultural policy in the sense that no gains can be made in the area of language acquisition and normalization if the language is not in widespread use across the cultural spectrum. However, by making linguistic concerns the key drivers of cultural policy, CiU effectively advocated a *strong* form of *cultural* normalization which was actually predicated on a *weak* form of *linguistic* normalization. The aim of supporting only those cultural forms that used Catalan was designed to back up a linguistic policy that actually had a reciprocal duty to back up cultural policy, but was unable to do so effectively. Many of the controversies over cultural policy during the years of CiU government were directly related to this mismatch between the two core policy elements that were in theory supposed to be in harmony with one another. The disparity between them allowed critics various points of attack, whichever group's rights they claimed to represent, and contributed to the mixed messages that were being sent to the public about the progress of the normalization campaign. In turn, these attacks then strengthened CiU's resolve to keep plugging the seemingly ineradicable link between language, culture and identity, taking the matter back to square one.

NOTES

[1] 1. El castellano es la llengua española oficial del Estado. Todos los españoles tienen el deber de conocerla y el derecho a usarla. 2. Las demás lenguas españolas serán también oficiales en las respectivas Comunidades Autónomas de acuerdo con sus Estatutos. 3. La riqueza de las distintas modalidades lingüísticas de España es un patrimonio cultural que será objeto de especial respeto y protección.

[2] 1. La llengua pròpia de Catalunya és el català. 2. L'idioma català és l'oficial de Catalunya, així com també ho és el castellà, oficial a tot l'Estat espanyol. 3. La Generalitat garantirà l'ús normal i oficial d'ambdós idiomes, prendrà les mesures necessàries per tal d'assegurar llur coneixement i crearà les condicions que permetin d'arribar a llur igualtat plena quant als drets i deures dels ciutadans de Catalunya. 4. La parla aranesa serà objecte d'ensenyament i d'especial respecte i protecció.

[3] 'cal advertir de la fal·làcia de la llibertat total quan coexisteixen dues llengües, una més forta, l'altra més feble.'

[4] 'El català, com a llengua pròpia de Catalunya, ho és també de la Generalitat i de l'Administració territorial catalana, de l'Administració local i de les altres corporacions públiques dependents de la Generalitat.'

[5] 'un dels millors exemples de patriotisme i de sentit de responsabilitat que s'han donat des de fa anys a Catalunya'.

[6] Decret 75/1992, de 9 de març.

[7] Ley Orgánica 10/2002, de 23 de diciembre, de Calidad de la Educación.

[8] 'como corresponde a un país socialmente bilingüe'.

[9] The survey is from Viladot (1993) *Identitat i vitalitat lingüística dels catalans*, Barcelona: Columna.

[10] 'una ficció que ens volem creure'

[11] 'Doncs bé, la identitat de Catalunya és en gran part lingüística i cultural. [. . .] Hi ha molts components en la nostra identitat, n'hi ha una pila, però la llengua i la cultura en són l'espina dorsal. Per tant, si la llengua i la cultura fossin greument afectades la personalitat de Catalunya ho seria també'.

[12] 'Qui atenta a la llengua d'un poble, atenta a la seva ànima i la fereix en les fonts mateixes de sa vida.'

[13] 'la seva pretensió que la política lingüística es deriva lògicament d'un principi superior'.

[14] '*mentre els catalans ho vulguin així*, el català serà la llengua predominant de la vida pública'.

[15] 'els últims vestigis de nacionalisme ètnic'

[16] 'aduana lingüística'

[17] 'La exigencia de proteccionismo lingüístico revela, en realidad, la formación de sistemas de proteccionismo social, político, laboral o económico garantizados por la lengua particular antes que por la común y no resultarían populares opiniones o medidas que lesionaran esa circunstancia'.

Chapter Three

High Culture

As we have seen, it is the opportunities for the use, rather than the acquisition, of the Catalan language that have been the more difficult aspects to address. It is for this reason that the boundaries between language planning and cultural policy have been broken down, and any form of culture that requires the use of language has become an element in the strategy for the normalization of Catalan. However, there are risks involved in allowing this to happen. Firstly, there is the danger that cultural policy becomes so focused on the task of linguistic normalization that its other potential functions are ignored. This might mean putting to one side issues such as equality of access to culture, the stimulation of creativity in whatever form this appears, or the promotion of the cultural industries as part of an economic development strategy. Secondly, in any multilingual community, a policy that only recognizes culture produced in one language risks alienating those whose natural preference is for culture in another language. Thirdly, and in consequence, it is possible that culture produced in the chosen language becomes firmly associated with 'the establishment' (in whatever sense – educational, political etc.), inviting the development of alternative cultures that use different languages or non-standard varieties, and the association of particular socio-cultural groups with these alternatives – not for linguistic reasons, but because they reject the political messages of the institutions themselves.

A further complication relates to the way in which governments select the aspects of culture they wish to prioritize. Whether the criteria relate to social inclusion, profitability, 'taste', national identity, or international renown (etc.), decisions inevitably have to be taken about how limited resources can best be allocated. In the case of CiU, its policies initially showed a clear preference for forms of high culture, which can be traced to the general development of Catalanism since the nineteenth century but is also a specific part of their ideological heritage as a party. The rebirth (*Renaixença*) of interest in Catalonia's identity in the mid nineteenth century was firmly centred around the educated middle classes and their high-cultural tastes. Political Catalanism then flourished in the early twentieth century at the same time as important Catalan achievements in the arts – for which Antoni Gaudí's name has come to stand as shorthand – and significant movements such as *Modernisme* and *Noucentisme*. During the Franco dictatorship, when political Catalanism was forced underground, the arts continued to perform a rearguard, or perhaps 'guerrilla', function that was crucial to the continuation of a sense of Catalan identity among the social groups from which there would emerge the political leaders of the 1970s. Jordi Casassas and Josep Termes sum up the effect of this legacy when they note:

> the constant return to intellectuals, artists, etc., that every great declaration of Catalanism uses as a formula for self-ennoblement, linking its need to adapt to the ever-changing present with an inheritance from the past, an inheritance that compels it to keep up a Catalanizing cultural action and not just political interventionism. (Casassas and Termes, 1997: 72–3)[1]

By highlighting Catalanism's need to adapt, this comment also points to the problem that the late twentieth century was a very different cultural environment from the one in which Catalan culture had flourished decades before. Literature, art and intellectual life were easy totems to hold up when there was little else; even cinema, radio and the advent of television did not have much bearing on this since there was no opportunity for programming in Catalan. In the 1980s and 90s, however, television, video games, the internet, pop music, cinema and the press were all clamouring for attention, not just from the Catalan public but from the policymakers. Not only could these now be used as 'normalizing' tools by the language planners, which would make them legitimate candidates for financial backing, they were also attracting a mass audience in a way that literature and the arts simply were not. Catalonia was experiencing the same phenomenon that was affecting the rest of Europe, since as Tim Edensor puts it, 'forms of cultural authority have multiplied and fragmented, and can no longer masquerade as being of national importance' (Edensor, 2002: 16). Nevertheless:

> National elites, governments and patricians continue to perpetuate the idea that 'high' culture is something that the nation must be associated with, as a form of international prestige. The national badges of high culture – national galleries, opera houses and international concert halls, national theatres, learned societies and high cultural institutions – remain marks of status. (Edensor, 2002: 15)

This means that the Catalan autonomous government is not alone in continuing to pay attention to high culture, even if it has particular reasons for doing so that go deeper than concerns about 'international prestige', or even Barcelona's rivalry with Madrid.

It is not possible to cover here all the different aspects of CiU's policy on high culture. Instead, this chapter will focus on literature and the theatre. Literature was the *sine qua non* of Catalan culture from the *Renaixença* to the Transition and still plays a very important part in the rhetoric surrounding Catalan identity, but the reality of life for contemporary authors, critics and publishers is less rosy than might be expected, partly because of the limitations on the Catalan literary field. On the other hand, theatre, which in many ways used to be lumped in with literature in terms of the cultural canon, has become sharply differentiated from it in the last quarter century, enjoying a national and international visibility that neither narrative nor, certainly, poetry have been able to emulate thus far. The performance and 'industrial' elements of theatre have made it more suited to the current climate, and it also gives scope for creating 'badges of high culture' such as the *Teatre Nacional* which had its official opening in 1997. Nevertheless, in both cases there have been criticisms from practitioners that the cultural policy of the *Generalitat* under Pujol put institutionalization above creativity and symbolic value above quality.

Literature and Identity

The association of literature with Catalan identity is a very deep one. In part, of course, it comes from the clear relationship between language and identity, so that writing in Catalan is, like the use of the language in any other context, an expression of identity/ difference and a marker of cultural continuity. However, there are other aspects specific to literature that have traditionally given it a privileged position above other cultural forms.

One of the keys to understanding the importance of literature is the process by which interest in Catalan culture and identity was revived in the mid nineteenth century. *La Renaixença*, as it came to be known, was a period in which the educated middle classes of Catalonia began to take an interest in the language and history of the region after a long interlude in which Catalan had been denied any prestige or institutional support. There were two major influences in this revival: romanticism, which invited an interest in history and local 'colour', and therefore in the distinctive culture and character of Catalonia; and the vigorous economic development of the region, which encouraged the Catalan bourgeoisie to distance themselves from the political and economic chaos of the rest of Spain. These led certain sectors of Catalan society to believe that the Catalan language was more than a low-status vernacular and to start to explore its possibilities as a vehicle for high culture. The main expression of this revival was in poetry, with the symbolic date of the start of the *Renaixença* (chosen with hindsight, of course) being the publication of Bonaventura Carles Aribau's poem '[Oda a] la Pàtria' ([Ode to] the Fatherland) in 1833. The writing, reading and sharing of poetry in Catalan became a fashionable pursuit in middle-class houses, although, as Joan-Lluís Marfany reveals, it was an activity undertaken with more enthusiasm than talent (Marfany, 1995: 276). Despite this, the production of poetry, then narrative and theatre, became an integral part of the revival of Catalan identity in the nineteenth century and eventually gave rise to writers who could compete with the best that Spain, or even Europe, had to offer. The key point here, then, is that the revival of interest in Catalan identity in modern times began as a form of cultural regionalism which had literature at its core.

This cultural regionalism transformed itself in some circles into cultural and then political nationalism, producing different nuances and groupings as it went. By the early twentieth century, when political Catalanism was making its mark within both the region and the state, Catalan culture was also flourishing and had taken a significantly different direction to the rest of Spain. A wide range of literary, artistic and popular cultural forms were on offer and had more than respectable numbers of takers. However, the civil war and its consequences cut short this time of creativity and individuality: henceforth, Franco decreed, there would only be one unified Spanish culture expressed in the Spanish language. This is where the second major element of the relationship between literature and identity came into play, because literature became one of the few tools with which Catalans could fight Spanish cultural hegemony. Even this was difficult at first, since censorship prevented the free circulation of books in Catalan, but at least in private writers could continue to write and trusted friends could continue to share books and opinions, and some writers managed to get their work published overseas. When publishing in Catalan began to re-emerge in the 1960s, this private world could once again become public. However, during this hiatus Catalan literature had, as previously, become the domain of a few enthusiasts, since circumstances had forced a retreat back into the more rarefied forms of high culture that had also been the mainstay of Catalanism in the nineteenth century. Crucially, the majority of these writers saw themselves as shouldering the full responsibility of preserving the Catalan language and, therefore, a distinctive Catalan identity.

The result of this was both positive and negative. On one hand, the Catalan language did survive as a high-status written language, and some of the best works of Catalan literature were produced at this time despite the adverse circumstances of the Franco dictatorship. On the other hand, the retreat into literary and linguistic perfectionism meant that a void developed in the layers of written culture that should have been occupied by popular or more experimental forms. For this reason, the new generation of writers who emerged in the 1970s found little in the work of their immediate predecessors that inspired them; theirs was a different reality in which the memory of Catalonia's pre-war glories played little part. Instead, they had grown up with television, overt political protest and increasing access to the world outside Spain. They were more willing to be experimental, even playful and disrespectful, in their writing, because unlike those before them they had not been charged with saving a culture from extinction. Even so, there was still no mass audience for their work.

By the time the autonomous government was active and the tools of cultural policy could be employed to help literature recover a more favourable position, circumstances were very different from any that had surrounded Catalan literature before. The main changes that affected writers in the 1980s and 90s were to do with the conditions of the publishing industry rather than more aesthetic or even nationalistic concerns (Berrio, 1998: 960). Literature is now a cultural commodity to be bought and sold. Small publishers that had been instrumental in keeping the production of Catalan literature going during the dictatorship have been forced to close or merge as the result of competition from big multimedia groups. The market for literature has shrunk because of a general decrease in interest in reading, which is partly attributable to the success of audio-visual media; authors have increasingly found it necessary to be part of these media themselves, maybe to promote their work or to supplement their income by such activities as scriptwriting. Most importantly, Catalan literature is trying to compete with Spanish literature on the same market-based terms, and this can never be a fair fight. It was therefore felt necessary that some form of protection should be offered to Catalan writing through the cultural policy of the *Generalitat*, and it is important to note that this was not just because of the link between the promotion of the Catalan language and the need for a healthy range of publications that use that language. The ideological track of CiU's centre-right Catalanism runs from those poetry enthusiasts of the *Renaixença*, through to the literary resistance of the Franco era, and on to the continuing belief that the achievements of Catalan literature signify something fundamental about Catalan identity.

Policy and Institutional Support

Despite – or possibly because of – this certainty about the importance of literature to Catalan identity, one of the most difficult questions that writers, critics and policymakers have had to grapple with over the last few decades is apparently the most basic: what counts as Catalan literature? There are two main dimensions to this debate. Firstly, there is the influence of the cultural rupture between the different autonomous communities where Catalan is spoken, which means that some people take the term Catalan literature to refer only to that produced by writers from the autonomous community of Catalonia, preferring to see writers who live in other areas as producing Valencian literature, Majorcan literature, and so on. Other people would regard literature written in any variety of Catalan to be Catalan literature. Secondly, there is the ambiguous position of writers who live in Catalonia but who choose to write exclusively or mainly in Spanish. In this case, they are normally referred to as Catalan writers within the Spanish literary world but as Spanish writers within the Catalan literary world. It is not my intention to examine these debates in detail here, as I have done so elsewhere, as have others (Crameri, 2005; King, 2005a; King, 2005b). However, some elements of the issue are particularly relevant to the cultural policy decisions of the Pujol era because the definition of Catalan literature employed by the *Generalitat* and its associated institutions was crucial in deciding how to support this element of Catalan culture.

On the question of the language used by writers, the *Generalitat*'s position was perfectly clear, and consistent with the history of the relationship between language, literature and identity outlined above: Catalan literature was literature written in Catalan. This meant that virtually all institutional support was directed at the production, publication and promotion of books in Catalan. This position seems entirely logical, since there was a necessary link between a successful linguistic policy and the need for reading material of all kinds to be available to the general public. Spanish publications were readily available and therefore required no special treatment. On this cultural–linguistic basis, then, the *Generalitat*'s approach was understandable. However, when we add a sociopolitical dimension to the issue, matters become much more complicated. As democratically elected representatives of the residents of a particular territory, it can be argued that the *Generalitat* has a responsibility to recognize the cultural plurality within Catalan society and to support cultural contributions produced in both the official languages of the autonomous community. As Terenci Moix (1998) said, 'language is irrelevant when it comes to paying taxes. [. . .] Spanish-speakers pay the salaries of *Generalitat* employees too'.[2] The counter-argument to Moix's point is that Spanish-language writers have support from the more powerful institutions of the Spanish state, including international promotion through the *Instituto Cervantes*, which during the period of CiU's government only showed a token interest in the elements of Spain's literary production that were not written in Spanish. For this reason, the argument goes, it was fair that the more limited money and influence of the *Generalitat* should have been directed entirely to the promotion of literature in Catalan. While this might be pragmatic, it does appear to suggest that writers like Juan Marsé or Eduardo Mendoza have been working in some kind of parallel universe, and that their presence on Catalan soil and their interaction with Catalan writers on various levels (personal, social, professional) does not imply any kind of reciprocal cultural influence, which of course is not the case. These writers are a part of Catalan culture, in the broadest sense of the term.

Although concerns for the viability of Catalan literature without some form of institutional protection are well founded, there might also be deeper reasons for attempts to keep such writers out of the Catalan compound. As will be demonstrated later, the reception of translated works from Catalan in the rest of Spain is much less enthusiastic than might be expected. This means that the majority of Spaniards form their impressions of Catalonia from those authors who write in Spanish. In the introduction to a volume entitled *Peripheral Visions,* Ian Bell gives the example of northern English writers in the 1950s and 60s who were:

> unwittingly absorbed into the greater national consciousness, becoming a tokenist presence rather than a fully realized identity. The prevailing image of nationhood, paradoxically, was consolidated by the incorporation of these alternative voices, which then became the authorized way of imagining 'the North', impeding any attempts to write of the experience differently. (Bell, 1995: 3)

This could help to explain why there is Catalan resistance to Spanish-language writers in Catalonia: they are seen to collude with this kind of creation of an 'authorized' way for Spaniards to imagine Catalonia. This is especially the case for works which make no mention of the Catalan language and therefore seem to suggest that Spanish is the normal language of all Catalans. Salvador Cardús certainly seems to be worrying about these effects when he says that to accept the idea that it is possible to produce Catalan culture in Spanish is to buy into a regionalist vision of Catalonia's position within Spain 'in which the region contributes elements that belong to the single national culture of the state' (Cardús, 1992: 426).[3]

There therefore exist two polarized stances as to whether Catalan writers who use Spanish should be supported by the *Departament de Cultura.* The crux of the issue is that while the term 'Catalan literature' can very reasonably be declared to apply only to literature written in Catalan, the phrase 'Catalan writer' cannot unambiguously denote someone who writes in Catalan, since this depends on whether you take it to mean 'a writer who uses Catalan' or 'a Catalan who writes'. While CiU opted to ignore anything that was not 'literature in Catalan', the left-wing government that followed them opted for the more 'social' definition of the Catalan writer and immediately broadened the remit of their cultural policy while still trying to protect literature in Catalan from the ravages of the market. This is in many ways a more ambitious project than CiU's because it attempts to acknowledge and deal with complexities that CiU preferred to ignore, as if they hoped the problem would go away. On the other hand, to say, as the PSC did in their *Llibre blanc de la cultura a Catalunya*, that 'all literature written by authors born or permanently resident in Catalonia is Catalan literature' (Mascarell, 1999: 195)[4] is to muddy the waters too much. It is probably more helpful to work from the basis that both Catalan literature (i.e. literature in Catalan) and literature written in Spanish by Catalans are part of Catalan *culture*. Whatever one's stance on this issue, it is clear that the matter of language is the crux of the struggles in the Catalan literary field, in which, as in any literary field, 'what is at stake is the power to impose the dominant definition of the writer and therefore to delimit the population of those entitled to take part in the struggle to define the writer' (Bourdieu, 1993: 42).

Having decided to support actively only the production of literature in Catalan, there were two basic aspects to the Pujol-era *Generalitat*'s policy: support for the publication of books in Catalan, and for the promotion of Catalan books and authors once published. As far as aids to publishers were concerned, the main mechanism was what was called 'generic support' (*el suport genèric*). This involved a commitment by the *Generalitat* to buy between 150 and 300 copies of eligible books which it would then donate to libraries, thereby guaranteeing a minimum sales level that would take away some of the risk associated with covering production costs. (This also fed into general policy on the improvement of Catalonia's libraries, and the promotion of Catalan culture through foreign universities.) The eligibility criteria included, of course, the stipulation that the book be written in Catalan, but also that the print run not exceed a certain number of copies and that the cover price not be too high. Clearly, this was meant to ensure that books that were commercially viable on their own would not receive unnecessary subsidy. However, the author Quim Monzó was of the opinion that in practice this meant that the only books receiving support were those that under normal circumstances would not have been considered worth publishing (Monzó, 1998: 160–2)! In other words, he felt that the availability of subsidies interfered with 'quality control' aspects of the market rather than just redressing the balance on purely financial grounds. The counter-argument to this was that in order for Catalan culture to function 'normally' it must give rise to the same wide variety of publications that would be available in any other language, and it would not be viable to produce these if they had to rely on the market alone. If this meant letting through a few poor-quality items, it was felt to be a price worth paying.

Another strategy of the *Generalitat* was to commission and publish texts itself through the *Entitat Autònoma del Diari Oficial i de Publicacions de la Generalitat de Catalunya* (EADOP). These cover a wide range of subjects from popular culture, literature and education to tourism, agriculture and transport. The 2004 catalogue listed nearly 4,500 titles in print, which could be bought, among other outlets, at the *Generalitat*'s own book shops in Barcelona, Lleida, Girona and Madrid. Many of the books I have used while researching this study were published by the *Generalitat*, since the primary purpose of its publications is to provide information about Catalan life and culture that would not be available if the matter was left to commercial companies. The different departments commission books in areas they feel should be covered, and the *Departament de Cultura* is of course one of the key instigators of publications, as is the *Departament de la Presidència*. Some of these aim to teach residents or foreigners about basic aspects of Catalan history, culture and identity. One example of this would be the publication *Conèixer Catalunya* by Josep M. Puigjaner, which is also available in French, Spanish, German and English (*Getting to Know Catalonia*). This general introduction to Catalonia's symbols, geography, history, language, culture, institutions, economy, society, education etc. has a foreword by Jordi Pujol, who describes the three main objectives of the book: to affirm that Catalunya is a nation, to show that Catalonia has a lot to offer the world (e.g. through its economic strengths), and to tell the world how Catalunya came to be where it is and where it is going (Puigjaner, 2000: 11). In other words, these kinds of publications serve as a means of transmission not only of knowledge about Catalonia but also of the particular Catalanist message of the party in power in the *Generalitat* itself.

It is certainly the case that the *Generalitat* has supported book publication in Catalan in a wide range of genres, including educational texts. However, the association of Catalan identity with particular forms of high culture has been reflected in the decision to pay particular attention to literary creation, which is supported through an entity called the *Institució de les Lletres Catalanes* (ILC). This was first created in the 1930s (during the civil war, amazingly enough), and was resurrected in 1987 as a body under the umbrella of the *Departament de Cultura*. Its main jobs are to distribute subsidies, to organize promotional activities, and to make available data about publications and information about authors. One of its key aims has been to encourage Catalans to read in Catalan, and to this end it has concentrated a lot of its efforts on schemes involving visits by authors to schools and community groups throughout Catalonia. It has also been involved in activities to promote Catalan literature abroad, for example by attending book fairs, although it now shares this task with the *Institut Ramon Llull* (IRL) since its creation in 2002.

Another area in which the ILC and the IRL shared responsibility after 2002 was in encouraging and subsidizing translations of literary works into Catalan (ILC) and out of Catalan (IRL). Translation into Catalan has always been important for Catalan writers, for a number of reasons (Crameri, 2000). Since the *Renaixença*, many authors have translated as well as writing their own original works in order to give their fellow writers access to the best of foreign literature, to bring foreign works to a general Catalan-speaking readership, to make some extra money, or simply out of a love for the texts they chose to translate. When publishing in Catalan started to recover in the 1960s and 70s, a number of translations were produced even though, once again, these were most often undertaken by writers rather than by trained translators, some of whom were not particularly proficient in the language from which they were translating. This situation changed in the 1980s and 90s when universities – particularly the Universitat Autònoma de Barcelona – started to produce adequate numbers of professional translators, and publishing in Catalan became an industry rather than a form of struggle against the Spanish system. However, this professionalization has brought other problems. Translators complain that their pay is lower than that received by their colleagues in other European countries and that their work therefore appears to be undervalued. There is also a concern that the publication of translations is contributing to the constant flooding of the market with new titles, making it difficult for individual works (either originals or translations) to make their mark and build up their sales to a respectable level. This is particularly apparent around the time of the St George's Day book fair, which will be examined in detail later. One bookseller was of the firm opinion that 'today's translations into Catalan, because of overproduction, are not of such good quality, and home-grown authors are finding themselves occupying less and less space on the stands for new titles' (Deltell, 2002: 32).[5] Despite this, it is the official policy of the *Generalitat* to encourage translations so that Catalan readers can choose to read Proust, Graham Greene or J. K. Rowling in Catalan rather than having to resort to the Spanish version.

As far as translations out of Catalan are concerned, it is necessary to look separately at the question of translations into Spanish before considering other languages. Although few Spanish texts are translated into Catalan, Catalan publishers do make every effort to ensure that Catalan texts reach a Spanish-speaking audience, thus hugely increasing the market for the authors' work. Or at least, this would be the theory. In practice, Catalan writers complain of an almost pathological rejection by Spanish speakers. A text that is visibly identifiable as a translation from Catalan will not attract Spanish buyers in the numbers one might expect. Quim Monzó (1998: 49) complained of people at a book fair in Madrid rejecting his books with a grimace of disgust when they realized he was Catalan; Matthew Tree (2002: 5) calculates that Monzó should by rights sell twenty times more copies of his work in Spanish than he actually does; and Baltasar Porcel traces the beginning of the problem to the mid 80s when there was a generalized reaction against Pujol and against Catalonia's attempts at linguistic normalization (Ayén, 2001). Nevertheless, efforts to interest a Spanish-speaking audience have become more urgent and sophisticated over the years, with some authors producing a Spanish version themselves, and publishers trying to gain as much of a marketing advantage as possible by publishing Spanish and Catalan editions of some texts simultaneously.

If translation into Spanish is not without its perils, then translation into other languages is even more complex because the Catalan publisher has much less influence in the process. This is why the institutions of the *Generalitat* have tried to encourage foreign publishers to buy the rights to Catalan works, either through subsidies or promotional activities such as attending international book fairs. The problem is that however much Catalans might want to be translated, they can only achieve this if a foreign publisher sees the text as saleable. As Gideon Toury says, 'translations are facts of target cultures; on occasion facts of a special status, sometimes even constituting identifiable (sub)systems of their own, but of the target culture in any event' (Toury, 1995: 29). In other words, publishers within the target culture must convince themselves to commission a translation through their own commercial and cultural logic; the source culture's arguments for getting a text translated are not relevant. However, it is clearly the case that passing information to foreign publishers about Catalan writing will keep it in their minds as a possible source when it comes to looking for translatable texts. The offer of a subsidy might also sway a publisher who is in two minds as to whether to take a risk on a text, although the system requires that the publisher take the decision to translate and then make an application for a grant, which is assessed in competition with other applications. In 2003, the IRL gave money towards the translation of seventy-two titles into a total of seventeen languages, including Hebrew, Hungarian and Icelandic. In terms of what might be considered more prestigious languages, French and Italian publishers seem more receptive to Catalan texts than British or American editors, no doubt partly because of the general lack of interest in translations shown by English-speaking audiences. It should also be noted that Catalan texts that have already been translated into Spanish have the advantage of greater visibility to foreign publishers looking for viable translations.

In general, the aim of the support provided by the *Generalitat* and its associated institutions was to counteract the effect of the distortions introduced into the Catalan publishing industry by its subordinate position within the Spanish market. Without a protectionist policy, it would be difficult to encourage Catalans to see choosing texts in Catalan as the normal option, especially if the particular European classic or American best-seller they wanted was not available. Equally, Catalan authors would find it difficult to have any influence on European literary trends or any recognition outside their own limited circle. However, many writers felt that the *Generalitat* had in fact only paid lip service to these aims. In the late

1990s and early 2000s, the amount allocated to support for literature through the *Departament de Cultura*, including the ILC and *el
suport genèric*, amounted to only around 3.5 per cent of its total
budget (ICIC, 2002: 99). Other areas such as theatre, cinema and
music were prioritized over support for literature. The main reason
for this seems to have been that literature was perceived as needing
less support than other cultural forms. In a way, this was a recognition of the quality of writers such as Quim Monzó, Jesús Moncada,
Carme Riera and Baltasar Porcel, whose works were able to tri-
umph on their own merits. Why should the *Generalitat* put money
into supporting Catalan literature when it was quite able to create a
good reputation without their help? However, many authors felt
that the real reason for the lack of substantial investment was that
Pujol and those around him had no interest in culture except in so
far as it symbolized Catalan identity and the *fet diferencial* (Bru de
Sala, 1999: 146). This meant that as long as plenty of books in
Catalan ended up on the shelves, there was little interest in providing further backing.

The Book and the Rose

One of Catalonia's best-loved traditions is intimately connected with
literature and was seized on by the *Generalitat* as a way of promoting
the identity and culture of Catalonia. St George is the patron saint of
Catalonia and so 23 April has been a special date in the Catalan
calendar since the Middle Ages, although it is not now a public
holiday (Soler i Amigó, 2000). In the 1920s, an initiative to link
23 April with the promotion of literature – since the date is also the
anniversary of the deaths of Cervantes and Shakespeare – failed to
prosper in the rest of Spain but took hold in Catalonia where the
date already had traditional significance. As a result, it is customary
to give books on the day, as well as the roses whose symbolism of love
is derived from the original legend of Saint George, and book fairs
are held all over Catalonia. In 1995, the tradition was given another
new twist when the *Generalitat* and Catalan publishers persuaded
UNESCO to declare the date 'World Book and Copyright Day'.

This success provided a raft of marketing opportunities for the
Generalitat, the most international of which was a series of advertise-
ments in foreign newspapers explaining the origins of World Book
Day. In Britain, *The Times* was chosen for these full-page adverts,

and one appeared there each year on or near 23 April from 1996 to 2003. These were sometimes part of a colour supplement on Catalonia or on World Book Day, although the latter had to cease when the British unsportingly decided to move the date of their book day celebrations to fit in better with the school term. The text of the first advert, used in 1996 and 1997, explains the tradition and illustrates the kind of message the *Generalitat* hoped to project. The main image is a drawing of William Shakespeare, underneath which is the strapline 'Today he is Catalan'. As well as describing the roots of the custom and its transformation into World Book Day, the text explains the location and characteristics of Catalonia, drawing on both cultural and economic strengths to interest the British public in the idea of Catalonia as a distinct entity.

> As of this year one of the most deep-rooted Catalan traditions is spreading throughout the world. Today, April 23rd, St George's Day, has been declared by UNESCO, as World Book and Copyright Day. Consequently, we dare to say that even today Shakespeare would feel Catalan. [. . .] For many years, Catalonia has celebrated St. George, our patron saint, as Book and Rose Day. And on this day we all give, to the most dear, a book and a rose [. . .] Catalonia is a country, with 6 million inhabitants, having its proper language, culture and personality within Spain. A progressive Mediterranean country, with a strong economic development, made up of people with initiative and mentality for the future. (*The Times*, 23 April 1996, 24.)

Unfortunately, the message is rather undone by the poor English that is characteristic of the *Generalitat*'s translated attempts at international projection at this time.

Although the 'Today he is Catalan' advert is probably the best known of the series, and won an international advertising prize, it is the text accompanying the image used in the 2001 advert that best expresses the ideology behind the promotion of Catalonia through literature:

> Books. Books and roses. These are the gifts that we, the Catalans, exchange to celebrate our most important festival, Saint Georges [sic] Day, the Patron Saint of Catalonia. In 1995 UNESCO declared the same date, 23 April, *World Book Day*. In Catalonia the book has been the main protagonist of our festival for the last 75 years, and we have been exchanging roses on the same date since the Middle Ages. We are proud of this tradition for it is a sign of sensitivity and cultural interest and above all, because we believe that what distinguishes a

modern, truly civilised nation is unquestionably its love of books.
(*The Times*, 23 April 2001: Catalonia supplement, 14)

This last sentence, although an elegant piece of rhetoric, seems to be begging to be deconstructed. While the terms 'modern' and 'civilized' may be words which are expected to elicit a positive reaction from an audience conditioned to accept these attributes as obviously good things, in this context they also raise questions. Does 'modern' here mean 'of the 21st Century', or given the place of literature in our current cultural climate does it actually suggest 'belonging to the period of modernity as opposed to that of postmodernity'? Is the degree of civilization of a nation only demonstrated by a love of literature if civilization itself is supposed to hang on liberal humanist principles of personal and national improvement through high culture? Would a contemporary Western observer, when asked to define a civilized nation, not talk of democracy, justice, high standards of living and good international relations before worrying about the inhabitants' reading habits? In fact, books are highlighted here precisely because they provide one of the few ways that CiU could claim a distinctive form of civilization for Catalonia, rather than because of any universal definition of the term.

A further question raised by the text is the extent to which Catalans really do love books. The *Sant Jordi* celebrations are unquestionably focused on the book, with the streets of the major cities filled with stalls and buzzing with buyers. However, there are two serious challenges to claims about the significance of the *Dia de Sant Jordi*. Catalans are not in fact avid readers when compared with other Europeans. A survey in 2003 showed that fewer Spaniards read for pleasure than the European average (39.4 per cent as opposed to 44.8 per cent), with fewer than half of Spaniards having read a book of any kind in the last twelve months.[6] (Comparisons show that in recent years Catalans have either been slightly above or below the average figures for reading in Spain as a whole, which means that it is fairly safe to generalize on the basis of statewide data.)[7] This general lack of interest in reading has led Adolf Tobeña to comment that a particular trait of Catalans is to 'buy books on just one day of the year and never actually read them' (Tobeña, 1998: 84).[8] A second problem is that the '*Sant Jordi* effect' artificially alters the market for books in Catalan since publishers rush to produce new titles to sell on the day. This leads to an overabundance of new books on the stalls and in the shops which makes it very difficult for individual authors to make their mark, or for buyers to make informed choices about which books to buy. The press is also implicated in this confusion since they publish large St George's Day supplements which can nevertheless high-light only a limited number of the new titles. As a result, authors and publishers who have not been successful at getting their products noticed find that instead of being able to create a steady build-up of interest, unsold copies are quickly returned to the warehouse or confined to the bargain bin. It could therefore be argued that a national love of reading is actually an insignificant element in the sale of books on St George's Day.

Critics and Plaudits

The problems revealed by the St George's Day 'experience' raise the question of the role of critics and scholars in helping the public to acquire an interest in Catalan writers. While this is not an area in which the cultural policy of the *Generalitat*, or any other elected body, has much direct influence, it is an important part of the context in which literature operates within Catalan culture and therefore worth looking at. Issues to do with criticism are also linked to the question of literary prizes, which do have an institutional dimension.

Although recent years have seen indications of change, in general it is true to say that academics working in Catalan departments in universities have mainly busied themselves with the study of works of literature by dead white males (with a few female exceptions such as Mercè Rodoreda, Montserrat Roig and Caterina Albert/Víctor Català), while contemporary literature is the domain of the media, non-university critics, and scholars working outside Catalonia. This division introduces imbalances into the critical milieu within which contemporary authors operate because their work is only appraised superficially in short reviews, interviews, or media debates between critics and writers. In-depth studies of the texts themselves are few and far between. This does not mean that there is no interest in evaluating the significance and quality of the works being produced – on the contrary, the subject of the quality of Catalan literature is a perennial favourite of critics and commentators. However, it does mean that the pool of reviewers and critics is fairly small and there are not many opportunities for thorough criticism of specific works, which is not ideal as far as achieving a plurality of views and a diversity of ideas is concerned.

Xavier Bru de Sala explores these issues in a text entitled *El descrèdit de la literatura* (The Disrepute of Literature), published in 1999. He argues that the division between academic and media critics (for want of a better term) means that Catalan literature is stuck with an old, stale canon that needs to be renewed, but that the lack of depth in criticism of contemporary authors means that there is currently no one capable of constructing a new one. If a new canon could be devised:

> Catalan writers and readers, instead of having to choose between taking on a tradition that will weigh them down or bypassing it to go straight to the storehouse of universal literature, would have the chance to incorporate into the latter the works from their own tradition that really deserve it. [. . .] Nothing looks more like a dead canon than an overloaded canon, and no tree has more chance of sprouting again than the tree that has been severely and diligently pruned. (Bru de Sala, 1999: 127–8).[9]

While it is certainly true that a more robust critical context that helped the reading public to make informed choices about what to read would be a worthwhile development, it is interesting that Bru de Sala is thinking specifically in terms of a literary canon. In some ways, he seems to regard it much in the way that Harold Bloom does, as a source of personal enrichment for readers and of constructive literary influences for authors, rather than as a 'programme for social salvation' (Bloom, 1996: 15–41; 29). (Presumably he has either overlooked or rejected Bourdieu's view of canon-formation as an act of 'symbolic violence' that 'gains legitimacy by misrecognizing the underlying power relations which serve, in part, to guarantee the continued reproduction of the legitimacy of those who produce or defend the canon' (Johnson, 1993: 20).) Nevertheless, a national element is clearly present in Bru de Sala's thinking: it matters that these works are Catalan rather than Spanish, French or American. In other words, he still views national literatures as 'hosting exemplary species of national genius' (Edensor, 2002: 141). The problem with this, as expressed by Tim Edensor, is that 'in contemporary times, the consensus

around canon formation and the universal recognition of excel-
lence is no longer tenable'. Literature is no longer a privileged site
for the representation of the nation simply because it is no longer a
privileged cultural form, at least as far as the general public is
concerned.

The desire for a Catalan canon that would also provide some of
the great works of world literature has also been partly responsible
for the obsession with quality on the part of Catalan critics.
However, more universal forces are at work here too, and have
prompted a reappraisal of the relationship between 'quality' literature and 'popular' literature. The Catalan public – released from
years of censorship, better educated, and now able to enjoy the full
range of publications available to Western readers – has shown
itself to be just as interested in genre literature and popular
best-sellers as in catching up with the authors that had been hidden
to them under the Franco regime. Of course, the majority of these
were available in Spanish rather than Catalan, which is one reason
why translation of foreign best-sellers has been encouraged. The
broader implication, however, was that there needed to be Catalan
authors who were capable of interesting the reading public even if
what they were demanding was romantic, detective or science
fiction. Joaquim Molas (1990: 154) recognized this in the early
1980s, and called for a diversification of book production so that
the 'elite' authors at the top of the pile would be supported by a
continuum of other writers and a general public that was at least
used to reading something – anything – in Catalan. He warned that
if this did not come about, Catalan culture would continue to be 'a
big head with no body'.[10] Twenty years later, there had certainly
been an opening out of literary production, so that different
genres were represented on the shelves, female authors (and
readers) had made more of a mark, and writers such as Quim
Monzó had achieved a level of popularity that was partly founded
on their ability to write for a wide sector of the public. However, the
discussions about quality continued unabated, with many critics
berating both writers and readers for preferring transient gratifica-
tion (*literatura 'light'*) over lasting self-improvement.

In 2002, Matthew Tree, who writes narrative in both Catalan and
English, tackled the subject of popular literature in an article
published in the *Journal of Catalan Studies*. He points out that any
contemporary culture necessarily hosts fewer top-quality authors
than popular but low or mid-quality writers. He also says, as Molas

had, that Catalan literature in the 1920s and 30s was perfectly normal in this respect, with a vast range of popular offerings on the book stalls. However, the task of preserving the Catalan language during the Franco regime, which led to the association of literary and linguistic quality with the potential for survival of the culture, problematized the production of popular literature. This means that even though there has been such a flourishing of new writers since the 1980s that, according to Tree, 'we can happily assert that the most recent Catalan narrative, by new authors, is now at the same standard as the rest of Europe' (Tree, 2002: 3),[11] these few superstars are not enough to declare that Catalan literature is 'normal again':

> Because 'literary normality' means [. . .] the existence of literary genres that straddle the vulgar and the cultured; it means – to use examples taken from contemporary Scottish literature – the possibility that someone who starts off by reading Irvine Welsh can end up reading Alasdair Gray or even John Burnside, *and* vice versa. If these conditions do not materialize, we will end up with a literature that is polarized between a pile of cultured authors huddled up at one end of the cultural spectrum, and four best-sellers, most of them media-derived, selling like hot cakes at the other, without there ever being any point of contact or common ground between the two. (4)[12]

Tree says that part of the problem lies in the lack of support for contemporary literature given by the academic world, which has been lulled into a false sense of security by the visible quality of recent production by a few key authors and does not feel it necessary to intervene. As mentioned above, the *Generalitat*, and Pujol personally, have been the target of similar criticism.

One of the elements that plays into this feeling of security is the phenomenon of literary prizes, and here critics, academics, writers, publishers, and political and cultural institutions combine to perpetuate a rather deceptive feel-good factor within the literary world. So many prizes are now on offer for works written in Catalan that some commentators joke that there will soon be enough for every unpublished work to receive at least one! A study carried out by the *Departament de Cultura* in 2003 showed that in the period 2000–1 there were 1,249 prizes for works in Catalan or Aranese, or works written in Spanish but produced in Catalonia (Departament de Cultura, 2003a: 4). The total prize money was over five million euros, although the amount for each individual prize varied greatly. The vast majority, whether open to works in just one language or more than one, accepted submissions in Catalan (95.8 per cent), with 32 per cent taking Spanish manuscripts, and less than one per cent accepting Aranese (10). The prizes also stipulated other criteria, including a variety of specifications related to genre, theme, length, age and/or place of residence of the author, and whether the manuscript was published or unpublished. The question of juries is also important. The study found that only 255 of the prizes declared the names of jury members in advance, and these gave a total of 857 different names, 68 per cent of whom were male (36). It is therefore hard to know how much overlap there might be between jury members for prizes in similar areas. The *Generalitat* was involved in the prize-giving process itself, the most important being the *Premi Nacional de Literatura* which was given to individuals rather than specific works, although the *Departament de Cultura* also awarded prizes for submitted works in specified genres from 1981 to 2000; these were managed by the ILC from 1988 to 2000.

Strangely, the study draws no conclusions from its findings. However, in 1997, Josep-Anton Fernàndez wrote that literary prizes had expanded out of all proportion, so that they:

> have ended up having the opposite function to the one they fulfilled at the point where they became an institution: from being an alternative mechanism for creation of the literary canon (in the sense that it was one of the few available resources to guarantee a minimum level of cultural reproduction, some degree of public presence, of institutionalization, and the continuation of a sense of literary tradition), the prizes have gone on to relativize not just the value of the books that are chosen, but also that of the Catalan literary institution as a whole. And however much we may complain about it, the role of literary prizes in the Catalan cultural field will never be redefined while authors continue to submit their works and while other authors and critics continue to sit on the juries, perpetuating, in consequence, the most perverse aspect of the Catalan cultural field.[13] (Fernàndez, 1997)

In other words, having started out as a necessary form of compensation for the difficulties of the Catalan literary world, the prizes are now a honeytrap that stifles creativity and actually lowers the absolute standards of Catalan writing. In many cases, they have also generated controversy because juries are open to accusations of favouritism or allowing the institution that funds the prize to influence their decision in some way.

All this points to the fact that the best Catalan authors of the period 1980 to 2003 seem to have produced good literature in spite, rather than because, of the policy on literature devised by the *Generalitat*. Designed to compensate for the limitations of the Catalan market and the unbalancing effect of the overlapping Spanish market, the basic mechanism of the *suport genèric* was too much of a blunt instrument. It was substantially reformed by the new government's *Consellera de Cultura*, Caterina Mieras, in 2005, shortly after it was discovered that more than two hundred thousand books paid for under the scheme had never found their way into libraries and many of them were likely to be pulped. (The scheme was changed so that although the subsidies would continue – with an increased budget – they would no longer be predicated on the *Generalitat* automatically receiving copies of the books.) The ILC, an equally important part of CiU's attempts to support literature, found its efforts hampered by a lack of funding, and once again Mieras stepped in to double their budget for 2005. Only time will tell whether these changes are effective, especially since there appear to be structural shortcomings in the Catalan literary world that cannot be addressed through *Generalitat* policy. The main problem seems to be its intrinsic smallness, which limits potential readership and economic viability, and also contributes to the tendency for critics, authors and academics to end up bound together with each other, and with policymakers and the media, in a somewhat claustrophobic network. It may be that only more far-reaching reforms – broadening the interests of academics, creating more interest in the subject of literature on the part of the audio-visual media, equipping potential readers with the desire to read in any language and only then worrying about whether they read in Catalan – will have a genuine impact on the overall success of literature in Catalan.

Theatre

Catalan theatre suffers from some of the same contextual impediments as literature and has given rise to some of the same heated debates, but these often have different outcomes. So, for example, we could rehearse here some of the same arguments about whether

Catalan theatre means 'theatre in Catalan', and could draw parallels such as the fact that both novelists and theatre companies often produce versions of their works in Castilian for the Spanish market and require translation into other languages for the international market. However, on the question of language, one statistic is significant enough to cut through these discussions. In 2001, 69 per cent of those who had been to see a theatrical production in the last twelve months stated that the last one they saw was in Catalan (Institut d'Estadística de Catalunya, 2003a: 139, 53). In contrast, only 33.2 per cent of those who had read a book in the same period said that the last one was in Catalan. Statistics show that there is no significant difference between the socio-economic and occupational status of book readers and theatregoers, which rules out any kind of explanation for this based on ethno-linguistic background and therefore ability to read Catalan rather than to understand it when spoken (49 & 138). The main factor seems to be that the public is used to having its theatre in Catalan: around 80 per cent of the productions put on by established Catalonia-based theatre companies are in Catalan (Cubeles and Fina, 1999: 60; Berger, 2005).[14]

Today, theatre is one of Catalonia's most successful cultural forms, but this has not always been the case. As far as modern dramatists are concerned, only Àngel Guimerà stands with the great Catalan novelists and poets of the late nineteenth and early twentieth centuries. This lack of a solid dramatic tradition is partly explained by the stress on poetry that was evident during the *Renaixença* and then returned during the era of *Noucentisme*, although in the latter period too there was one crucial contributor, J. M. Sagarra (George and London, 1996: 13; Terry, 2003: 97). The genre was unable to flourish after the civil war because of restrictions on performances in Catalan, and it was not until the 1960s that significant numbers of performances, whether original works or translations, could be staged (Gallén, 1996: 19–27). At this time, only the private companies could contemplate putting on these productions, which meant that it was their willingness to take risks that was crucial to reviving any kind of dramatic tradition in Catalan (Bru de Sala, 1987: 91), especially since the safest way to escape the censors was to stage the production for one night only (Salvat, 2005). There are also significant developments during this period such as the founding of performance groups, including *Els Joglars* (see below).

However, it was after the death of Franco that theatre blossomed in earnest, both in terms of the quality of writing and the development of companies and institutions. One of the most significant features of this development has been the sheer variety of dramatic forms and performance arts that have found their way into Catalonia's theatres. While the more highbrow forms still exist, there are many companies that are inspired by traditional and popular forms of performance and/or incorporate contemporary mime, dance, music and circus skills into their productions (Saumell, 1996). This gives them a broad entertainment appeal, and allows them to move flexibly between large theatres, small venues, the street, and television. It is these kinds of companies, such as *Els Joglars, Comediants, La Fura dels Baus* and *La Cubana*, that have come to represent what is innovative and distinctive about theatre in Barcelona. As María Delgado says, 'it is in Barcelona where innovative theatrical forms have taken root before shifting along to the rest of the [Spanish] nation' (Delgado, 2003: 7). Not only this but actors, performers, directors and technicians who train in Barcelona are in demand both nationally and internationally. Much of the support for this has actually come from the *Ajuntament de Barcelona* and the *Diputació de Barcelona*, both of which have put significant effort into backing all aspects of the performing arts. Concentrating here on the policy of the *Generalitat*, then, does not by any means imply that this has been the only significant source of support for theatre, although it has generated some of the most hotly debated controversies.

There were two main aspects of CiU's support to theatre and the performing arts in general: subsidies, and the creation of an adequate infrastructure for both training and performance. Subsidies were not restricted to one aspect of theatrical production and could be paid to individuals, companies, venues or producers to support training activities, one-off productions, travelling productions or festivals. So, for example, a company wanting to take its production abroad might receive help with travel costs, or a theatre in a small town might receive money to help it attract travelling productions. In 2001, public money accounted for 28.2 per cent of the total funding for theatre and dance companies in Catalonia (Departament de Cultura, 2003b: 153), and the *Departament de Cultura* spent 16.2 per cent of its total budget on theatre and dance. Significantly, 85 per cent of this money went to supporting publicly owned facilities (ICIC, 2002: 137). These found around 65 per cent of their income from public investment, whether from the *Generalitat* or other entities, whereas for private companies this figure was only around 5–10 per cent. This imbalance led privately run theatres to complain of unfair market conditions (Berger, 2005: 128–9).

The stress on public ownership of theatrical infrastructure is very much to do with the status-giving potential of grand institutions. The expense is justified by the need for Barcelona to compete on cultural terms with the other great cities of Europe, but also by the desire to endow Catalonia with the same national institutions as a nation state would have. Although not the only project that has been conceived as a response to these desires, the *Teatre Nacional de Catalunya* (TNC) has come to symbolize them, and the controversies to which it has given rise are indicative of the different positions they have generated (Orozco, 2006: 214–5). The project was first mooted in the 1980s and was to involve the building of a state-of-the-art complex that would also have architectural and environmental merits, and the creation of a resident national theatre company that would perform in Catalan and pay due attention to dramatic works originally written in Catalan. The idea had many supporters, although some thought that the *Generalitat* would do better to build on existing facilities such as the *Teatre Lliure*, which is now run by a private foundation and has received money from the *Ajuntament*, the *Diputació* and sponsors such as *TV3* as well as the *Generalitat*. Other more vocal critics were wary of the institutional elements of the project from the outset. Further disagreements surfaced as work – slowly – progressed, including controversies over the process of finding a director for the company and the *Generalitat*'s apparent attempts to influence artistic decisions.

The degree to which this was an institutional rather than an artistic project is clear from the priorities set by the *Generalitat*. First of all, although the TNC was constituted as a Public Limited Company (*Societat Anònima*), the *Generalitat de Catalunya* was to be the sole shareholder. This gave the *Generalitat* clear financial control of the theatre not only in the initial period of development but also once it was up and running. Secondly, the theatre itself was to be a landmark building. A site was chosen which was in need of regeneration and would allow the theatre plenty of space, so that it was not hemmed in by other buildings and would have a strong presence. The architect selected to design the theatre was, of course, a Catalan – Ricard Bofill. His design was appropriately monumental, with classical Greek influences that metaphorically reinforced the idea that the theatre would deserve its own place within the great European cultural tradition. This has provoked criticism both from those who see the design as inappropriate for the building's setting, making it seem rather unwelcoming and inaccessible, and those who disapprove of the pretensions symbolized by the design: Albert Boadella of the performance group *Els Joglars* went as far as to call it a Catalan 'Valley of the Fallen' (Delgado, 2003: 166).

Another key decision for the *Generalitat* was who was to take charge of the artistic direction of the new company that would make the *Teatre Nacional* its home. Having selected the actor Josep Maria Flotats, no trouble or expense was spared in securing him for the post, and his contract was said to be worth a total of 265 million pesetas (Delgado, 2003: 166). Flotats trained as an actor in France and spent some time with the *Comédie Française*, which was exactly the kind of institution the *Generalitat* wished to emulate. He then returned to Barcelona in 1984 to form his own company, on the understanding that this was the antecedent of the company that would take up residence in the TNC – it was heavily subsidized by the *Generalitat* on this basis. Flotats was highly enthusiastic about the idea of a national theatre company for Catalonia, although he did not necessarily share the vision of CiU and others that its primary purpose should be to showcase dramatic works by Catalans (Gallén, 1996: 34). For more than a decade, he helped prepare the ground for the opening of the TNC and was closely involved in planning even the technical and administrative aspects of the project (Buffery, 2006: 199). Eventually, though, he chose as the company's first production, in 1996, not a Catalan play but *Angels in America* by Tony Kushner.

The official inauguration of the main auditorium took place on the suitably nationalistic date of 11 September 1997 (Catalonia's national day) with a suitably Catalan performance: Santiago Rusiñol's *L'Auca del senyor Esteve*, directed by Adolfo Marsillach. However, by the time Flotats's second production was up and running that same month – Chekhov's *The Seagull* – he had already been told that his contract would expire at the end of June 1998. He was sacked ostensibly for bad management and lavish over-spending, although Flotats himself cites 'artistic differences' with the new *Conseller de Cultura* Joan M. Pujals, who wanted to dictate 'which works had to be staged, with whom, and how' (Buil i Feliu, 2003).[15] In short, having been the lynchpin of the *Generalitat*'s theatre policy, he had then been unceremoniously dumped by the establishment. The actress Núria Espert, a staunch supporter, reminded Flotats that 'when you're in a public theatre it's obvious that you've been hired by a politician and the same politician can fire you' (Sotorra, 1999).[16] Flotats moved to Madrid to set up a production company, while the TNC was forced to start over again without its founder.

As María Delgado says, during the period he spent at the TNC 'Flotats was to repeatedly stimulate debate about what a national theatre should do and how it should function within Catalonia' (Delgado, 2003: 276). Possibly the second most important contributor to this debate was Albert Boadella, whose disapproval of the architectural design of the TNC has already been reported above. A high-profile critic of the *Generalitat* and Pujol, Boadella even went as far as to create a work entitled *El Nacional*, which played from 1993 to 1994, in which he tackled the subject of the damage done to theatrical creativity by bureaucratic intervention and neo-liberal cultural nationalization (Boadella, 1993). Although this was not solely directed at the creation of the TNC, and was in fact inspired by the company's experiences of working in Paris, it was nevertheless part of a concerted campaign against the TNC that included the rival registration of the name *Teatre Nacional de Catalunya* as an umbrella for a coalition of independent companies. Even though it has occasionally benefited from subsidies awarded by the *Generalitat*, Boadella's company, *Els Joglars*, has come to stand not only for what is innovative about Catalan theatre but also, politically, for the very opposite of the institutionalization of the theatre that was at the heart of CiU's policies (Feldman, 1998: 42–8).

Lourdes Orozco (2004) sums up the aim of these policies as 'the facilitation of theatre produced by the *Generalitat* itself', which means traditional, realist theatre based on texts in Catalan and translated into Catalan, as well as 'a bourgeois perception not only of the theatre as a phenomenon but also of the act of going to the theatre'.[17] Not only this, but she makes it plain that in the world of Catalan theatre, there is no such thing as a free lunch: 'subsidies [. . .] are not given expecting nothing in return, but in exchange for a certain level of fidelity to those who have provided them'.[18] As a result, according to many critics, Catalonia's public theatres have become unwilling to take risks because of their dependence on their political paymasters. As Juan Carlos Olivares (2004) put it, 'the enormous resources required by a public theatre are only justifiable when it offers added value within the theatrical panorama of its country'.[19] Critics of the TNC and of the effects of the *Generalitat*'s subsidies claim that this aim had patently not been achieved during Pujol's presidency. Rather than having a commercial, private theatre that responds to audience demand and a subsidized, public theatre that has the freedom to innovate or to challenge, Catalonia has ended up with a comfortable 'pipe and slippers' public sector that is not actually filling the gaps left by the private sector and, commercially, is even treading on its toes. Instead, these gaps are the domain of the precariously positioned 'alternative' sector, which, according to the distinguished writer and director Ricard Salvat (2005) is currently stuck in a contradiction: 'The truth of the theatre can perhaps be found at this moment in its most marginal spaces. But right now no one is paying any attention to them' (see also Buffery, 2006: 197–8).[20]

If this account of the *Generalitat*'s theatre policy seems to have kept the stress firmly on Barcelona, this is an accurate reflection of the imbalance between access to the arts in the capital and elsewhere. In part, this is caused by the sheer number of public authorities that are involved in maintaining Barcelona's theatrical infrastructure. The *Generalitat* treats Barcelona as the capital of the nation, requiring flagship facilities that are supposed to represent all Catalans, but the *Ajuntament de Barcelona* is also heavily involved in supporting the performing arts in the city, as is the *Diputació de Barcelona*. The *Diputació* coordinates the *Institut del Teatre* which comprises a number of prestigious training institutions for skills related to the performing arts. Since 2000 the Institute has its headquarters in the state-of-the-art *Ciutat del Teatre*, an ambitious project in partnership with the *Ajuntament de Barcelona* that was clearly designed to rival the TNC and has caused controversies of its own (Delgado, 2003: 183). While all this means that Barcelona can now boast international prestige and more than two million visits to the theatre each year, it does beg the question of what is happening in the rest of Catalonia. In the 2000–1 season, performances in Barcelona accounted for 56.3 per cent of the total for Catalonia, and the municipality with the second highest number of performances was Lleida with an astonishingly paltry 1.9 per cent (Departament de Cultura, 2003b: 147). Much of the responsibility for promoting theatre outside Barcelona falls to the *Ajuntaments*, and the three other provincial capitals at least have a respectable offering, including touring productions from Barcelona and the rest of Spain, supported in many cases by public funds. However, the concentration of facilities, personnel and money in Barcelona leaves the rest of Catalonia in a very poor position in comparison, something that the *Generalitat* did little to address in practice despite holding the general view that an overly strong Barcelona was bad for Catalonia.

The essence of CiU's policy on theatre, then, was the same as its policy on literature. The emphasis was on works in Catalan that could be seen as part of a long cultural tradition, privileging the elite end of the cultural spectrum over more popular forms, and institutionalizing culture to give it legitimacy and visibility.

Conclusion

In an essay on theatre in Spain in the ten years after the dictatorship, Francisco Ruiz Ramón (1988: 110) praised the success of Catalan theatre and compared this with what he saw as the poverty of theatre in Galician and Basque. The blame for this, he says, rests with the fact that the Galicians and Basques were using theatre above all as a way of promoting their language and identity. He warns that, as a result, 'their theatrical maturity will only be able to begin once they have got over this juvenile stage of the search for identity, that is to say, when the *real* story and the *narrated* story coincide, instead of conflicting with one another'.[21] Whatever the Galicians and Basques might have to say about this criticism, it implies that the Catalans – even this early – had managed to get over this tendency and to see theatre as more than just a way of imagining the country they would like to inhabit. Ironically, it seems to have been partly the lack of a deep rooted tradition of elite theatre in Catalan that allowed this to happen. As Helena Buffery puts it, the history of Catalan theatre 'is full of breaks, gaps, and sutures, where the difficult, differential location of Catalan culture is always evident at the surface' (Buffery, 2006: 198). One of the positive consequences of this was that the architects of the revival of the 1960s, 70s and 80s were able to take their influences from a very broad field that included traditional and popular forms of performance, and international developments in all aspects of the performing arts, as well as more highbrow Catalan, Spanish or global dramatic traditions. Even though being able to perform in Catalan was a significant requirement for many companies, this did not necessarily mean that they were only interested in using theatre to be able to say something about *being* Catalan. In other words, the contemporary development of Catalan theatre has primarily been about exploring the rich possibilities of theatre as a genre, not about exploring Catalan identity. This made the theatre less susceptible to the nationalizing and institutionalizing pressures coming from the *Generalitat*, although of course it did not exempt theatre professionals from having to engage with them.

If we compare this with what Bru de Sala says about Catalan literature, we can see a clear link with Ruiz Ramón's comments, above, which suggests that the opposite has been true for literature. In the prologue to *El descrèdit de la literatura* he says:

> Catalan literature's definitive submission to the politics of Catalanism, which has in turn abandoned it, cuts off at the root any possibilities for a dialogue with society, because it forces literature to populate the imagination of a desired country instead of reflecting the real country.[22] (Bru de Sala, 1999: 13)

When he talks about Catalan literature, Bru de Sala is clearly thinking about it as an institution rather than as a collection of individual works and writers. Because of this, it is helpful to apply Bourdieu's ideas of habitus and field to Bru de Sala's argument. The parameters of the Catalan literary field are quite narrow because of the difficult circumstances surrounding the evolution of the relationship between literature and Catalanism over the last two centuries. When CiU came to power it saw no reason to widen the parameters because it had inherited the ideologies that had generated them. The introduction of an active cultural policy by the *Generalitat* – which functions as a quasi-state in cultural matters – set the boundaries even more firmly, conditioning the habitus of the individual writer, critic or scholar and limiting the way in which Catalan literature could be defined and explored. It could also be argued that the main form of misrecognition engendered by this control is the idea that Catalan identity can be damaged by attempts to broaden the field; Bru de Sala is clearly of the opposite view, that damage is done by the limitations imposed on it.

One of these limitations relates to the institutions' stress on the more highbrow end of the artistic spectrum. This has been evident in the way that CiU's cultural policy privileged traditional text-based forms of theatre over contemporary performance art, for example (Orozco, 2006: 218). It is clear that the working definition of culture which drove policy was based on a bourgeois perception of its functions within society. This meant that the rhetoric about widening access to culture, valuing diversity and increasing participation that is so familiar in European cultural policy was either absent from CiU's policy or reduced to a pledge to equip more people with the ability to read and understand Catalan, thus theoretically giving them the choice to participate in Catalan culture, although only as this was defined by the dominant centre-right Catalanist ideology. Even the supposed commitment to bring access to culture to those outside Barcelona was honoured more in the breach than the observance, as can be seen from the small budget given to the ILC to take authors into communities, or in the stark contrast between public theatre provision in Barcelona and the rest of Catalonia. In other words, questions of access were limited to attempts to cultivate the public, and the social function of culture was reduced to a Catalanizing function.

One of the clearest factors complicating this approach as time went on was a growing awareness of the economic function of culture, and this is the subject of the next chapter. Even though it was not until the late 1990s that there was a concerted attempt to grapple with the challenge of culture as an industry, as early as 1988 Salvador Cardús was able to suggest an approach to high culture not based on identity or nationalist ideology but on economic potential: 'in a fairly small country like ours, it is precisely the *specialized* forms of culture that have a brighter future, even if they are more expensive' (Cardús, 1988: 78).[23] In his view, it was unlikely that Catalonia would ever produce a new Beatles or Spielberg; 'On the other hand, poor as we are, we excel in the most elitist of the arts.'[24] This attitude, and the strength of both the publishing industry and the theatre within Catalonia's core economic activities, meant that high culture remained on the agenda when it came to discussion of how best to capitalize on Catalonia's cultural industries, although, as we shall see, the marriage of liberal economic strategies with a bourgeois preference for high culture and a nationalizing form of identity politics brought to light some interesting paradoxes within CiU's ideological approach to cultural policy.

NOTES

1   'el constant retorn als intel·lectuals, als artistes, etc., davant cada gran
     declaració del catalanisme, com una fórmula que aquest té per a
     ennoblir-se, per a lligar la seva necessitat d'adaptació al present
     canviant a una herència de passat, a una herència que l'empeny a
     continuar fent acció cultural catalanitzadora i no solament interven-
     cionisme polític.'

2   'a la hora de tributar no hay idioma que valga [. . .] también los
     castellanohablantes mantienen a los empleados de la *Generalitat*'.

3   'en el qual des de la regió s'aporten elements propis a l'única cultural
     nacional de l'estat'.

4   'tota la literatura realitzada per autors nascuts o residents de manera
     estable a Catalunya és literatura catalana'

5   'les traduccions que es fan ara al català, a causa de l'excés de produc-
     ció, perden qualitat i els autors d'aquí cada vegada ocupen menys
     espai al taulell de novetats'

6   'Hábitos de lectura y compra de libros en España año 2003', study
     carried   out   by   PRECISA,   *www.federacioneditores.org/0_Resources/*
     Documentos/Presentacion_2003_9_03_04.ppt,   accessed   12   February
     2007, slide 71.

7   See, for example, 'Hábitos de lectura y compra de libros en Catalunya
     año 2001', study carried out by PRECISA, *www.gremieditorscat.es/*
     AdArch/Bilio/Ftp/Habits_2001_Catalunya.pps, accessed 17 February
     2005, slide 17.

8   'comprar llibres un sol dia de l'any i no llegir-los mai'.

9   'els autors i els lectors catalans, en comptes d'haver d'optar entre
     assumir una tradició enfarfegadora o bé prescindir-ne per anar
     directes al bagatge universal, tindrien l'oportunitat d'incorporar al
     segon les obres de la pròpia tradició que de veritat s'ho valen [. . .] No
     hi ha res que s'assembli més a un cànon mort que un cànon recarre-
     gat, ni arbre que tingui més possibilitats de rebrotar que l'arbre
     esporgat amb severitat i diligència'.

10   'un gran cap sense cos'.

11   'es pot asseverar tranquil·lament que la narrativa catalana més actual,
     d'autors nous, ja està a l'alçada de la mitjana europea'.

12   'Perquè 'normalitat literària' significa [. . .] l'existència de gèneres
     literaris a cavall entre el vulgar i el culte; significa – per posar exemples
     trets de la literatura contemporània escocesa – la possibilitat que algú
     que comenci llegint Irvine Welsh pugui acabar llegint Alasdair Gray o
     fins i tot John Burnside, *i a l'inrevés*. Si aquestes condicions no es
     donen, acabarem amb una literatura polaritzada entre un munt
     d'autors cultes arraulits a un extrem de l'espectre cultural i quatre
     best-sellers, la major part derivats mediàtics, venent-se com xurros a
     l'altre, sense que hi hagi cap punt de contacte, cap espai comú, entre
     els dos.'

13   'han acabat complint la funció oposada a la que feien en el moment en
     què es van convertir en una institució: de ser un mecanisme alternatiu

de formació del cànon literari (en el sentit que era un dels pocs
recursos a l'abast per tal de garantir uns mínims de reproducció
cultural, una certa presència pública, una certa institucionalització, i
la continuació d'un sentit de tradició literària), els premis han passat a
relativitzar no només el valor dels llibres premiats, sinó també el de la
institució literària catalana en el seu conjunt. I per molt que ens en
queixem, el paper dels premis literaris dintre el camp cultural català
no es redefinirà mentre els autors s'hi continuïn presentant i mentre
altres autors i crítics continuïn formant part dels jurats, i en conse-
qüència perpetuant la part més perversa del camp cultural català.'

[14] This figure of course falls when productions by visiting companies
from outside the region are factored in, although only to around 60
per cent (Departament de Cultura, 2003b: 132).

[15] 'qué obras había que hacer, con quién y cómo'.

[16] 'quan s'està en un teatre públic és evident que t'ha contractat un
polític i que aquest polític et pot treure'.

[17] 'la potenciació del teatre produït per la mateixa Generalitat'; 'una
percepció burgesa no només del fenomen teatral sinó de l'acte d'anar
al teatre'.

[18] 'la subvenció [. . .] no es dóna a canvi de res sinó a canvi d'oferir una
certa fidelitat cap a qui la concedeix'.

[19] 'Els enormes recursos que necessita un teatre públic només es justi-
fiquen quan ofereix un valor afegit al panorama teatral del seu país'.

[20] 'La veritat del teatre potser es troba en aquest moment en els espais
més marginals. Però ara ningú no els fa cas'.

[21] 'Su madurez como teatro podrá sólo empezar cuando se haya
superado esa etapa juvenil de búsqueda de la identidad, es decir
cuando la historia *real* y la historia *contada* coincidan, en lugar de
enfrentarse.'

[22] 'La submissió, en definitiva, de la literatura catalana a la política del
catalanisme, que al seu torn l'ha abandonat, li escapça d'arrel les
possibilitats d'interlocució social, ja que la força a poblar l'imaginari
d'un país esperat en comptes de reflectir el país real.'

[23] 'en un país prou petit, com és el nostre, són precisament les *cultures
especialitzades* les que tenen més futur, ni que siguin més cares'

[24] 'En canvi, pobres com som, excel·lim en arts summament elitistes'

Chapter Four

The Cultural Industries

The success of the publishing industry in Catalonia was a source of pride – and revenue – for the *Generalitat*, and the worry that Madrid might lure companies away was a real concern. However, although there were some signs in the mid to late 1990s that Catalonia was losing market share (ICIC, 2002: 88), it was not publishing that was the primary factor in the *Generalitat*'s growing interest in the cultural industries, but more 'contemporary' forms of culture such as the audio-visual sector. Jordi Vilajoana, who became *Conseller de Cultura* in 1999, had a background in advertising and had been director general of the body that runs Catalan television and radio – the *Corporació Catalana de Radio i Televisió* (CCRTV) – which meant that he had a very good idea of the issues facing this area. Although he was not the first *Conseller* to worry about the position of Catalonia's cultural industries, it was he who oversaw the creation of the *Institut Català de les Indústries Culturals* (The Catalan Institute for the Cultural Industries – ICIC), which is to be the main focus of this chapter.

Created through an act of the Catalan parliament in 2001, this body was made responsible for putting into practice the policy of the government in relation to the cultural industries. It is still in operation, as one of the very few of CiU's initiatives to be cheerfully retained by the new left-wing government after 2003. The preamble to the law of 2001 makes it clear that the ICIC has to promote both the symbolic and the economic benefits of Catalan culture, as can be seen from the very first sentence:

> The cultural industries of a country are today seen not only as a factor of economic progress, but also as a way of guaranteeing the presence

of its own cultural products, that is to say, to present its own creativity and point of view in the universal cultural marketplace.[1]

The first task of the ICIC was to carry out a review of the status of the cultural industries in Catalonia, and the resulting publication – 'The Handbook of the Cultural Industries in Catalonia' (*Llibre blanc de les indústries culturals de Catalunya*) – surveys their current state, pointing out strengths and weaknesses in each specific area and making recommendations for the way forward. It also highlights the challenges of reconciling symbolic and economic prerogatives, especially in an era of cultural and economic globalization.

The ICIC's remit is a broad one, as defined both by the law that created it and the *Llibre blanc*. Its responsibilities include the areas of books, the press, cinema, new 'multimedia' technologies, television, radio, the recording industry, the visual arts, the performing arts and live music. In the words of the introduction to the *Llibre blanc*, this mixture of different kinds of cultural enterprise means that the aim of the ICIC has to be to:

> consolidate a business fabric in all the cultural sectors of Catalonia that will allow local creation to be connected to international circuits and cultural consumption to be increased. This means that in some cases it is a matter of strengthening the traditional cultural industries, while in others it is about realizing the potential of the commercial aspect of the other cultural sectors. (ICIC, 2002: 4–5).[2]

It should be noted, however, that the ICIC has chosen to focus on *cultural* industries, rather than the broader *creative* industries (Hesmondhalgh, 2002: 14). If we compare the definition of the creative industries used in the second *Creative Industries Mapping Document* produced by the British government's Department for Culture, Media and Sport around the same time as the ICIC's *Llibre blanc*, we can clearly see the difference in emphasis (see also Garnham, 2005). Some of the areas covered by the British document, such as designer fashion, the antiques market and advertising, do not feature in the Catalan *Llibre blanc*. The *Creative Industries Mapping Document* is concerned with 'those industries which have their origin in individual creativity, skill and talent and which have a potential for wealth and job creation through the generation and exploitation of intellectual property', and this definition clearly shows a different emphasis in the British case (DCMS, 2001: 5). Catalonia may have been ahead of the rest of Spain in paying particular attention to the cultural industries, but the *Generalitat*'s approach already seems somewhat restricted when compared with the British document. It is interesting, in this regard, to note that in an essay on 'Creative Enterprises' published in 2005, Stuart Cunningham dismisses cultural industries policy as having had its heyday in the 1980s and 90s, only being concerned with 'rebadging' established industries, and having a narrow focus in the nation state rather than stemming from a broader conception of the relationship between the global and the local (Cunningham, 2005: 284–5).

Despite these limitations, the ICIC as a unit that answers directly to a Department of Culture does reach beyond the areas normally associated with this kind of governmental intervention in the cultural industries. According to cultural policy expert Mark Schuster (2002: 1):

> The Institut Català de les Indústries Culturals has a rather unique mandate. It is to concern itself, first and foremost, with the *production* of cultural goods and services. Thus, it will focus its attention on organizational and industry activities in the profitmaking sector, the nonprofit sector, and perhaps even the governmental sector. (Yet its mandate appears to stop short of considering production in the unorganized and noninstitutionalized amateur sector.) This mandate goes well beyond what is normally suggested by the phrase "cultural industries" as it is used in the cultural policy literature; typically, this phrase has been used to describe those fields whose focus is on large scale *reproduction* of cultural *products*, a field firmly rooted in the for-profit sector of the economy. Thus, ICIC is being asked to undertake a set of tasks that are not normally packaged together in the design of government cultural policy agencies.

The implication is that this could either turn out to be an innovative move on the part of CiU, or a recipe for confusion. By attempting to influence the conditions for cultural production, the *Generalitat* would put itself in a position where it might be directly responsible for stimulating or stifling particular forms of cultural creation. Not only this, but by focusing on production, the ICIC might be ignoring what Nicholas Garnham describes as 'the key locus of power and profit' of the cultural industries, which is 'cultural distribution, not cultural production' (Garnham, 1993: 58).

Even if the focus had been solely on the industrial conditions for the reproduction of cultural products, Miller and Yúdice explain that state governments normally avoid making the cultural industries a target for *dirigiste* cultural policy because 'the market is declared the proper venue for the culture industries, while heritage [. . .] is administered by the state' (Miller and Yúdice, 2002: 16). In the Catalan case, however, the need to promote and protect the Catalan language and identity meant that the market could not be left entirely to its own devices. Garnham's definition of the cultural industries is helpful here, as he highlights the fact that cultural commodities also have to be regarded as symbols: the cultural industries are 'those institutions in our society which employ the characteristic modes of production and organization of industrial corporations to produce and disseminate symbols in the form of cultural goods and services, generally, although not exclusively, as commodities' (Garnham, 1993: 55). The institutions that control Catalan cultural policy are perhaps more aware than most of the fact that they are dealing in symbolic values as well as commodities, but it is precisely here that the biggest conundrum presents itself: how to balance the two given the limited resources available and the limited powers afforded to Catalonia under the present political system. Furthermore, Allen J. Scott believes that 'The production of culture in contemporary society has [. . .] become far too closely interwoven with the very fabric of capitalism itself for the blunt exercise of administrative authority – except in the most extreme cases – to be politically feasible or workable' (Scott, 2000: 215). In this context, CiU's approach raises interesting issues about how far a nationalist strategy firmly based on cultural differentiation can successfully be combined with market-led development of the cultural industries.

In order to illustrate the problems raised by this kind of intervention in the cultural industries, this chapter will take as its examples two forms of audio-visual culture that have enjoyed contrasting fortunes in Catalonia since 1980: television and cinema. While Catalan television is regarded by many as the most successful area of CiU's cultural policy, cinema in Catalan has been struggling and the *Departament de Cultura* has achieved little with its attempts to help it. As usual, the question of the Catalan language is key here, but it is not the only consideration. It is now recognized that support for the processes of creation, production and distribution is vital if audio-visual culture in Catalan is to have any chance of triumphing over its rival in Spanish. Conversely, CiU also came to the conclusion that audio-visual culture was a field that could contribute substantially to the region's economic growth if its products were made for the Spanish or international markets. The next two sections will therefore look at the development of television and cinema, respectively, during the twenty-three years of Pujol's government, as a way of introducing the discussion of CiU's cultural industry policy which is to follow.

Television

Even as late as the start of the 1980s it seemed as though literature would retain its place as the main medium for introducing old and new Catalans alike to the full possibilities of the Catalan language and culture. However, by the end of the decade it was clear that it was actually television that now had this power. This change is partly related to the pluralization of Spanish television as a whole after the end of the dictatorship, which gave rise to new channels and contents, allowing the public access to forms of information and entertainment that had previously been denied them. As part of this relaxation of control, legislation passed in 1983 gave the autonomous communities the right to run their own 'third channel' (after the two statewide channels that were the only ones in existence at the time). However, the scope of this legislation was limited and did not allow the Catalans the level of freedom they would have liked. Also, the situation of autonomous communities with their own language was not taken into account when private television franchises were being awarded in the 1990s, which meant that there was no requirement for the new statewide channels to cater for the needs of different regions. As a result, the autonomous channels faced increased competition for viewers and advertising revenue without the compensation of seeing their efforts towards linguistic and cultural normalization being backed up by other, more powerful, players. These limitations meant that Spain remained a 'single market' as far as the audio-visual sector was concerned, a fact which led Josep Gifreu to comment in 2003 that until this situation changed, any initiative by the Catalans to create their own audio-visual space would continue to be fatally undermined (Gifreu, 2003: 17).

Nevertheless, regular broadcasts of the public Catalan channel TV3 began in January 1984, and only three years later one commentator stated that it was 'difficult to imagine this country or how it would have evolved culturally, politically and socially without the existence of this medium, whose creation – and I think I am representing a fairly widely held opinion here – is the most important work of government the *Generalitat* has carried out' (Canals, 1987: 192).[3] A second public channel, Canal 33, began broadcasting in 1989.[4] Not only was television able to reach a wider cross-section of the public than written cultural forms, it also allowed the creation of a mass Catalan imaginary. News, current affairs, sport, fiction, gossip and debate could all be framed within a Catalan context and contribute to the generation of a sense of identity and social cohesion. However, on a less noble level, it would also allow Pujol and CiU access to a powerful medium through which to diffuse their policies and swing public opinion in their favour (Antich, 1994: 94).

Having realized the full potential of the television project shortly after he came to power, Pujol was in a hurry to see it in action and took a very personal interest in its progress. It was apparently Pujol's decision that from 1982 the *Departament de la Presidència* should take charge of it rather than the slow-moving *Departament de Cultura,* and that Alfons Quintà would be its director (Cortacans, 2003: 20–1). Stung into action by the director general of *RadioTelevisión Española* (Spain's public television and radio company – RTVE), who had commented that television produced by the autonomous communities should be 'anthropological and complementary' (Cendrós, 2003), the Catalans set about creating a channel that had professionalism and innovation as part of its core mission and would eventually surpass the viewing figures for *Televisión Española* in the region. RTVE's unwillingness to cooperate also meant that the *Generalitat* had to build its own network of transmitters, at a substantial cost. Although some revenue would come from advertising, it was accepted that public money allocated by the *Generalitat* would form the main funding mechanism for the body with overall responsibility for public television and radio in Catalonia, CCRTV, whose head would be appointed directly by the *Generalitat.*[5] In other words, the establishment and management of Catalan television was subject to the direct influence of CiU throughout its period in power, not just as a result of the implementation of a cultural policy per se but through broad political authority which could be exercised either overtly or covertly.

The questions of expenditure and political control have been the main areas for criticism of CiU's actions. The law which created

CCRTV was approved unanimously by the *Parlament* in May 1983, but the enthusiasm its members felt for the general idea seems to have blinded them to some of the problems that would result from the way the company was set up and run. The accounts for 2003 show that CCRTV received 89 million euros in transfers (Generalitat de Catalunya, 2004b: 25), and had benefited from another 390 million in loans for which the *Generalitat* acts as guarantor (Corporació Catalana de Ràdio i Televisió, 2003: 8). Public television was therefore a major drain on the *Generalitat*'s resources, and although it did not expect to make a profit, the extent of the annual loss was worrying to say the least. By 2002, CCRTV had accumulated debts of 763 million euros (Cendrós, 2003). Part of the problem is of course related to the fact that Catalan television has to compete for advertising with statewide Spanish channels which offer a much wider coverage, and these channels are also fighting among themselves to attract advertisers. However, the grand ambitions of the *Generalitat* and its appointees, and their refusal to contemplate a radical rethink of CCRTV's structure and mandate when the debts began to mount, are also responsible for the situation.

There were also calls for structural reform for political reasons, which again went unheeded during CiU's period in power. The board of CCRTV was constructed in much the same way as that of RTVE: in both cases, the members of the board were political appointees, elected by the relevant parliament. In this sense, the situation in Catalonia merely mirrored the Spanish state's control over RTVE, which had been a subject of constant controversy including some well-founded accusations of pro-government bias in RTVE's news coverage. Pujol's successor Artur Mas even felt able to claim that although there was political influence over Catalan television at least it was not as bad as the kind of influence exercised by other political authorities over the media they manage (Cendrós, 2003). Nevertheless, one of the side effects of this control was to constrain news coverage and programme making within limits that reflected CiU's vision of Catalan society and the mission of Catalan television.[6] Another – rather paradoxical – result was to restrict the coverage of Catalan high culture and intellectual activity, partly because of the perceived need to make 'popular' television, and partly because of CiU's general distrust of intellectuals.

It was decided that TVC would operate in Catalan to the largest possible degree, without any programming in Spanish, and making concessions only to interviewees who could not speak Catalan, for example. This idea was opposed by some left-wing members of the *Parlament* who were of the opinion that TVC should be a television for all Catalans and should reflect real linguistic usage; indeed, this debate resurfaced after the left-wing tripartite government was elected in 2003. However, the decision to make Catalan the default language of TVC had important consequences for the process of linguistic normalization, not just in improving people's command of Catalan but in opening their eyes to the broad usefulness of a language that had for too long been artificially confined to domestic or high cultural domains. The case that is always cited to illustrate this is the decision to screen *Dallas* on TV3 after it had been dropped from the schedules by TVE, just before the infamous 'who shot J.R.?' storyline. A dubbed episode of *Dallas* was part of the schedule for TV3's inaugural broadcast in 1983, and the rest of the series was shown when regular programming began in 1984. According to José Antich, this masterstroke can be attributed directly to the *Generalitat* itself, since Lluís Prenafeta, who ran the *Departament de la Presidència*, went personally to New York to secure the rights to the series (Antich, 1994: 98). Not only did the presence of *Dallas* in the schedules draw in a larger audience than might otherwise have been found, it also made people realize for the first time that wealthy Texans could speak Catalan just as easily as they could speak Spanish. The idea that Catalan was appropriate for any communicative situation was therefore reinforced through the dubbing of foreign imports as much as through home-produced programming such as news and sports broadcasts, although it is also said that giving people no option other than to watch *Barça* games with a Catalan commentary played its own significant role.

Television, especially in the 1980s, therefore helped significantly with the status planning aspect of linguistic normalization, but it also gave rise to disagreement in areas related to corpus planning and linguistic standards. Televisió de Catalunya (TVC) put an enormous amount of effort into assuring the quality of the Catalan used in its programmes, with a *Comissió de Normalització Lingüística de Televisió de Catalunya* and a linguistic advisor for each area of its programming – six for news programmes (Faura, Paloma and Torrent, 1998: 5, 12). In 1995 it published its own 'Style Book' which was meant to provide detailed guidance for anyone working in Catalan television. Possibly the most controversial decision TVC made was the choice of central Catalan as the standard model to be followed unless there was some very good reason not to. There is of course more natural variation in spoken language than in formal written language, which meant that TVC would have had a tougher job than, say, the press or literary correctors if they had wanted to ensure correctness but still allow a plurality of accents and dialects to be used. In the end, it was thought that plumping for one variety would ensure consistency, and central Catalan was felt to be the most 'neutral' of the alternatives. On the other hand, the lack of plurality in the use of the different varieties of Catalan has been one of the constant criticisms levelled at TVC over the years, especially by viewers living outside the zones where central Catalan is spoken. Not only this, but a study of the language used on TVC published in 1998 found that the obsession with correctness was also constraining scriptwriters in their use of style and register, meaning that little differentiation was seen in the Catalan spoken in supposedly informal settings, such as domestic scenes in soap operas, and more formal uses such as news items (Faura, Paloma and Torrent, 1998: 135). There have been more attempts in recent years to broaden the use of Catalan in television, and the variety of styles and registers seems to have improved (Cendrós, 2003). It could be argued that the initial insistence on standardization and correctness was appropriate for the overall linguistic situation of Catalan at that time, whereas with more of the population now formally educated in Catalan and able to manipulate the language in a variety of communicative situations, greater flexibility is both possible and desirable.

TVC's mission to provide a linguistic model for the public is probably also related to its desire to produce good quality, innovative television that can compete with the best in Europe. While initial efforts were focused on providing good quality news programmes, well-dubbed imports and films, children's programmes, and plenty of sports coverage, over the years there has been a significant increase in the number of serials, documentaries, game shows, and 'magazine shows' commissioned specifically by TV3 and made either in-house, by independent producers, or as co-productions. Oriol Cortacans (2003: 24) comments that even in the early days, TV3 was able to teach TVE a thing or two about how to produce innovative and professional news programmes, even in the simplest detail such as making sure they began on time! In the 1990s, popular serials like *Poble Nou* and *Nissaga del Poder* were not only vital to TV3's audience figures but also made their own mark on this emerging genre in Spain. The presenter and academic Mònica Terribas, when asked to evaluate TV3 over its first twenty years of existence, also highlights the fact that it devised innovative formats of its own, some of which were 'revolutionary' or 'unimaginable' within the scope of Spanish television at the time (Roma M., 2003: 34). TV3 has not only produced a 'star system' of its own and a standard of programme making for others to emulate, it has also contributed to a general recognition of the quality of Catalan television professionals and production companies. It is therefore not surprising that one of the conclusions of the *Llibre Blanc de les Indústries Culturals* is that 'TVC is a pillar around which a large part of the Catalan audio-visual industry has emerged' (ICIC, 2002: 42).[7] One of the key successes of the *Generalitat*'s cultural policy in the 1980s was therefore the creation of a public television that provided the impetus for the development of an entire audio-visual sector in Catalonia that would have had very limited prospects if it had had to depend solely on statewide channels.

In cultural terms, then, the *Generalitat*'s policy on television was a demonstrable success, which was no easy achievement given the obstacles placed in its way by the state and its media institutions. TV3 is the most-watched station in Catalonia and the simple presence of the Catalan language on television is no longer a matter worthy of comment. Despite political interference and the cost to the public purse, TVC continues to be regarded as an indispensable element of the *Generalitat*'s activities. So why has the position of cinema proved so different?

Cinema

In 2001, only 4.3 per cent of the people surveyed by the *Departament de Cultura* said that their last visit to the cinema had been to see a film in Catalan, whereas for 90.8 per cent it had been in Spanish. This shocking figure is even more surprising when contrasted with the 69 per cent whose last theatre visit was to see a production in Catalan, or even the 33.2 per cent whose last book read was in Catalan (Institut d'Estadística de Catalunya, 2003a: 131, 139, 53). Linguistic competence cannot be the deciding factor here given that virtually all long-term residents of Catalonia understand spoken Catalan. The reasons for the situation are complex and explained by a number of different factors, some of which might plausibly have been affected by a suitable cultural policy from the *Generalitat*, and some of which seemed completely out of its reach. To try to simplify the discussion, I will begin with the issues that reflect the particular cultural situation of Catalonia before moving on to look at how the conditions of the Spanish and international markets constrain the development of cinema in Catalan.

One of the main internal problems seems to be that there has been no revolutionary moment, comparable to the screening of *Dallas* on TV3, to convince the public that it is normal to watch films in Catalan. This is especially the case for dubbed films, and here a particularly Spanish mentality is at work (not just a Catalan one). All Spaniards have grown up with dubbed films and many are not impressed with the idea of subtitles. Under the Franco dictatorship all foreign films had to be dubbed because this facilitated censorship, and in any case audiences were not all literate enough to follow subtitles. The habit became ingrained, so that nowadays fewer cinemas in Spain show foreign films with subtitles than their dubbed versions, and those films that are only available subtitled are normally low-budget productions that do not attract big enough audiences to warrant the cost of dubbing. Catalan audiences have become used to hearing only Spanish in their cinemas, and they even associate particular Spanish voices with particular foreign actors. All this means that the average cinemagoer has a mental block when it comes to conceiving of cinema in any language other than Spanish. This will change as technologies such as DVD introduce more people to the concept of subtitling, but Catalan cinema cannot afford to wait a generation for this to happen.

A second internal problem relates to the very small numbers of feature films that are made originally in Catalan. Although twenty-eight of the new films shown in the cinemas in 2003 were made by Catalan studios, only one of these was actually in Catalan (Cendrós, 2004). Given the viewing statistics and the linguistic preferences of cinemagoers outlined above, the decision to make a film in Catalan implies acceptance that not only will it reach a very small audience in the original version, it will have to be dubbed or subtitled in Spanish to have any widespread impact at all. The logical decision is therefore to make your film in Spanish in the first place. This is of course one area where subsidies given by the *Departament de Cultura*, and later by the ICIC, were able to make some difference to the industry as a whole, even if this is hardly reflected in the number of actual feature films made in Catalan. In the year 2000 the *Departament* gave nearly 836 million pesetas (roughly 6 million euros) in subsidies to cinema and television production, which were directed at films or series made by Catalan producers, in Catalan (Departament de Cultura, 2000: 269). The money could be sought to cover different expenses associated with making, distributing, showing and promoting any feature-length or short film in Catalan. By 2003, when the area came under the remit of the ICIC, the amount had risen to 8 million euros (Departament de Cultura, 2003c: 333). The subsidies were designed to compensate the industry for the loss of revenue involved in choosing Catalan, but could not guarantee an audience for the films once they were made.

On top of this, other sums were given under the heading of Linguistic Normalization for the dubbing of films into Catalan; the production, subtitling or dubbing of DVDs; or to cinemas that showed films in Catalan. Some of the companies benefiting from these seem surprising at first, since they include giants of the film industry such as Warner, Columbia Tristar or UIP. However, this is where we head into the murky waters of international production and distribution, which is the area in which the *Generalitat* has least influence. Hollywood companies care little for linguistic pluralism and, while they are quite happy to provide dubbed versions for a huge Spanish-language market, they feel no compulsion to do this for Catalan. Paying a proportion of the costs for the dubbing or subtitling of popular films themselves is the only way the *Generalitat* can persuade them. Twenty-three films received subsidies in 2003, including *Finding Nemo*, *Terminator 3* and *Harry Potter and the Chamber of Secrets*. However, even this does not guarantee a substantial presence of the Catalan version in cinemas. Only ten copies of *Harry Potter and the Chamber of Secrets* in Catalan were distributed for use in cinemas, eight of which were for Catalonia and two for the Balearic Islands (Cester, 2002). Although this was an improvement on the first instalment of the series, which had only been subtitled, it still limited dramatically the public's access to the Catalan version.

In an ideal world, to engineer a situation in which this kind of blockbuster was available only or mainly in Catalan might allow something of the *Dallas* effect to rub off on cinema (Gifreu, 2003: 37–9). However, this was beyond the *Generalitat's* control, as they quickly found out when they claimed the right to impose linguistic quotas on cinema as part of the Linguistic Policy Act of 1998 (Article 28 (3)): it seemed that Hollywood, and its Spanish distributors, would prefer not to have a market in Catalonia at all rather than have to dub everything to be shown there at their own expense. Not only was the then *Conseller de Cultura* Joan Maria Pujals forced to fly to the USA to try to negotiate personally with the American companies – which seemed rather an act of desperation –, but a Decree passed in 1998 setting out the quotas and sanctions envisaged in the law had to be repealed after a two-year battle in the *Parlament* and the courts about its legality.[8] Even though the availability of subsidies and the greater awareness of American distributors about the linguistic situation of Catalonia have meant more films are now being dubbed, this was a painful period in the history of CiU's cultural policy, which for many is emblematic of a general failure on their part.

The criticism most often levelled at CiU was that in the area of cinema they had confused cultural policy with linguistic policy to such an extent that this imposed artificial restraints on the growth of the sector. Lluís Bonet Mojica (2000), for example, complains that the amounts spent dubbing US imports would have been better targeted at supporting the film industry in Catalonia. He also points out that by ignoring production in Spanish the *Generalitat* made it logical for many up-and-coming or respected professionals to move to Madrid, even though in the 1970s it had been Barcelona that was the incubator for much Spanish cinema (see also Gifreu, 2003: 55). This was not helped by the fact that the state's focus on Madrid in its support for culture gave the capital more resources to attract them. Àngel Quintana states that the Spanish *Ministerio de Cultura* and its own mechanisms of support for filmmakers were the main points of reference even for those that remained in Catalonia, and comments that the rising national and international profile of Spanish film in the 1990s left Catalan cinema even more marginalized (Quintana, 1999: 332, 333; see also Smith P. J., 2003: 118–20). It was not until the late 1990s that the *Generalitat* seemed to wake up to the situation and take a real interest in the potential of Catalan cinema as a whole rather than just as another tool for linguistic normalization.

Xavier Bru de Sala et al. make the point that Catalan culture never seems to thrive when it requires some kind of industrial network to support it, and this is certainly demonstrated in the different degrees of success of theatre and cinema in Catalonia (Bru de Sala et al., 1997: 27). Although for the public there might seem to be little difference between going to see a play or a film, the production and distribution network required for cinema is many times more complex than for the theatre. This means that there are many more points at which the production of Catalan films can be stymied by financial or logistical considerations. Unless something could be done to reach these intermediate domains as well as the initial process of creation and the final stages of exhibition, the *Generalitat* would be unable to have any significant impact on cinema. The *Llibre blanc de les indústries culturals* diagnosed several problems in these areas, including the fact that the distribution of Catalan films was often carried out in a fairly haphazard way by small distributors, a lack of investment by large multimedia corporations, and a general negativity on the part of the media which hampered efforts to promote films (ICIC, 2002: 17). Improving these would both increase the chances of success for films in Catalan, and allow Barcelona to start to compete with Madrid as a centre for cinematic production.

A Trial Separation for Language and Culture?

It should be apparent from the above discussion that, at least up until the late 1990s, CiU's policy on the audio-visual sector was not strictly speaking a cultural policy, but a language policy. Although in the case of television this produced clear benefits in linguistic terms, the failure to engage with other aspects meant that even here the full potential of the medium was untapped. This of course has been the main criticism of those associated with the audio-visual sector who felt that the definition of what constituted Catalan culture, and could therefore be supported with *Generalitat* funds, was too narrow, and stifled some important areas of creativity. It is not clear whether this criticism in itself was enough to turn CiU's thoughts towards the economic potential of culture, but a combination of this and other factors did change their perspective during the 1990s. For example, the Catalans became more involved in European regional affairs, including the Committee of the Regions and partnerships such as the 'Four Motors', which meant a greater awareness of the possibilities of regional economic development through culture. Within Catalonia, the general influence of the PSC's ideas on cultural policy also grew in this later period, especially once they published their *Llibre Blanc de la Cultura a Catalunya* (Mascarell, 1999). There were also some indications that Catalonia was beginning to lose its advantage over other areas of Spain in the cultural industries. According to a survey published in 2001, Catalonia's contribution to Spain's culture industry in the 1990s was growing more slowly than that of many other regions, especially Madrid. The report especially highlighted Catalonia's 'inability to export its products, which generates a closed market with no external promotion' (Ramos, 2001).[9]

One other major influence on CiU's thinking at this time was the growing debate about globalization and its effects on regional and local identities. The topic of globalization is dealt with in more depth later in this volume, but also needs to be mentioned here as part of the context for the ICIC. CiU's concerns about globalization and its relationship to culture as an industry can be briefly introduced by looking at what Joan M. Pujals, *Conseller de Cultura* before Vilajoana, had to say about it. In 1998 he published a book entitled *Les noves fronteres de Catalunya* (Catalonia's New Borders), one of the aims of which was to show that globalization does not have to mean loss of identity (9). Instead, 'now more than ever it is right to think globally and act locally' (10), because 'a solid identity is the best way to understand and participate in a world that is as global as it is diverse' (45).[10] He goes on to stress that this identity is based on culture, which is Catalonia's main asset (104). In other words, Pujals was arguing that a strongly defined cultural identity would give Catalonia more chance of retaining its character in a globalized world. He went on to develop this argument in the specific context of culture as an economic asset in a speech given in 1999 and published under the title *Economia, llengua i cultura* (Economy, Language and Culture). Pujals was convinced that Catalonia had both the creativity and industrial infrastructure necessary to allow it to become a centre of the global culture industry, but needed to construct a distinctive 'brand' in order to do so (13, 15). As forward-looking as Pujals's words may seem, the usual caveat is applied: in order to achieve this goal 'we will continue with a cultural policy that, while not being confused with linguistic policy, will not forget the importance of the Catalan language in Catalonia' (15).[11] In other words, they would be trying to improve Catalonia's capacity to export its products while at the same time retaining their ideological commitment to one of the main barriers to cultural exports, the Catalan language itself.

This commitment is evident in the pages of the *Llibre blanc de les indústries culturals* published a few years later. It contains a separate section on language which gives statistics on the use of Catalan in various sectors of the cultural industries and then makes six main recommendations. The very first of these is that there should be a deliberate policy of positive discrimination in favour of products in Catalan. This recommendation is put forward rather apologetically, and begins:

> Although the fundamental objective of this Handbook is to strengthen the creative and business structures for the totality of culture produced in Catalonia, independently of the language in which it is expressed, we cannot deny the importance of production, and the market, in the Catalan language in preserving an autochthonous space for expressive, symbolic and identity-related purposes. (ICIC, 2002: 377)[12]

So, Catalan-language products would continue to be considered central to the ICIC's mission, which gives rise to a number of contradictions and difficulties that are highlighted by the non-Catalan contributors to the Handbook. Two experts had been asked to provide papers that comment on the *Llibre blanc* and the future role of the ICIC, and both were wary of the planned attempt to put culture in Catalan first. Andy Pratt of the London School of Economics warned that the tradition of supporting Catalan culture as a 'good thing' in its own right could confuse and complicate the task of making the same cultural sectors part of a new industrial policy (ICIC, 2002: 437). Mark Schuster of the University of Chicago said that, because of the primacy of language in the Catalan context, 'It may be that cultural industry policy is really language policy, though in a slightly different guise.' If so, 'There is substantial opportunity for policy confusion here, especially since other governmental agencies exist to deal with the regularization and promotion of the Catalan language, with economic development in Catalunya, and with the arts and culture and heritage of Catalunya' (ICIC, 2002: 432).[13]

The overall thrust of the *Llibre blanc* indicates an attempt to move away from a cultural policy that is too strictly driven by linguistic concerns, even though the recommendation that products in Catalan should be accorded more importance – an echo of Pujals' caveat – lurks behind the business-speak. To see precisely how the attempt to broaden the perspective of the policymakers was supposed to apply in practice, we can return to the audio-visual sector and the diagnoses and recommendations regarding television and cinema made in the *Llibre blanc*. Four main points stand out from these recommendations:

(1) The need to engage fully and enthusiastically with the Spanish audio-visual sector as a whole – and for it to engage with Catalonia!

This recommendation seems to spring from a realization that the Spanish audio-visual sector is potentially the best ally for the Catalans, and that to ignore it or to attempt to bypass it would be fundamentally counterproductive. The reality of the situation is that audio-visual production and distribution companies are concentrated in Madrid, and Catalan companies need to be able to market and promote their products there, which might mean using public funds to do so. Co-productions between companies based in Madrid and Barcelona would also help to put Catalan output on a more solid footing and there might be ways of devising financial incentives for this. However, it is not just a case of Catalans engaging with the industry in Madrid: TVE carries out part of its programme-making in Sant Cugat del Vallès, most of which is for its own (limited) transmissions in Catalan, although a small amount is in Spanish for statewide use. The ICIC document highlights the fact that TVE, as a company that represents and broadcasts to the whole of the Spanish state, has a responsibility towards Catalan culture that should include a greater willingness to use the talents of Catalans and commission programmes from Catalan independents.

(2) The need to find niche products in which the Catalans can excel.

In a sense, this is a difficult symbolic issue for a government committed to cultural normalization. While it might be desirable for Catalonia to produce the 'normal' range of audio-visual culture, this might be a bad strategy from a business perspective. The report identifies two particular niches where the Catalans are beginning to carve out a solid reputation:

documentaries and animation. If these can be strengthened so that Catalan companies become the default choice for programme commissioners, it will have a knock-on effect on the audio-visual sector as a whole as well as increasing regional GDP. The implication is that the ICIC will have to make some hard choices about funding, prioritizing these areas over others when it comes to allocating resources. However, the symbolic power attached to having a flourishing feature-film industry is greater than that attached to being a market leader in the production of cartoons for the under tens. It would therefore be desirable that Catalan culture should succeed in the 'right' niches and not just any niche, which implies that funding decisions cannot be entirely dictated by objective consideration of the likely return on investment.

(3) The need to work with Barcelona city council to make Barcelona a centre for audio-visual production, professional training and the development of related technologies.

Again, this might imply some difficult choices for the *Generalitat* as any attempt to privilege Barcelona will fuel criticisms from other parts of Catalonia that the capital is over-provided with cultural facilities and financial–industrial infrastructure. In fact, Jordi Pujol himself was always clear that if Barcelona was allowed to become too dominant this would be to the detriment of the rest of Catalonia, and he did not wish to see the rest of the autonomous community subsumed into a 'city state' of Barcelona (Muñoz, 2002). On the other hand, the need for interdependent firms in a particular sector to be reasonably close together, and near to relevant educational and social facilities, is a key part of most regional development strategies. Allen J. Scott (2000: 36), speaking specifically about image-producing industries, points out that not only are 'agglomerations of technologically dynamic firms' a distinct competitive advantage, but creativity itself depends on 'places where qualities such as cultural insight, imagination, and originality are actively generated from within the local system of production, and put into service in the shaping of final outputs'. Scott goes on to say that 'these qualities can be theorized not so much as the outward expression of inscrutable psychological processes as the determinate efforts of a many-sided economic and geographic system of production'. In other words, the Catalans cannot rely on their inherent creativity alone (despite Vilajoana's high estimation of this as expressed in his prologue to the *Llibre blanc*), but must generate physical, social, educational and economic networks of support for it.

Barcelona city council has already invested a fair amount of its own energies in supporting the audio-visual sector with initiatives such as the *Barcelona Plató* Film Commission and *22@bcn*. *Barcelona Plató*, created in 1996, is an office that provides a number of services aimed at encouraging people to film in Barcelona, including free or low-cost use of spaces in the city, and comprehensive free information about the available facilities. *22@bcn* is the name for an urban regeneration project in the Poble Nou area which aims to make this a centre for technological research and development. (This project is in keeping with the *Ajuntament*'s general strategy of linking cultural events or the provision of new cultural facilities to wider urban regeneration.) Even though the list of sectors they hope to attract to the area is long, and includes information technology, telecommunications and publishing, the audio-visual sector is one of their key targets, and part of the development is set aside as a *Campus Audiovisual*. One of the reasons for the city council's attempts to create a more professional framework for the audio-visual sector is its succinct diagnosis that 'the city's independent producers are situated more within an ideological project than a business one' (Institut de Cultura, 1999: section 5.3.1),[14] meaning, presumably, that making money is not as important to them as making cinema in Catalan. The *Ajuntament* sought to change this attitude, but clearly attributed part of the blame for it to the *Generalitat*, which it claimed had failed to fulfil its responsibilities as a catalyst and coordinator, and had not dedicated sufficient resources to the area. The *Llibre blanc* at least recognizes that not enough has been done to capitalize on the developments in Barcelona that have been instigated by the city council (ICIC, 2002: 43), although it blames this more on the lack of interest shown by private companies than on anyone's cultural policy.

(4) The need to attract private investors.

The need to use public funds strategically in order to generate private investment in the cultural industries is one of the general themes of the *Llibre blanc* and is specifically highlighted in the recommendations for the audio-visual sector. There is a perception that the Catalan bourgeoisie has not shown enough interest in the investment opportunities presented by cinema, television and the media and has tended to stick to more traditional areas of activity. Many of the success stories of the audio-visual sector in Catalonia actually have largely 'Spanish' or international shareholders (e.g. Gestmusic, a Barcelona production company that is now part of Dutch-based Endemol, whose majority shareholder is the Spanish telecommunications company Telefónica). This means that their products are primarily aimed at the Spanish market. As with publishing, the process of incorporation of Catalan businesses into Spanish or international companies has accelerated in the audio-visual sector in the last few years, resulting in the de-prioritization of products for the Catalan market (Aguilera, 2005).

Devising specific measures to attract the interest of Catalan investors became a major concern only quite late in the Pujol administration, despite a limited attempt during the time of the ill-fated *Pacte Cultural* (Giner, Flaquer, Busquet and Bultà, 1996: 171). For the first few years after the autonomous government was established, public investment in culture was low simply because there was not enough money being transferred from central funds; however, there has been a general trend for the amount invested in culture to rise each year. In 1996, Pujol warned that this reliance on public money would have to come to an end and private money would have to be found wherever possible: 'We are looking to find this balance in everything, and especially in the area of culture' (Generalitat de Catalunya, 1999: 28).[15] The move to strengthen the cultural industries in Catalonia followed swiftly on the heels of this statement. This decision was not entirely to do with budgetary limitations and the need to reconcile competing demands on public funds. It was also related to a general perception that private companies are better placed to offer competitive cultural products for the global market, because they are inherently more flexible and therefore more able to act with entrepreneurial flair (Du Gay, 1996: 154–6). However, for this strategy to succeed, the *Generalitat* would have to 'let go' of culture to some extent, leaving the market to its own devices even when this had a negative effect on linguistic normalization.

Discussion of CiU's Approach

All of these recommendations demonstrate the intention of looking beyond the rather isolationist stance of the *Generalitat* up to that point, although they would certainly not mean the abandonment of subsidies to production in Catalan under the heading of Linguistic Normalization. However, this renewed attempt to kick-start the market for Catalonia's cultural industries gives rise to some interesting challenges and contradictions. Some of these have already been mentioned above, such as the unusual decision to intervene in the production of culture as well as its reproduction (Schuster, 2002: 1), which is related to the temptation to apply a *dirigiste* cultural policy to areas that are more normally left to the market (Miller and Yúdice, 2002: 16), and the difficulty of separating out overlapping and potentially conflicting language and cultural industries policies.

Two other considerations should be added to the list here. Firstly, Miller and Yúdice (2002: 16) draw a distinction between 'culture as fun (via the market) and progress (via the state)', which means that governments do not normally intervene in cultural products that are viewed strictly as entertainment, but concern themselves only with cultural forms that are believed to have an educational or social value. However, this distinction did not apply in the context of CiU's approach to Catalan culture: 'culture as fun' could not be left to the market because it was central to the survival of the Catalan language. Forms of entertainment were seen instead as 'culture as [linguistic] progress', and regulated as such by the Catalan quasi-state. Secondly, as Jordi Busquet reminds us, the linguistic distinction between Catalan and Spanish products actually represents an oversimplification of a more complex problem that we have already touched on in the case of literature: 'It is precisely when we come to analyse the cultural industries that we see the difficulty of speaking about *Catalan culture* or *Spanish culture* as if they were unrelated facts' (Busquet, 1998: 882).[16] A cultural industries policy that aimed for economic growth in areas such as cinema and television would necessarily call for a more flexible definition of what constituted a Catalan cultural product than had been provided in the past by the application of linguistic criteria. Yet by embracing the idea that Catalan culture could employ Spanish (or English, or Japanese. . .), or might involve products with no clear cultural provenance at all, CiU would have opened

themselves up to accusations of abandoning the core of their
nationalist ideology in favour of simple money-making.

Salvador Giner, Lluís Flaquer, Jordi Busquet and Núria Bultà
(1996: 40) express the key element of these dilemmas by using the
terms 'sacred' and 'profane' to analyse different approaches to
Catalan culture: 'the strong modern process of secularization has
reached its limits: the national community, among others, has
become the house of the sacred, and its most fundamental manifestations draw on this new sacredness and transcendence'.[17] In other
words, essentialism is still present in modern attitudes to national
culture and identity (61). This means that a nationalist party
cannot risk a purely 'managerial' approach to cultural policy – one
that treats culture as just another aspect of the public sector to be
rationally and efficiently administered – because their supporters
will see this as a profanation of the essence of their culture and
identity (203, 205). Nevertheless, other modern processes such as
globalization and the commodification of culture, coupled with
the prosaic day-to-day realities of government and administration,
mean that some form of managerialism is now an inevitable part of
any cultural policy (202, 216): 'Managerialism means that culture is
profaned, but is also choosing survival'.[18] Finally, the authors
suggest a 'third way' between the profane (managerialism) and the
sacred (essentialism) which involves a return to the cooperative
spirit of the *Pacte Cultural* and a recognition of the plurality of
Catalan culture, even in terms of the language in which it is
expressed. It is not clear how this would work in practice, but their
ideas do point forward to the position that the left-wing tripartite
government would adopt after November 2003. As far as CiU's time
in government is concerned, the authors note a clear preference
for essentialist approaches in the early 1980s under Max Cahner
(134), a swing towards managerialism after the failure of the *Pacte
Cultural* (135), and a return of essentialism from 1993 to 1996 when
relations with the central state were particularly strained (77). We
could add that it is also the tension between essentialism and
managerialism that appears to have shaped CiU's cultural industries strategy from 1996 to 2003.

This tension manifests itself particularly in the policy of subsidies
for certain producers and forms of culture that has already been
illustrated above. In effect, the *Generalitat* was carrying out a form of
patronage, which was perceived by many cultural practitioners as a
significant issue during the Pujol years and led to it being known as

'la repartidora', a term which could be loosely translated as 'the distributor'. Salvador Cardús describes the effects of 'la repartidora' as 'generating both profound gratitude and eternal dissatisfaction at the same time' (Cardús, 1988: 7).[19] This is because patronage necessarily involves a form of selectivity that is unlikely to be based on purely artistic criteria. As Bourdieu remarks, 'art and cultural consumption are predisposed, consciously and deliberately or not, to fulfil a social function of legitimating social differences':

> Explicit aesthetic choices are in fact often constituted in opposition to the choices of the groups closest in social space, with whom the competition is most direct and most immediate, and more precisely, no doubt, in relation to those choices most clearly marked by the intention (perceived as pretension) of marking distinction vis-à-vis lower groups [. . .] (Bourdieu, 1984: 7, 60)

In the context of Catalonia in the late twentieth century, one of the keys to this form of differentiation was the split between supporters of CiU and PSC, especially in Barcelona where the PSC's control over the *Ajuntament de Barcelona* gave it a great deal of cultural influence. Many artists, intellectuals and business people came to be associated with one or other of the groups, maintaining personal friendships with politicians and/or contributing their opinions to the media in ways that endorsed the approach of one party or the other. As we have seen from the case studies of Catalan literature, theatre and television, many important postholders in the cultural field were also appointed directly by politicians. Not only did all this lead to suspicions of favouritism in the granting of subsidies, posts and prizes, it also made it difficult for anyone wanting to be successful in the cultural field to remain politically neutral. Even though the PSC insisted after taking power in the *Generalitat* that such exclusive practices would no longer be the norm, Mark Schuster points out that the 'small pond' of Catalan culture might not in any case be a good place to attempt a truly objective system of selection.

> In a place such as Catalunya it is likely that all of the major players in a particular subsector know and interact with one another. Moreover, their links to government are likely to be close and personal. How is it possible, then, to develop a policy that will be built on hard choices, on saying yes to some and no to others? Will the network of interpersonal relationships be so strong as to undo the effect of any policy initiative [. . .]? (Schuster, 2002: 10)

In other words, the inherent conditions of the Catalan cultural field make it particularly susceptible to political influence, whether in the form of essentialist criteria being applied to cultural policy decisions, or *dirigiste* intervention in the market.

Another problem that is indirectly highlighted by Schuster's comments relates to the position of the consumer – a figure who has not yet played much of a role in this discussion. The small world of Catalan culture lends itself to a rather claustrophobic relationship between creators and policymakers which actually seems to exclude consideration of the consumer. This may be partly caused by the tendency, that has already been discussed in other chapters, for culture in Catalan to be seen as elite culture. It would be counterproductive to allow this elitism to influence policy on the cultural industries, whose products must necessarily be directed to a mass audience to achieve the maximum return on investment. Even so, the stress on normalizing 'prestige forms' such as the feature film suggests that elements of elitism are still present, which in turn will limit the potential for expanding audiences. Salvador Cardús warned against this in 1988: 'The daily reality faced by every cultural agent is, fundamentally, one of *scarcity of demand*. And, logically, a cultural policy would be silly to base itself on a low level of demand and should instead be built on an explicit desire to *stimulate it'* (Cardús, 1988: 94).[20] This is especially true in the case of the cultural industries, since, as Nicholas Garnham explains, 'in general the costs of reproduction are marginal in relation to the costs of production [. . .] Thus, the marginal returns from each extra sale tend to grow, leading in turn to a powerful thrust towards audience maximization as the preferred profit maximization strategy' (Garnham, 1993: 57). In the case of the Catalan cultural industries, it is necessary to draw a distinction between what we might call internal and external audiences. Internal audiences, in this case, would be residents of Catalonia who are to be encouraged to choose cultural products in the Catalan language, wherever language is a factor, or by Catalan producers wherever it is not. External audiences would be Spanish, European or global consumers who would be encouraged to buy Catalan products either as part of a strategy of profit maximization or, if the products were recognizably Catalan in some non-linguistic way, as part of a desire to increase awareness of Catalonia's cultural distinctiveness. The ICIC's remit included both of these groups, but this gave rise to the danger that internal audiences would end up consuming Catalan products on the same basis as external audiences unless cultural policy could shape internal demand as well as supply.

During CiU's period in power the main policy areas that related to the creation of internal cultural demand were education and linguistic normalization. However, these primarily addressed Catalans as citizens and only secondarily as consumers: i.e. as 'the *national* subject' rather than 'the *rational* subject' (Miller and Yúdice, 2002: 73). This gave rise to the danger that Catalans would feel they had done their duty as citizens by becoming proficient in Catalan and being prepared to use it in the domains that seemed to have been marked out for it by the *Generalitat:* administration, education, high culture, supporting *el Barça.* . . This would then leave them free, as consumers, to choose from the vast range of mass cultural products being offered to them in Catalan, Spanish and (increasingly) English. CiU appeared to be worried that if the cultural industries in Catalonia started to produce more material for an undifferentiated Spanish market, this would send the wrong signals to Catalans both as citizens *and* consumers, and this is why the ICIC's *Llibre blanc* was unable to ignore linguistic constraints in favour of a fully market-based cultural industries strategy. Protectionism towards the internal market was to be retained whatever effect this might have on the external market, and this decision can be understood most easily if it is related to the role of the cultural industries in producing symbols. These symbols affect group identity and are therefore instruments of power. As David Hesmondhalgh puts it, 'the cultural industries are those industries most directly involved in the production of social meaning, because they make and circulate texts, artefacts that are primarily intended to inform and/or entertain. This is the key to understanding the particular role of the cultural industries in relationship to economic, political, social and cultural power' (Hesmondhalgh, 2002: 264). It is Hesmondhalgh's contention that 'The study of the cultural industries has to incorporate the consideration of texts; and the study of texts has to take seriously analysis of the cultural industries'. The Catalan case demonstrates the truth of this statement.

The discussion here has very much centred on the problem of the overlapping Spanish and Catalan cultural markets (and consumers), with only a nod to the wider world and Catalonia's cultural relationship to it. The final chapter corrects this oversight by addressing two phenomena, globalization and immigration, that force Catalonia's cultural policy to operate within an even more complex environment than has been acknowledged here. However, before we can tie up the discussion in this way it is also necessary to look at cultural policy in areas that were not driven primarily by linguistic concerns (although these played their part too) but by other elements of the historic identity of Catalonia. While the cultural industries might have been seen as the 'cutting edge' of Catalan cultural production, history and tradition could not be abandoned and needed to take on innovative features themselves in order to be in a position to respond to those very same challenges of globalization, immigration and commodification.

NOTES

1   'Les indústries culturals d'un país són percebudes avui no només com un factor de progrés econòmic, sinó també com la via de garantir la presència de productes culturals propis, és a dir, de presentar la creativitat i el punt de vista propis en el mercat cultural universal.' Llei 20/2000, de 29 de desembre, de creació de l'Institut Català de les Indústries Culturals.

2   'consolidar un teixit empresarial en tots els sectors culturals de Catalunya que permeti connectar la creació local amb els circuits internacionals i incrementar el consum cultural. En alguns casos es tracta, per tant, d'enfortir les indústries culturals tradicionals, i en altres, de potenciar el vessant mercantil de la resta de sectors culturals.'

3   'difícil d'imaginar aquest país o quina hauria estat la seva evolució cultural, política i social sense l'existència d'aquest mitjà, la creació del qual – i em crec portaveu d'una opinió bastant generalitzada – és l'obra de govern més important que ha dut a terme la Generalitat.'

4   Canal 33 was restructured in 2001 and renamed K3/33: its broadcasting was split so that children's programmes fill the daytime schedules ('K3'), with cultural and educational programmes for adults from 8pm ('33'). An international service via satellite was rolled out from 1997, and a news channel, 3/24, was inaugurated on 11 September 2003.

5   CCRTV (Corporació Catalana de Ràdio i Televisió) is also responsible for four radio stations: Catalunya Ràdio, Catalunya Música, Catalunya Informació and Catalunya Cultura.

6   There was a further struggle for political control that went outside Catalonia's borders and which cannot be treated here for reasons of space. The prejudices and unhelpfulness of RTVE have already been mentioned, but this was nothing compared with the blocks that were put in the way of TV3, mainly by the Spanish state, when it tried to

broadcast to Valencia and the Balearic Islands. For details see the special edition of *El Temps*, no. 1003 (2–8 September 2003).

[7] 'TVC és un pilar al voltant del qual ha emergit bona part de la indústria audiovisual catalana'.

[8] Decret 237/1998, de 8 de setembre, sobre mesures de foment de l'oferta cinematogràfica doblada i subtitulada en llengua catalana; Decret 172/2000, de 15 de maig, pel qual es deroga el Decret 237/1998, de 8 de setembre, sobre mesures de foment de l'oferta cinematogràfica doblada i subtitulada en llengua catalana.

[9] 'la incapacidad para exportar sus productos, lo que genera un mercado cerrado sin promoción externa'

[10] 'Ara més que mai és convenient de pensar globalment i d'actuar localment'. 'Una identitat sòlida és el millor camí per entendre i participar en un món tan global com divers'.

[11] 'continuarem fent una política cultural que, sense que es confongui amb la política lingüística, no oblidi quina és la importància de la llengua catalana a Catalunya'.

[12] 'Malgrat que l'objectiu fonamental del Llibre Blanc és potenciar les estructures creatives i empresarials del conjunt de l'oferta cultural produïda a Catalunya, amb independència del seu idioma d'expressió, és innegable la importància que té la producció i el mercat en llengua catalana per tal de preservar un espai expressiu, identitari i simbòlic autòcton.'

[13] 'Pot ser que la política de la indústria cultural sigui veritablement una política lingüística, tot i que en una forma lleugerament diferent.' 'Hi ha una oportunitat substancial de confusió política aquí, en especial perquè d'altres agències governamentals existeixen per tal de tractar la normalització i la promoció del català, amb el desenvolupament econòmic de Catalunya, i amb les arts, la cultura i el patrimoni de Catalunya.' (The English version reproduced in the text is taken from the original English version of the paper, 'Catalunya and its Cultural Industries: Policy Pitfalls and Policy Opportunities' (Schuster, 2002: 10).)

[14] 'Les productores independents de la ciutat estan més situades en un projecte ideològic que no pas empresarial.'

[15] 'Mirem de trobar aquest equilibri en tot, i especialment en el camp de la cultura'.

[16] 'És precisament en analitzar les indústries culturals quan es constata la dificultat de parlar de *cultura catalana* o *cultura espanyola* com a fets aïllats'.

[17] 'el fort procés modern de secularització ha trobat els seus límits: la comunitat nacional, entre d'altres, ha esdevingut la casa del sagrat, i les seves manifestacions més fonamentals, participen d'aquesta nova sacralitat i transcendència.'

[18] 'Amb el gerencialisme la cultura resta profanada, però al mateix temps opta a la supervivència'.

[19] 'generadora de profunds agraïments i d'eternes insatisfaccions alhora'.

[20] 'La realitat quotidiana amb la que topa tot agent cultural és, fonamentalment, la de *l'escassedat de la demanda*. I, lògicament, una política cultural mal faria de refiar-se d'una demanda escassa, sinó que s'ha de bastir sobre un desig explícit d'*estimular-la*.' (Italics in the original)

Chapter Five

History, Tradition and Heritage

This chapter will take as its central theme the use of tradition and heritage by CiU in its cultural policy and nation-building strategies. One of the clear priorities of the new autonomous government in 1980 was to counter the effects of the systematic distortions of history that had been perpetrated by the Franco regime. Younger generations of Catalans (and Basques, Galicians, Majorcans . . .) had been subjected to a historical education that had robbed them of any contact with their own community's past and subjected them to tales of the glory of the Spanish nation. Lucia Graves, educated in Majorca after her father took the family to live there in 1946, gives an especially eloquent account of this form of brainwashing, during which 'We wrote endless dictations about the glory of the Spanish flag and the greatness of the Empire, and were told that democracy was the ruin of a nation' (Graves, 2000: 62). Not only this, but physical traces of the past had also been erased by changing the names of streets and buildings, removing statues and monuments, and destroying or restricting access to books and archives. Traditions were repressed if the regime considered them potentially subversive; those that survived without risk to the participants were either saved by their religious content, which was then stressed above all other meanings, or whimsical enough to be regarded as nothing more than local colour. After the dictatorship, all the buried manifestations of Catalonia's difference could be restored to public view: heritage and history were to be re-Catalanized, while traditions would be rediscovered or modernized.

Centre and right-wing Catalanism has tended to have an ambivalent relationship with Catalan traditional and popular culture. Catalanists between the late nineteenth and early twentieth centuries saw literature (especially poetry) and 'art' in its broadest sense as the backbones of Catalan culture, with only a cursory nod in the direction of popular culture in the shape of the *sardana*: a dance that was reinvented in the mid nineteenth century, ironically enough by an Andalusian immigrant. During the Franco dictatorship, traditional culture was important because the manifestations of it that were still possible functioned as a point of connection between Catalans and their history and identity, even if the regime did its best to contextualize these events as rather outmoded demonstrations of local Spanish culture.[1] After the end of the dictatorship, traditional culture was part of the celebration of democracy and autonomy, while also providing a significant vehicle for protesting and articulating demands during the negotiations that characterized the Transition. This, then, is where traditional culture found itself in 1980: newly resurgent, after a period of repression during which both habit and defiance had kept certain aspects of it alive.

As far as heritage was concerned, it was now possible to reclaim for Catalonia elements of built heritage that had been appropriated by the regime. Statues, monuments and street names could be restored, while major buildings could be given back to Catalan institutions, including the parliament building in the Ciutadella park, and the *Palau de la Generalitat*. The provisions for autonomy enshrined in the Spanish constitution of 1978 led to the systematic devolution of control over museums, libraries, archives and historic buildings to lower tiers of government, whether local or regional: the *Generalitat* is responsible for those that are considered important to Catalonia as a whole, and are therefore tagged as national assets in the Catalan sense. This was of course just the beginning of the story, since one of the side effects of the Franco regime had been a serious neglect of Catalan heritage that left many buildings and institutions crumbling, poorly run and underused, especially in the case of museums (Garcia, 1999). A great deal of time and expenditure has been necessary to restore them to a fit state and equip them for mass public use. The *Museu Nacional d'Art de Catalunya* (MNAC) at Montjuïc, for example, was officially created from the neglected *Museu d'Art de Catalunya* in 1990, but the project to update the building, infrastructure and collection of the museum was to last until 2004 and cost 122 million euros (Serra, 2004: 54). Another challenge has been to coordinate the complex network of responsibilities generated by the division of competencies between local, autonomic and state actors, which was also deemed to be a factor in slowing down progress on the MNAC.

It is worth remembering that this effort to recuperate the heritage, tradition and history of Catalonia must also be seen within the Spanish context of revival and repositioning after the dictatorship. Edward Stanton speaks of a general 'return to tradition' in Spain which includes a 'festive escalation' that is a direct result of political decentralization (Stanton, 1999: 52–3). The task of taking over responsibility for museums and built heritage has fallen on every autonomous community and local authority in Spain, however ill-prepared they felt for the challenge (Holo, 2000). Difficult decisions about how best to spend public money, and how to attract revenue from tourists without compromising the meaning of the site or tradition for the local community, are common to all places and all administrations. However, it is those communities that felt a specific grievance against the Franco regime for robbing them of their distinctive identity that have been keenest to capitalize on the possibilities offered by autonomy.

Opportunities have been seized to recover lost aspects of history, or to produce alternative historical narratives, not only through cultural policy but also through education. The education system that resulted from the Spanish law on education (LOGSE) of 1990 allowed for up to 45 per cent of the history curriculum to be decided by the autonomous communities themselves, and Catalonia took greater advantage of this than any other region (Segura, 2001: 34, 36). These institutional arrangements were backed up with other initiatives in publishing and the media, some of which were directly generated by the *Generalitat*, through advertising and publishing or thanks to its influence over publicly owned Catalan media. Catalan television (TV3) even produced a cartoon version of Catalonia's history, in thirty-nine episodes, aimed at children (Artigas, 1989). This was shown in 1988 to coincide with the celebrations of the millennium of Catalonia's birth as a separate political entity – a commemoration which, as well as providing an opportunity to teach Catalans about their history, was also a conscious attempt to strengthen the legitimacy of the *Generalitat* as an institution (Salrach, 1988).

These kinds of initiatives have not been uncontroversial, as we can see from three examples. Firstly, in 2000 there was a review of history teaching in Spain carried out by the *Real Academia de la Historia* that suggested that the Catalans and some other autonomous communities were failing to pay due attention to the history of Spain as a whole in their textbooks and syllabuses (Segura, 2001: 37). This led to something of a moral panic in the media, fanned by the *Partido Popular*'s general paranoia about any lack of 'constitutional patriotism' from Spain's regions and nationalities. Their criticisms were met by angry reactions from Catalan historians, politicians and educators (Segura, 2001: 36–7; Martí Font, 2000). Secondly, the pages of the Catalan history journal *L'Avenç* are continually occupied by articles and opinion pieces exploring issues of tradition, heritage, history as an academic discipline,[2] museums and cultural policy, within the specific context of Catalan autonomy and identity. These articles have proved invaluable in my research for this chapter and are a useful barometer of the debates in these areas. Thirdly, we should not forget the 'Salamanca papers', the archives of the *Generalitat* during the Second Republic, and of other Catalan institutions, that had been removed from Catalonia to Salamanca at the end of the civil war and were used to identify and 'incriminate' Catalans who were considered enemies of the regime. The papers were the object of fierce arguments between those who wished to see them returned to Catalonia (as most eventually have been) and those who felt they should remain in Salamanca as part of a national – Spanish – heritage. These kinds of debates feed in to cultural policy as it 'produces zones of public memory and learning, organized by rules and colored by debates in historiography, that regulate the past, in a way that is determined by the concerns of the present' (Miller and Yúdice, 2002: 23).

Furthermore, as Stephen Reicher and Nick Hopkins point out, 'The real significance of these arguments lies in their action-orientation. It is practical politics – the organization of collective action through the grounding of strategically organized identity constructions – which shapes these speakers' forays into the past' (Reicher and Hopkins, 2001: 151). This means that history can only be truly useful in building a sense of national identity if it is embodied in particular projects with specific objectives. This is why this chapter will not draw a strict distinction between tradition and heritage but look at both in terms of the practical use that has been made of history as a part of CiU's cultural policy. In fact the Law of

Catalan Cultural Heritage passed in 1993 includes tradition under the umbrella of heritage,[3] and so, implicitly, do Graham, Ashworth and Tunbridge (2000: 2) in their 'straightforward definition of heritage as the contemporary use of the past'. However, while the definition of heritage might be straightforward, its management through cultural policy is far from simple. Tradition and heritage in Catalonia, as in any other nation, have different uses, users, and means of support, and these often conflict with one another (Miller and Yúdice, 2002: 22–3). These conflicts might involve different interpretations of history, or of the symbolic value of an artefact, site, tradition or myth. On a more practical level, there has also been an ongoing problem of coordination between different levels of government. This chapter will trace these issues through various examples of policy concerning tradition and heritage, while also bearing in mind the general context in which these policies were made and the debates they have provoked.

Legislation and the Basis of Policy

Although linguistic normalization was very much the priority for the *Generalitat* when they first began to legislate on cultural matters, traditional culture and heritage were not forgotten. Various laws were passed during the period that CiU were in power, concerning popular and traditional culture, libraries, archives, museums, and architectural, artistic and archaeological heritage. The general aims of these laws were to establish the responsibilities of the different layers of government in each area and to encourage cooperation between them, to safeguard important aspects of Catalonia's heritage and traditions, to improve access to these forms of culture for all residents, and to establish favourable conditions for them to flourish (Holo, 2000: 166–9). However, critics of the laws point out that in many cases the provisions they included were never put into practice, competences remained unclear, cooperation between administrative bodies was patchy at best, and funding was insufficient (Fancelli, 2003; Mascarell, 1999: 41–52, 68–71).

To get an idea of the spirit of the laws we need only look briefly at two, beginning with the 1993 law on popular and traditional culture (*Llei 2/1993 de 5 de març, de foment i protecció de la cultura popular i tradicional i d'associacionisme cultural*).[4] The preamble to the law starts by stressing the importance of civil society and participation in cultural associations, before making the following general statement about the importance of traditional and popular culture in Catalonia:

> Traditional and popular culture, as the totality of the past and present manifestations, knowledge, activities and beliefs within the collective memory, is the reference point out of which society's initiatives are framed in a context that configures Catalonia as having its own national identity rooted in plural forms of popular expression and, at the same time, in a firm desire to project itself into the future.[5]

This assumption that Catalan identity must be well rooted if it is to have a meaningful future is key to the cultural rhetoric of the *Generalitat* and of Jordi Pujol himself, and it is well illustrated by this particular law. Many of its provisions are related to the need to have a written inventory of the cultural forms covered by the law (which include *festes* and customs, traditional music, crafts, and cultural associations), and to categorize the most important of these as being 'of national interest' or 'of cultural interest'. Cultural forms can therefore be protected by being described and catalogued, and decisions on the allocation of funding can be taken more easily as a hierarchy of importance to the national culture will have been established.

The cultural heritage law (*Llei del Patrimoni Cultural Català*)[6] passed in the same year, takes a similar position regarding heritage and allows for certain historic items or sites to be declared as being 'of national interest'. Once again, the preamble to the law made it clear that Catalonia's cultural heritage is to be regarded collectively as an affirmation of the nation's identity above all other things: the first sentence reads 'Cultural heritage is one of the fundamental witnesses to the trajectory of the history and identity of a national collective'.[7] For the purposes of the law, a wide definition of cultural heritage was employed that included natural and built heritage, collections of material culture and documents, as well as forms of traditional and popular culture. One of the main provisions of the law was to make sure that all heritage was properly catalogued and classified: searchable inventories of such things as built heritage and popular festivals are now available on the *Generalitat*'s website.[8] Also, article 57 of the law made provision for what came to be known as 'l'1 per cent cultural', since it declared that 1 per cent of the budget for public works should go to projects related to conservation, restoration, excavation, etc. An exhibition catalogue published in 2003 (Generalitat de Catalunya, 2003a) showed that by that stage more than 300 projects had been funded with this money, most of them with comparatively modest budgets and often involving a partnership with the local authorities. The works were scattered around Catalonia and often involved small towns or villages rather than cities, although some projects were city based, such as a contribution to the restoration of the façade of the Basilica of Santa Maria del Mar in Barcelona (nearly 240,000 euros), and a joint project with the *Ajuntament de Girona* to restore the city walls and incorporate them into a public walkway (at a total cost of around 784,000 euros). These projects, along with the catalogues of sites, collections and traditions, are among the most tangible outcomes of the law.

History and Heritage

CiU's approach to heritage conservation raises a number of issues, including the problem of conflicting agendas in the management of heritage. This problem has two main aspects: the fact that heritage can have both commercial and symbolic uses, and the complications added by the existence of different layers of government and administration, with different priorities and areas of responsibility, operating within the same territory.

Graham, Ashworth and Tunbridge, in their book *A Geography of Heritage* (2000), stress the fact that heritage should be properly viewed as a resource that is used for contemporary purposes rather than as some kind of frozen reflection of the past. Heritage is used to promote tourism and development, 'But heritage also helps define the meanings of culture and power and is a political resource; and it thus possesses a crucial sociopolitical function. Consequently, it is accompanied by an often bewildering array of identifications and potential conflicts, not least when heritage places and objects are involved in issues of legitimization of power structures' (Graham, Ashworth and Tunbridge, 2000: 17). In the Catalan case, this process of legitimization is at the heart of cultural policy, in the sense that the aim of that policy was to reduce the potential for bewilderment and conflict by steering the public towards particular visions of heritage that would legitimize CiU's own versions of Catalonia's past, present and future. Even so, the policymakers and administrators could not avoid the problem of what Graham, Ashworth and Tunbridge call 'heritage dissonance'. They define this as 'the mismatch between heritage and people, in space and time' and go on to say that 'it is caused by movements or other changes in heritage and by migration or other changes in people, transformations which characteristically involve how heritage is perceived and what value systems are filtering those perceptions. The most pervasive source of heritage dissonance lies in the fundamental diversity of societies' (Graham, Ashworth and Tunbridge, 2000: 93). The radical transformation of Catalan society that began with the mass movement of people from other areas of Spain in the 1950s and 60s, and continues today as Catalonia becomes an evermore attractive destination for international migrants, presents a clear challenge when it comes to using heritage as a way of recuperating a particular version of Catalonia's past.

One project has come to be emblematic of the practical problems of reconciling different cultural priorities and different layers of institutional responsibility: the construction of a provincial library in Barcelona on the site of the disused Born market (Menéndez and Pastor, 2002). A large steel and glass construction, the market was built in the 1870s and closed in 1971. The building had seen a series of temporary uses since then, so it seemed like an ideal choice for redevelopment as a library, especially because of its favourable position on the edge of the *Ciutat Vella* (Old City). The library was to be a joint project between the Spanish *Ministerio de Cultura*, the *Generalitat* and the *Ajuntament de Barcelona*, and was part of a statewide initiative to build provincial libraries – only Barcelona and Bilbao were left without one at that stage. The responsibility of each party initially seemed clear enough: the Ajuntament would supply the site (free of charge), the state would cover construction costs and capital investment in equipment etc., and the *Generalitat* would eventually be responsible for running the library. However, the project, which should have been completed in 2005, was thrown into confusion when it emerged that archaeological remains that were known to be buried under the market were more extensive and potentially more important than first thought. The site held the remains of a suburb that was constructed in the fourteenth Century and then destroyed in 1716 to make room for a military citadel whose purpose was to stamp the state's authority on the people of Barcelona after their defeat in the War of Succession. While some held that the remains were not so old as to be of great significance, and others feared their preservation as some kind of propagandistic monument to Catalan resistance, many politicians, archaeologists, historians and citizens did feel that it was necessary to reach a compromise whereby the library could coexist with the preservation and conservation of the remains.

It was at this point that serious tensions arose between the different parties. If the provision of the library was eventually found to be incompatible with the preservation of the remains, which should prevail? The *Ministerio* said that it was happy to use another site if one could be provided, but there were no obvious alternatives. Despite some reservations about noise and disruption, the district council did not want to lose the opportunities presented by having a major library on its doorstep and so asked for it to be built there while conserving the remains to the greatest possible extent. Many historians, archaeologists and museologists argued that anything less than full preservation of, and public access to, the remains would be a crime against Catalonia's history and heritage. This left the *Generalitat*, the *Ajuntament* and the *Districte de Ciutat Vella* (the district council) to fight over the rights and wrongs of the case, with the *Generalitat* seeming the least willing to put forward a clear point of view on the issue. (An application for the site to be declared to be 'of national interest' under the terms of the cultural heritage law was dealt with remarkably slowly!) Eventually, the architects proposed a solution in which the library would be built on the site as planned, incorporating some conservation and display of the remains but involving a certain amount of destruction of them in the laying of the foundations, and resulting in the reburial of up to 75 per cent of the site. However, the strength of the protests against this compromise forced the authorities to step back from their initial guarded acceptance of it and think again. Members of the public joined interested intellectuals and professionals in condemning the compromise as ill-conceived and unacceptable.

Finally, following a proposal from the then mayor of Barcelona, Joan Clos, in October 2002, the decision was taken to abandon the market as the site of the new library and to build it instead on land belonging to the nearby railway station, the *Estació de França* (thus appeasing the residents by keeping the library in the same district). A provisional plan was soon in place for the restoration of the market, the preservation of the remains, and the development of exhibition spaces to chronicle the archaeological work in progress. The fact that this project would be under the control of the PSC-led *Ajuntament* no doubt allayed some people's fears about the remains being used as nationalist propaganda, even though in their electoral pledges CiU are still promising that, if they get the chance, 'we will develop the space offered by the Born as a historic symbol of our national identity' (Convergència, 2005: 27).[9] However, a delay in transferring ownership of the site back from the *Ministerio de Cultura* – blamed on slow bureaucracy – meant a long wait before any major work could begin. From May 2004 the excavation site was opened to visitors at weekends, although it was closed again in 2005 when the construction work finally started, not to build a library but a 'cultural centre' based around the stories told by the site. Meanwhile, the library project began in its new location several years behind schedule.

Clearly, economic considerations had to give way to other priorities during the wrangling over the future of the Born market. The preservation of the market building was always going to be a costly exercise in its own right (which is one reason why no one had taken on the challenge since it closed in 1971), but the even more substantial investment needed to excavate and preserve the ruins and then create the new cultural centre could not have been foreseen at the start of the process. The cost of this work will now fall primarily to Barcelona city council, and there is obviously a question mark over whether the project is viable in purely financial terms. Most projects that are subsidized from public funds are expected to prove their capacity to generate income, not necessarily to cover their own costs when they are fully operational, although this might be the case, but certainly to contribute to the economic growth of the area in which they are situated. For example, projects selected for funding with 'l'1 per cent cultural' have to demonstrate that they will have commercial or other benefits when finished, whether directly, by attracting tourist revenue, or indirectly, by enhancing the attraction of the locality so that shops and services can capitalize on the growth in visitors. The residents of the district, and the city council, will certainly be hoping that this is the case with the new cultural centre. However, it is the pressure to conserve the symbolic remains that has won the argument over the future of the site, and any financial concerns have had to take second place. Of course, the *Ajuntament* is not the only body that can be swayed by non-materialistic concerns: the *Generalitat* too is willing to relegate profit to second place when questions of identity are at stake, as can be seen from the case of the Museum of the History of Catalonia (MHC).[10]

The Museu d'Història de Catalunya

Not even contemplated in the museums law of 1990,[11] the museum project was set in motion in 1993 and it opened in 1996. It houses a permanent exhibition which takes the visitor through the story of Catalonia from pre-history to 1980, as well as hosting temporary exhibitions, which are often related to anniversaries or topical themes. Its purpose, as stated in Article 2(1) of the Decree which brought it into official existence,[12] was to 'conserve, exhibit and disseminate the history of Catalonia as collective heritage, and strengthen citizens' sense of identification with our national history'.[13] Interestingly, the person who had been commissioned to take the project forward, Carme-Laura Gil (a CDC member who later went on to be the minister for education in Pujol's last government), was happy to admit that she was responding to a political mandate and not to the need to house and exhibit a collection of artefacts.

> This museum is very unusual, since it didn't come into existence because there was a collection of pieces with historical value that was to be conserved and exhibited and perhaps used to explain the history of the country through it. What we have here is a political programme belonging to the party in power in Catalonia, the coalition Convergència i Unió, and in its programme on culture for this legislature it includes the creation of a Museum of the History of Catalonia, and this is the mandate that I have been given: to take this project forward.[14] (Casals, 1994: 58)

When asked about the motivations behind this political project, she replied that first and foremost its aim was to tell people about Catalonia's history, since there was a worrying level of ignorance amongst the public, but also that 'the museum and the knowledge of a common history helps social cohesion, especially because the History of Catalonia has never been an exclusive history'.[15] The museum was therefore supposed to function partly as a stimulus for integration, encouraging new residents to understand Catalonia's history and begin to forge their own personal links with it (Holo, 2000: 179). To do this, the MHC needed to act in parallel with education, political rhetoric, and cultural and linguistic normalization to project a sense of what one might call 'historical consonance' onto the new Catalan society. This meant that the main focus of its message was actually an 'internal' one, in the sense that it was targeted at residents of Catalonia and not at foreign tourists or other Spaniards.

In other words, this was primarily a nation-building project, and as such it has attracted criticism from various quarters. The PSC said that the creation of the MHC 'was not a response to any kind of museum-related necessity or social demand'[16] (Mascarell, 1999: 270), and the historian Ricard Vinyes described its purpose as to 'consolidate the mechanisms of national consensus of the centre-right'[17] (Vinyes, 2000: 35). Vinyes makes several interesting points in an article on the MHC in *L'Avenç*, two of which are worth mentioning here. Firstly, he says that since the MHC neither has a collection of its own nor carries out any form of in-house historical research, it cannot really function as anything other than a narrative that is based on a particular official discourse and explains the history of Catalonia to its citizens in official terms (35). As it was originally incarnated, then, the museum could derive only a very limited element of legitimacy by borrowing from discourses of history, archaeology and heritage conservation as 'objective' academic disciplines.

Secondly, Vinyes makes the observation that the version of Catalan history on which the museum's narrative is based derives from the work of Jaume Vicens i Vives (1910–60), who was one of the few authoritative voices on the subject during the Franco regime, partly because of the exile of so many left-wing intellectuals. Vicens i Vives's work on the political and economic history of Catalonia had a clear influence on those who sought a centre or centre-right Catalanist alternative during the Franco regime, not just through his published work but also through personal influence. Jordi Pujol himself has acknowledged a debt to Vicens i Vives, to the extent that he would sometimes ask himself what Vicens i Vives would have done in a particular situation (Muñoz, 1997: 385). Despite the respect that he enjoyed, Vicens i Vives was working in a difficult context that made it hard for him to carry out rigorous research and develop and test his methodologies. This, combined with his premature death, meant that some of his contributions to Catalan historiography can best be described as 'hypotheses' or 'theses' (Muñoz, 1997: 398). According to Vinyes, these 'unfinished hypotheses' became part of the ideological backbone of the centre-right and it was therefore logical that they should also inform the MHC's historical narrative (Vinyes, 2000: 36). However as a result the museum tells a story which is too coherent and reductive and does not leave room for alternative voices or interpretations, especially those of the left, which would have been key for projecting a true picture of Catalan history in the twentieth century.

Jordi Pujol has frequently complained that it is unfair to criticize Catalonia for creating these kinds of national institutions when every other capital city in the world has them (see, for example, Alay, 2003: 27–6), and of course on a simple level he is right. Nation states can and do indulge in this kind of historical reinterpretation. However, in the West most of these kinds of national museums were created during a historical period, the nineteenth century, in which it was commonly accepted that a museum should have a nationalizing, and even 'civilizing', function, and that this was best carried out by putting across one coherent message that would further the civic development of the visitor (Bennett, 1995: 47). To create such a museum today is to ignore the fundamental changes in museum practice that have taken place in the last few decades. John Urry describes these changes as responses to 'a changed conception of history', 'a decline in the strength of a given national history, which the national museums then exemplify', and 'a pluralisation and indeed a contemporisation of history' (Urry, 1999: 227). For example, newer institutions are more likely to eschew overarching narratives in favour of descriptive fragmentation, the juxtaposition of related or even contradictory 'bare facts' without commentary, the narration of subjective experiences and the posing of questions. In this sense, the MHC is a decidedly old-fashioned kind of museum, in which there is no 'negotiation of meanings and values between different cultures' (Bennett, 1998: 203) but instead an attempt to 'establish points of connection that [. . .] serve to incorporate the outer zones of the body politic into programs of civic education', which is how Tony Bennett describes one of the main purposes of the public museum of the nineteenth century (206).

At this point it is necessary to pause to consider whether the MHC is actually a museum at all. Kenneth Hudson (1999: 373–4),

debating the meaning of the term 'museum', states that much of
the difficulty of finding an acceptable definition derives from
changes in museum practice which mean that 'What a museum is
attempting to achieve has become more important than what it is',
a trend which 'makes the definition of a museum increasingly
difficult and perhaps increasingly pointless'. Even so, he is happy to
put forward one definitional element that is still valid despite these
changes: 'It remains true [. . .] that a museum is essentially an
institution in which objects – a better phrase, perhaps, is "real
things" – are the principal means of communication'. While we
might wish to raise questions about the definition of 'real things' in
this context, Hudson's main point stands: the objects themselves
should be the 'main carriers of messages'.[18] This is clearly not the
case in the MHC, for two reasons. Firstly, the MHC was not built
with the purpose of housing objects but of telling the story of
Catalonia's past. By 2004 the museum's collection amounted to
only 350 original objects (Aragay, 2004). This lack of objects can
almost be seen as a symbolic reinforcement of the idea that
Catalonia's history has been forcibly erased from the memory of its
people by successive Spanish regimes, and gives rise to the paradox
that the history told by the museum is actually characterized by its
own absence. Secondly, and in consequence, the 'carriers of messages' in the MHC are not the artefacts that are on display, which
are in any case mainly reproductions, but the written texts which
accompany each element in the sequential study of Catalonia's
history. In fact, the MHC as it was originally designed might be
better described as an exhibition of 'The Story of Catalonia' rather
than as a history museum.

Although the MHC does of course function as a tourist attraction, with its associated merchandise and entrance fee, its primary
purpose is sociopolitical and didactic rather than commercial.
This is exemplified by the fact that entry is free one Sunday a
month and on dates of national importance such as 23 April and
11 September, confirming the museum's role in strengthening the
national identity of Catalans. The *Generalitat* has of course been
subsidizing the museum: in 2002, the MHC received an investment
of 225,000 euros (which accounted for almost half of the total
direct investment in museums by the *Departament de Cultura* in that
year), with revenue from ticket sales and room hire amounting to
just over 106,000 euros (Departament de Cultura, 2002: 154, 202).
This support is given so that the MHC can carry out a form of

'correctional' didacticism that seeks to break Spain's monopoly on the telling of Catalan history. However, the narrative ignores even mutually beneficial aspects of Catalonia's relationship with Spain, virtually only acknowledging the state's existence when it can be blamed for some Catalan misfortune.[19]

A more detailed exploration of the layout and content of the museum is necessary in order to illustrate these points regarding the specific objectives that shaped the design of the permanent exhibition. It is housed on two floors, both of which have the same basic format: the history of Catalonia is told in displays that occupy the walls of rooms leading on one from another in 'correct' chronological order, inviting the visitor to take a linear route (Bennett, 1995: 43, 181–6), while the centre of the space is mainly occupied by reproductions or models of household, agricultural, architectural and industrial items from the period in question. Interactive elements are mainly confined to these central items, with the exception of push-button speakers which play music, fragments of speeches or readings from texts at appropriate points in the historical narrative. Each section is introduced by information boards in Catalan, Spanish and English, but individual displays are accompanied only by explanations in Catalan, in the form of small, plain texts on a white background situated in front of the displays. The displays themselves consist mainly of text, photographs, and reproductions of maps, books, and newspaper articles. In other words, it is as if a history book had been torn apart and its texts and illustrations stuck separately – although still in the correct order – on the walls. These are sometimes accompanied by artefacts which stand in front of the walls, between the plain explanatory text and the illustrated displays.

This layout raises interesting issues. First of all, there is a distinct separation between the historical narrative on the one hand and the objects in the centre of the rooms on the other. The visitor has the choice of how much of each to take in, but it would certainly be possible to take a route through the exhibition which largely ignored one of the two elements. In other words, visitors might choose to 'read the book' on the walls and ignore the central displays (in which case the experience has little more immediacy or appeal than reading a textbook), or they might skip the 'boring' texts in favour of admiring the life-sized models, pulling ropes and pushing buttons when the opportunity arises, and participating in 'fun' activities such as getting into knots attempting to make a stable archway out of the building blocks provided – in which case, these experiences will remain fundamentally decontextualized. Secondly, the labelling of the exhibits not only reinforces this separation but also gives the firm message that the MHC is only interested in reaching a Catalan-speaking public. Elaine Heumann Gurian (1991: 186) believes that good practice in museum label writing is based on the desire to be as inclusive as possible:

> Choosing to write label copy at a level that does not exclude children, the less well-educated, and those not fluent in the language in which the label is written helps make these groups feel included in a wider sense, whereas writing label copy that requires college-level fluency reinforces the notion that all others have come to the wrong place.

In the case of the MHC, the sole use of Catalan in detailed explanations – and a dry, formal Catalan at that – could make a whole host of visitors feel that they 'have come to the wrong place', including foreign tourists, Spaniards from non-Catalan-speaking areas, Catalans with only a limited ability to read the language, and children.

The version of Catalonia's history that is told in these labels is, as we have seen, controversial, because it presents one particular vision of 'the truth'. While publications and representatives of the MHC do often mention the need for the visitor to question their assumptions, the content of the museum gives the impression that the only assumptions that may legitimately be questioned are those that they bring in from outside. False ideas – especially those learnt at school by those educated under the Franco regime, which of course certainly did systematically mutilate reality for political purposes – can only be replaced by 'the truth' as told by the museum. However, as well as distorting the relationship between Catalonia and Spain, and failing to include left-wing perspectives on events in the twentieth century, there are other questionable elements in this version of the truth – for example in the choice of terminology used to describe the political entity of Catalonia at different periods. We might forgive the description of the period from the seventh to the thirteenth century as 'The Birth of a Nation' on the grounds of Pujol's argument that other national governments would no doubt also use the same terms about their founding period even though their ancestors had no awareness of being part of any such thing. However, to describe the period of the seventeenth and early eighteenth centuries as one in which 'Catalunya manté el seu estat propi' ('Catalonia maintains its own state') (Museu d'Història de Catalunya, 2003) – and, specifically, to talk of the defeat of the Catalans by Spanish forces in 1714 as 'la fi de l'Estat català' ('the end of the Catalan State'), as does one of the display boards – might well mislead members of the public, who will associate the term 'state' with its modern value and form a mistaken impression of the democratic credentials and level of independence of Catalonia at this time.

All the evidence suggests, then, that during the first years of its existence the MHC had a very specific visitor in mind – the Catalan citizen – and was not willing or able to broaden its appeal, even if that meant losing the opportunity to make non-Catalans more aware of Catalonia's history. Few obvious changes were implemented between the completion of the museum and the end of the Pujol era, although the temporary exhibitions of course changed regularly, and these did provide an element of plurality and diversity that counteracted the narrowness of the permanent exhibition (for examples of these see *www.mhcat.net/oferta_museal/exposicions_temporals*). Visitor numbers rose to 340,000 per year by 2004, but this is still not a particularly high number given the numbers of visitors to Barcelona – around 25 million per year (Generalitat de Catalunya, 2004b: 10) – and a total of 8 million museum visits per year throughout Catalonia (Departament de Cultura, 2005). In fact, around half of all the MHC's visitors currently belong to school groups, with senior citizens forming the second most important cohort. Groups may book a guided tour, which presumably releases them from the obligation to read many of the explanatory texts. This means that schoolchildren in organized groups will most likely feel 'included', as they will have a different kind of experience from children visiting with their families. On the other hand, foreign tourists form an insignificant part of the museum's audience, which is hardly surprising given the lack of enthusiasm shown by well-known guide books: the edition of the *Rough Guide to Spain* published in 2001 stated bluntly that the MHC was 'heavily nationalistic' and that 'the best part of the museum [. . .] is the fourth floor bar, which has a glorious view of the harbour and city skyline' (Ellingham and Fisher, 2001: 625)!

All this inevitably raises the question of whether those people that have not 'come to the wrong place' – Catalans – are addressed and represented by the museum as equals. It could be argued that the open invitation issued by the museum to residents to partake of their 'own' version of Catalonia's history constructs a Catalan citizenry that is undifferentiated by class, gender or origin, because it addresses the same story to them all, and moreover tells that story in a language, Catalan, which by excluding other groups reinforces the internal coherence of the group which it does address. However, we have already established that, according to Vinyes (2000: 37), those who lived through the Franco period and formed part of the left-wing resistance to the regime might not feel that their contribution had been recognized. Equally, first or second-generation Catalans who have connections to other parts of Spain might be uneasy about the lack of references to Spain as a whole and especially about the way the tale of immigration is told, as if these people only came into existence at the moment they stepped off the train. Both of these potential exclusions also have implications for the MHC's inclusiveness on the basis of class, since working-class Catalans are more likely to identify with left-wing political groups, or be of immigrant origin, or both.

In fact, the version of Catalan history told by the MHC is not only a nationalistic one, but a distinctly bourgeois one, and here again there are similarities with nineteenth-century museums, whose representations Bennett (1995: 97) describes as 'clearly articulated to bourgeois rhetorics of progress'. In the case of the MHC this again reflects the influence of Jaume Vicens i Vives, for whom the bourgeoisie was the key to understanding Catalonia's history as well as the best hope for its future. Vicens i Vives saw the feudal origins of Catalan society, the Catalan work ethic, the development of the merchant class and then of the bourgeoisie and petite bourgeoisie as the main forces that shaped Catalonia's subsequent character and direction. More specifically, he attributed the rise of Catalanism in the nineteenth century to the groundwork laid by the medieval bourgeoisie, who had displayed an 'intuition of the word nation in its modern sense' (Vicens i Vives, 1982: 74).[20] The intelligentsia and industrial classes were then able to construct a nation-building project on this framework, culminating in a brief period at the start of the twentieth century in which there was a coherent Catalanist elite with the same ability to engage ordinary Catalans in their project as had been displayed by that medieval oligarchy (Muñoz, 1997: 248). It was Vicens i Vives's opinion that only a new and dynamic Catalan bourgeoisie could lead political change in Catalonia. This gave a clear steer to Catalanists at the

centre of the political spectrum, as well as influencing their understanding of the historical processes that had formed their nation
(Balcells, 1994: 22, 124).

This understanding is reflected in the language and design of
the MHC. Two of the three sections into which the modern period
of the permanent exhibition is divided take elements of industrial
progress as their titles: 'Vapor i nació' ('Steam and nation' –
eighteenth and nineteenth centuries) and 'Els anys elèctrics' ('The
Electric Years' – 1900–39), and many of the objects displayed in
these sections are associated with industrial or commercial practices. Related to this is the fact that the historical narrative 'ended'
in 1980 with the first democratic elections to the autonomous
parliament, and of course the beginning of Pujol's first term as
president of the *Generalitat*.[21] Although this was a logical end point
in many ways, it does have the drawback of suggesting that these
events represent the culmination of Catalonia's historical development, especially given the 'bourgeois rhetoric of progress' that is
overtly deployed in the sections representing the modern period.
This kind of account of the relationship between past and present
seems to correspond to what Patrick Wright has called 'the complacent bourgeois alignment': 'Historical development is here conceived as a cumulative process which has delivered the nation into
the present as its manifest accomplishment. Both celebratory and
complacent, it produces a sense that "we" are the achievement of
history [. . .]' (cited in Bennett, 1995: 152). The MHC's narrative
orientation seems geared towards persuading Catalans that they
represent an achievement that has been orchestrated over time by
specific economic and political groups aligned with the Catalanist
centre and centre-right.

In other words, the MHC was an instrument of CiU's ideology
and cultural policy that acted directly on Catalan citizens. Its
intended effect was not only to disseminate a Catalan account of
Catalonia's history rather than the versions of it that had been
propagated by authoritarian and centralizing Spanish regimes. It
also legitimized CiU's particular vision of Catalan history, based on
narratives that were part of party members' own ideological formation during the Franco years and the Transition. Josep Llobera
contends that in order to foster a collective and productive sense of
national identity, 'to highlight certain episodes of history for political purposes may be permissible provided that it does not involve

blatant distortions' (Llobera, 1996: 203). Of course each individual's judgement on whether any particular historical element has been distorted, blatantly or otherwise, will depend on their own subjective position, based on their education, lived experience and ideological formation: what is a blatant distortion for one is gospel truth for another. This plurality of viewpoints is what the narrative of the MHC failed to acknowledge, and this failure is actually more significant than whether or not the narrative itself involves distortion.

The MHC constructs the visitor as a citizen at a time when contemporary museums increasingly address them as consumers (MacDonald and Silverstone, 1999: 424–7 and 430–2). The museum was designed to include those who can be labelled 'Catalan' and exclude (if only by not catering for them) others who might come as tourists seeking a leisure or educational opportunity. Because of this, the visitor to the MHC cannot be allowed to 'appropriate[s] curatorial power' or become the 'writer [. . .] of the museum's fictions', something that MacDonald and Silverstone (1999: 432) argue is increasingly the case in the contemporary museum because visitors normally have to be addressed as consumers. Even so, the museum takes advantage of the techniques of modern museums, especially in its interactive exhibits, and its designers therefore felt able to claim, with some justification, that the MHC represented an important step forward in museum practice in Catalonia (Hernández, 1997). In this sense, it has selectively incorporated some of the mechanisms for stimulating the interest of the visitor–consumer in order to address more effectively the visitor–citizen.

The permanent exhibition of the Museum of the History of Catalonia, as originally conceived under the direction of CiU, might therefore be best described as an innovative anachronism. It is with this paradox in mind that I intend now to turn to the subject of traditional culture in Catalonia.

Tradition

The official discourse of the Pujol-era *Generalitat* and its cultural institutions stressed the idea that there is something inherent in the Catalan people and their culture that gives them a strong basis for creating a future identity. Pujol himself said in 2001 that

Catalonia 'Lives off tradition, off what it has that is permanent, memory, the inheritance left by our grandparents [. . .] but constantly putting all this at the service of new adaptations' (Pujol, 2001a: 13).[22] It is this combination that makes the ideological basis and desired effects of CiU's cultural policy seem at once anachronistic and innovative. Francesc Roca, speaking specifically about traditional culture, uses a similar 'spin' when he claims that contemporary Catalonia enjoys a 'folklore no folklorista', i.e. a popular and traditional culture not based on stagnant practices but on things which relate to the 'forms and contents of the everyday life of almost everyone' (Roca, 2000: 188).[23] One of the six reasons he gives for this is 'Our capacity, which has been inherited and then expanded, to recreate and invent, working from a firmly documented basis, new cultural forms and even new traditions and new festivals' (189).[24] This kind of rhetoric stresses the organic nature of Catalan culture, since the cultural forms it generates are described as springing naturally from the innate resources of the Catalan people, although they evolve and develop to suit the changing circumstances in which they must attempt to flourish.

However, this openness to change is not without its pitfalls. In the early 1980s, Salvador Giner was able to say that 'Catalonia must be one of the very few industrial countries where the progress of technology and capitalism has not meant the relegation of a vast number of traditional festivities, dances and ritualistic games of all sorts either to remote rural areas, or to certain pockets of the popular classes' (Giner, 1984: 12). Just fifteen years later, according to Salvador Cardús, enactments of traditional Catalan culture had become either tourist attractions or museum pieces. 'The modern celebration – it is hard to call it a *festa* – no longer pertains to a place or a time, but to a commercial offering which can be celebrated anywhere and at any time' (Cardús, 1999: 30).[25] If we agree with Cardús's somewhat cynical opinion that popular traditions have lost their connection with the particular places and times that gave them their meaning as part of the life of a community, then they can no longer have an integrative function within that community except at a superficial and temporary level based on mutual enjoyment of a 'fun' activity.

There are many reasons for the progressive deterritorialization and commercialization of Catalan traditions since the early 1980s. When Giner gave his positive evaluation of the state of Catalan popular culture, it was still soon enough after the dictatorship for people to feel the excitement of being able to celebrate their traditions openly. Not only this, but the consumer boom of the late 1980s was still to come, the *Generalitat* and city councils were devoting less of their time to attracting tourists than they do today, and the process of professionalizing and categorizing traditional culture had only just begun. Circumstances had already changed markedly by the time the Catalan parliament passed its law to protect and promote traditional culture in 1993, and have changed again since then, partly as the result of the tourist boom which gathered momentum throughout the 1990s, due in no small measure to the positive effects of the Barcelona Olympics of 1992.

While Catalan culture since 1980 has obviously begun to feel the effects of the increased commodification of culture common to all contemporary Western societies, and to suffer from greater competition from more 'trendy' pastimes such as computer games and pop music, some of the responsibility for the deterritorialization and repackaging of traditions rests with the Catalan institutions themselves. Firstly, as we will see when we look at the examples of the *sardana* and *castells* (human towers), the spreading of traditions from one part of Catalonia to others has been encouraged. It is seen as beneficial because it increases the visibility and presence of Catalan traditions and allows them to be used as markers of a unified Catalan identity, and this is one reason why the *Generalitat* has passed laws declaring certain *festes* to be 'of national interest'. In this way, the *Generalitat* directs the ongoing process of 'inventing' Catalan traditions, especially 'those establishing or symbolizing social cohesion or the membership of groups, real or artificial communities' (Hobsbawm 1983: 9).

Secondly, cultural institutions are now also able to package Catalan traditions as forms of heritage and sell them as part of an enterprise culture which reflects Catalonia's strengths in business and tourism. This also has the advantage that it allows any embarrassingly 'backward' aspects of traditional culture to be presented as tourist attractions or curiosities. As Corner and Harvey put it, 'If the concept of "heritage" involves the construction and reconstruction of [the] past, the idea of "enterprise" promises all of the excitement of contemporaneity, modernity, and a vision of the future' (Corner and Harvey, 1991: 58). In other words, traditional practices become 'legitimate' commercial activities which in turn provide a stimulus for the modernization or revaluation of aspects of the country's past. On the other hand, this brings new pressures to bear on the organizers, who are increasingly forced to professionalize the execution of events, managing budgets, crowd control, marketing, insurance and the like. Worried organizers were offered help in the form of a manual published by the *Generalitat* in 2000, which explains their responsibilities under the relevant legislation, offers advice on everything from firework safety to the provision of toilets, and aims to convince the public that 'the festival, as an example of our living heritage, cannot isolate itself from more polished cultural forms and, beyond any doubt, must banish those quirks which, even now, too often link it with a certain image of carelessness and amateurishness' (Bertran and Nadal, 2000: 7).[26]

One of the reasons for this stress on professionalization has been the realization that traditional culture can be used to stimulate interest in Catalonia from other countries. The opening ceremony of the Barcelona Olympic Games provided a showcase for Catalan creativity which not only embraced the contemporary but also the traditional, for example in the dancing of *sardanas*. While this was viewed by millions around the world on television, there have also been attempts to take Catalan culture to smaller, live audiences in other countries, for example when hundreds of dancers, musicians, *castellers*, 'giants' and others took over Manchester city centre for a weekend in the summer of 2003: this event was sponsored by the *Generalitat* and was part of a series of annual visits to European countries that has run since 1988 (see chapter 6). These uses of traditional culture, as well as bringing Catalonia's cultural distinctiveness and creative spirit to the attention of non-Catalans, also legitimize tradition by reinscribing it within the global contexts of tourism and spectacle.

Another way of legitimizing traditional practices is to make them the object of academic study, and this is where the *Centre de Promoció de la Cultura Popular i Tradicional Catalana* (Centre for the Promotion of Catalan Popular and Traditional Culture) comes into play. The Centre was created as a result of the 1993 law on popular and traditional culture (see above) as part of the *Departament de Cultura*. It fosters the teaching of traditional skills, in music for example – thus contributing to the professionalization of the *festa* – and the academic study of traditional culture. One of its aims has been to explore the 'ethnological heritage' of Catalonia, a term which gained currency in the 1990s both because Catalan anthropologists wanted to make it clear that they had something to contribute to policy debates on heritage, and also because it helped to bring the *Departament de Cultura*'s own work up to date (Iniesta, 1995: 32).

Expenditure on culture by the Departament de Cultura in 2001

	Million Euros	%
Archaeology and heritage	8.6	5.5
Libraries and archives	28.3	18
Museums	28.0	17.8
Theatre and dance	25.5	16.2
Music	17.3	11
Cinema and video	8.9	5.7
Art	8.1	5.2
Books and newspapers	10.0	6.4
Traditional and popular culture	5.5	3.5
Linguistic Normalization	17.1	10.9
Total	157.5	100

Source: Departament de Cultura, 2003b : 171

These kinds of initiatives show that the *Generalitat* did take the question of traditional culture seriously, although it was not prepared to allocate huge resources to it. The area of popular and traditional culture was always at the bottom of the list of activities financed by the *Generalitat*, which in 2001, for example, allocated it only 3.5 per cent of its culture budget (see table). This of course led to complaints from those who felt that traditional culture was the poor relation in the cultural family, but this was not the only criticism voiced by the organizers of, and participants in, traditional culture, as has been noted by John Payne:

> They are not always at one with the 'official' version of popular culture put out by the Generalitat in its publicity material. These local activists feel that all too often the Generalitat stresses the extraordinary and the unique [. . .] And that there is insufficient stress on the importance of civil society appropriating public space for these festivities. Finally, they complain that all too often popular culture fails to address the interests of the new Catalans, both in sharing Catalan culture and in giving opportunity for public display

of other cultures from other parts of Spain and other parts of the world. (Payne, 2004: 186–7)

In other words, for most Catalans plurality is still an important feature of their traditional culture, and they are concerned that this should not be erased by the *Generalitat*'s desire to nationalize and catalogue. One of the clearest signals of this is the highly advanced use of web sites by *Ajuntaments*, cultural associations, festival committees and individuals to promote local events and explain their meaning to residents and visitors alike. In creating descriptions, histories and photo galleries of their *festes* for a web page, each organization or interested individual contributes to the ongoing project of documenting and reshaping Catalan traditional culture, thankfully in a more entertaining way than the *Generalitat*'s own database. The medium also allows for multiple voices to be heard and for the sheer enthusiasm of the participants to come through. Furthermore, the quality of design and technical expertise demonstrated by many of these pages is yet another testament to Catalan creativity.

However, one of the side effects of the continuing institutionalization and professionalization of traditional culture has been a tendency to sideline the contribution of civil society, or *associacionisme* (participation in associations). In an article in *L'Avenç* published in 1999, Eduard Delgado traces the history of cultural associations over the previous thirty years, and makes an important point that explains John Payne's comment, above, that many of his interviewees felt 'there is insufficient stress on the importance of civil society appropriating public space for these festivities'. Delgado maintains that the most obvious characteristic of Catalan culture is 'its social cohesion and civil participation' (Delgado, 1999: 63):[27] these attributes make it distinctive in the European context and result in 'a greater palette of colours that strengthens shared identities, collective expressiveness, transferable creativity and an inclination towards autonomy and self-sufficiency'[28] (64). According to Delgado, it is not just a question of civil society keeping Catalan culture going through the bad times, although this has certainly been true, but also the need to recognize that these associations are the primary motor of action and creativity in the good times as well (see also Andreu, 1999). Some of those who participate in *festes* feel that the institutionalization of traditional culture has sidelined their contribution and imposed forms of control that work against the spirit of such events.

This tendency could be regarded as one of the unfortunate consequences of attempts to nationalize the framework in which Catalan traditions are set. David M. Guss (2000: 13) describes what happens when this kind of process occurs:

> Events that were not only structured by local histories and conflicts but that also celebrated them now become symbols for a nation at large, a purpose for which they were never intended. To accomplish this has required that the hallmark of festive behaviour, its supera-bundance of symbols and meanings, be shrunk as much as possible to a handful of quickly and easily understood ideas.

Evidence that this has happened in the Catalan case is provided by Jesús Contreras Hernández (1998), who agrees with Salvador Cardús that the commercialization and deterritorialization of trad-itional culture has robbed it of a large part of its former signifi-cance. He points out that since the Transition there has been a radical reshaping of the spread of *festes* across Catalonia, in which some have disappeared unmourned, some have been so successful that they have been imitated everywhere, and some have even been suppressed 'because they were felt not to correspond with the Catalan personality'[29] (826). He also suggests that it was generally the *festes* most loaded with ritual and 'symbolic condensation' that could most easily generate a sense of identification throughout Catalan territory and whose expansion was therefore encouraged (824).

It is clear that, as with other areas of policy on heritage, CiU's treatment of traditional culture has given rise to much debate. The rest of this chapter will use examples of particular traditions to analyse the main tensions that cultural policy has either had to address or has in itself created. These can be summed up in a series of oppositions: professionalization vs *associacionisme;* 'top-down' stage management vs 'bottom-up' civil participation; commerciali-zation vs the preservation of symbolic and ritual contents; and the 'deterritorialization' of cultural forms vs the preservation of local roots, meanings and differences.

Commemorations: Political Uses of the Popular

I am first going to explore these problems in relation to the kinds of activities that specifically commemorate Catalonia's history. These fall into two basic categories: annual events, which have become traditions in their own right, and one-off events that bring together various aspects of tradition and heritage in order to bring a particular element of history to the attention of the public. Annual events include the *Dia de Sant Jordi*, and 11 September when the defeat of the Catalans in 1714 is commemorated. It could be argued that local festivals of religious origin also retain a subtext of historical commemoration, especially when they are connected to national symbols such as the Virgin of Montserrat. Some festivals such as Carnival were banned during the Franco regime, and this also gives the contemporary events a flavour of reconnection with the pre-Franco past, although as time passes fewer participants are able to make this connection from their own experience. One-off events include the celebration of major national anniversaries such as Catalonia's 'millennium' in 1988, or the birth or death of an important figure.[30] In both cases, the *Generalitat* can often have an important role in devising and/or supporting particular commemorations as part of its cultural policy and nation-building strategy.

One very striking example of this is the decision to declare 1988 the millennium of Catalonia's birth as a politically independent entity, and to mark this with a wide range of cultural and political events. Josep Llobera has summed up the usefulness of such commemorations in circumstances where 'the sense of continuity of a nation has been lost', saying in particular that they demonstrate 'a rupture with a certain undesirable past' and are 'useful when there exist divergent representations of time past and an unitary version of national identity is required' (Llobera, 1996: 197). More specifically, John Payne comments that the decision of the count of Barcelona to break his ties with the French king in 988 was 'conveniently timed' as far as the newly restored *Generalitat de Catalunya* of the 1980s was concerned (Payne, 2004: 32)! His implied cynicism is supported by an observation made by Josep M. Salrach: ordinary Catalans were apparently confused as to what the celebration was all about, especially since there had been none of the usual build-up to the event and it therefore seemed to come rather out of the blue (Salrach, 1988: 42). Pujol's decision to invite

King Juan Carlos to inaugurate the celebrations was also controversial. Nevertheless, the *Mil·lenari* went ahead with a series of events that was ceremonially launched by the king at the *Palau de la Generalitat* on 22 April 1988. Even if we can apply here Pujol's reasoning that nation states have this kind of commemoration and it is therefore legitimate for Catalonia to have them too, the rhetoric surrounding the event reveals a clear desire for it to confirm the political legitimacy of the new autonomous government. Salrach especially picks up on the fact that the celebration was supposed to commemorate 'the political birth of Catalonia and not simply the origins of Catalonia. It is as if the preoccupation of the political class regarding the distribution of powers in the State of the Autonomies had influenced (consciously or unconsciously) this choice' (Salrach, 1988: 43).[31]

These kinds of one-off commemorations have a clear nation-building function that is also present in some of the annual events in the Catalan calendar, especially the marking on the 11 September of the day in 1714 when Barcelona finally fell to the king's forces after a siege. This defeat spelled the end of Catalonia's opposition to Philip V during the War of Succession and the beginning of centralizing measures to bring Catalonia politically and culturally into line with the rest of Spain. Since 1980, this is Catalonia's official National Day, not so much because Catalans wish to dwell on the defeat but in order to commemorate their resistance, celebrate their determination to carry on despite the repression that followed, and remember that before 1714 Catalonia had a much greater degree of independence from Spain than it has had at any time since. Robert Surroca i Tallaferro dates the first act of commemoration to 11 September 1886 when a mass was held for the Catalan victims of the War of Succession (Surroca i Tallaferro, 2004: 37). More widely recognized as the origin of the present celebrations are the actions of a group of young Catalanists who placed a wreath on the statue of Rafael Casanova, one of the leaders of the siege, on 11 September 1901, attracting the attention of the police who beat and arrested them. This of course drew attention to their actions and stimulated others to emulate them in subsequent years, despite the hazards participants faced for most of the next eight decades. The first mass celebration since the days of the Second Republic took place in Sant Boi de Llobregat in 1976, since the authorities refused to sanction a gathering in Barcelona. The next year they relented and around one million people thronged the streets of Barcelona, using the occasion to demand a statute of autonomy for Catalonia. If nothing else, the history of the celebrations demonstrates the determination of many Catalans not to allow the threat of torture or imprisonment to overcome their desire to express their patriotism.

Today the 11 September is both an official holiday and a focus for Catalanist demands of various kinds. The preamble to the law of 12 June 1980 which declared this Catalonia's National Day makes it clear that the *Generalitat* had no role in 'inventing' the tradition, it is merely giving an official stamp to something that had grown sponta- neously as a result of many years of civic action: 'Now, as Catalonia steps back onto the path of freedom, the representatives of the People believe that the Legislative Chamber must sanction that which the Nation has already unanimously taken on board'.[32] Even so, the political nature of the event has continued to evolve and its symbolism is constantly debated and modified. It is customary for the president to make an annual speech in which he must refer directly to the events of 1714, but the message can of course be tweaked to suit his current political preoccupations. (Pujol used many of his speeches in the 1980s to remind Catalans how much work there was still to do in taking Catalonia forward into a prosper- ous and united future (Llobera, 1996: 200–1). Pasqual Maragall used his first speech in 2004 to draw a line under the Pujol adminis- tration and stress the importance of a new statute of autonomy for the future of all Catalans.)[33] The occasion also allows journalists, pundits, and politicians from other parties to make their own commemorative speeches or to publish articles on aspects of the tradition and its relevance to the present. In this way, the resonance of the day becomes far greater than whatever political or cultural events might take place during the celebrations themselves.

These kinds of wider resonances are also present in the St George's Day celebrations, and the way they have been capitalized on by CiU is particularly astute. I have already mentioned that the *Dia de Sant Jordi* has been used to promote Catalan literature both inside and outside Catalan-speaking areas, but there are also other important aspects of the day which should be considered. The first series of international advertisements may have concentrated on literature in an attempt to bring an awareness of Catalonia's cultural distinctiveness to inhabitants of other countries (as well as pointing out its business-related attractions) but some of the subsequent campaigns focused primarily on attracting potential investors. For example, in 1998 the advertisement was clearly aimed first and foremost at stimulating the growth of foreign business investment. Catalonia was described as both a 'Northern' European country, because of its work ethic and 'entrepreneurial spirit', and a 'Southern' European country, because of its favourable climate and lifestyle, as well as its culture and traditions (*The Times*, 23 April 1998: Catalonia supplement, 10). The advertisement for 2000 was even more squarely focused on attracting the attention of potential investors, associating the fact that 23 April had become World Book Day with Catalonia's international influence through its business links (*The Times*, 22 April 2000: Catalonia supplement, 6). In this sense, whatever was actually happening within Catalonia on the day itself, there was a separate dimension to the tradition which was indisputably modern and commercial, and which had little to do with the way ordinary Catalans experienced the event.

Nevertheless, the kind of didacticism that we saw in the case of the MHC is clearly present too in the way that Catalonia's national traditions are stage-managed. Thanks to the inclusion of teaching about these events in the school curriculum, vivid poster campaigns, extensive press coverage, and the *Generalitat*-sponsored publication of books on the subject, the exhortation to the public to share in these commemorations is as potent in Catalonia as it would be in any nation state. It is also clear that there is a geographical distinction between these kinds of commemorations and the local holidays or traditions that were the mainstay of Catalan traditional culture before autonomy. Saint George's Day, the *Onze de setembre* and one-off commemorations such as the *Mil·lenari* can be celebrated across Catalonia, do not require participants to return to their ancestral home, and belong to the nation as a whole, even if in practice this means that Barcelona becomes the centre of events (bringing of course a modern and cosmopolitan gloss to proceedings!). This chapter will now turn to traditions that did have specific local roots to show how these have been encouraged to spread outwards from their heartlands in order to play a similar kind of national role.

Sardanes and *Castells*: Deterritorialization and Professionalization

The contrasting fortunes of two of Catalonia's most emblematic traditions serve to illustrate both the advantages and disadvantages of nationalizing, or even internationalizing, Catalan culture. The *sardana*, a circular dance, and *castells*, the competitive formation of human towers, both developed in particular parts of Catalonia – the *sardana* in the north and *castells* in the south – and remained more or less confined there for some time before spreading further afield in the twentieth century. The major differences, however, are related to the timing and primary agents of this dissemination, since the *sardana* became the darling of Catalanists during the *Renaixença* whereas the *castells* found their time had come during the 1980s in a newly autonomous Catalonia.

The origins of the *sardana* are somewhat mysterious, but what is known for certain is that a dance of that name had been in existence in the Empordà region for some time when the famous Pep Ventura and his associates decided to alter both its choreography and its music in the mid nineteenth century in order to make it more attractive (Mas i Solench, 1993: 51–4). Even then, the popularity of the dance spread relatively slowly until its potential as a symbol of Catalanism was recognized, at which point it rapidly became a crucial element of the movement. Joan-Lluís Marfany describes in detail the process that led to this new role for the *sardana* and the passion the dance came to engender in its new champions, up to the point at which it seemed that 'the sardana had always been, since the remotest antiquity, *the* national dance, of *all* Catalans, the very expression of pure Catalanness' (Marfany, 1995: 325).[34] The circular dance in which anyone can participate was a suitable metaphor for the inclusiveness of Catalanism since all participants are equal and the circle can grow to accommodate as many as wish to join in (326). Despite suffering serious setbacks during the dictatorships of Primo de Rivera and Franco, the dance maintained this symbolic charge (now with an added element of resistance), and was able to carry it successfully into the new period of democracy and autonomy – only to see enthusiasm for the dance go into a steady decline.

On the face of it, the *sardana* continues to be an important symbol of Catalan identity. There are regular gatherings of dancers across Catalonia, and the tradition is maintained of dancing *sardanas* in symbolic places (such as outside the *Palau de la Generalitat* in Barcelona) or at meaningful times such as during *festes*. The evangelical character of the *sardanista* movement seems, if anything, to have increased, as is apparent from the words of Salvador Millet i Bel, the president of the *Fundació Universal de la Sardana* at the time of publication of Josep M. Mas i Solench's *La sardana: dansa nacional de Catalunya* (1993). Millet i Bel provides a prologue to the work in which he highlights that the main ambition of the Fundació is to 'extend [the *sardana*] little by little through-out the world, making it a dance for everyone, a universal dance that will unite all peoples in happiness and peace'.[35] Although this might have seemed like a more realistic prospect just after the success of the Barcelona Olympics in bringing Catalan culture to the world, the truth is that even Catalans are now losing interest in the national dance, especially the younger generations. According to Joan Soler i Amigó, the exaltation of the *sardana* as the national dance has led to it becoming segregated from other folk dances, which he sees as having negative consequences, because it has been artificially preserved from the currents of change that have allowed other traditional dances to remain relevant to younger Catalans (Soler i Amigó, 2001: 119). As a result, *sardanista* associations are finding it increasingly difficult to attract new recruits.

In contrast, the tradition of the *castells* seems to be growing in popularity and spreading fairly organically from its heartland, which lies in a triangle formed by the towns of Tarragona, Valls and Vilafranca del Penedés. Once again, the origins of the tradition are unclear but there is evidence that it may have originated in a dance which finished with the creation of a small human tower. Soler i Amigó (2001: 95) notes that there were two groups of *castellers* in Valls in 1805, and that the movement has had three 'golden ages': 1876–89, 1926–36, and 1960 to the present. The spread of the tradition was aided by the creation of a *colla* (group/team) in Barcelona in 1950 thanks to migrants from the region, although this expansion only became really significant in the 1970s and 80s. Now, performances are a part of the summer calendar in many towns and villages, and the press reports and records the outcome.

The *casteller* tradition seems to have shown a greater adaptability than the *sardana*. However, the element of sacredness bestowed on the *sardana* is missing, even though both traditions share the same imagery of inclusiveness and participation. Immigrants have been welcomed into the *colles* and have sometimes found participation a rapid route to acceptance within their new community. Social change has meant the acceptance of young girls into the groups, although few adult women form part of the main construction because they do not have the necessary physique. Also, a 'freestyle' variant of the *castells* known as *falcons* was introduced at the beginning of the twentieth century as a direct importation of a Czechoslovakian tradition, which was presumably accepted because of its closeness to the existing Catalan form, and today appeals particularly to teenagers. It is easy to see why the *castells* continue to thrive: it is a genuinely exciting event for both participants and spectators, with a clear element of competition not just with rival groups but also in trying to beat the former performances of your own *colla*. The element of risk brings excitement, there are many opportunities for participation at different levels, and the sight of a small child climbing fearlessly to the top of a tower is enough to earn the admiration of even the most tradition-averse spectator.

The changes undergone in the last two decades by the *casteller* tradition also illustrate the phenomenon of professionalization. In the nineteenth century, *colles* would walk from one town to another, leaving their homes for weeks at a time and relying on the hospitality and generosity of their hosts to make the trip financially viable. (If all else failed, at least the men had been fed at someone else's expense for that period.) For most of the twentieth century, the activity was characterized by its amateur status and the role of the *cap de colla* (the head of the group), who would be in charge of all aspects of the running of the group. These days, however, even leaving aside the obvious need for adequate insurance, running a *colla* is a complex affair that can involve large teams of people and fairly substantial sums of money, some of which has to be dedicated to marketing activities (Contreras Hernández, 1998: 828). The money itself comes from subsidies provided by the authorities, donations or subscriptions from individuals, and payment for some types of performances. This naturally means that the 'artistic control' of the *colla* is reduced as it must provide value for money to its paymasters, as is indicated by a report in *La Vanguardia* which recounts the disappointment of the organizers of the 2004 *festa major* (local festival) of Vilanova that neither of the two visiting *colles* they had contracted for the occasion attempted a nine-storey tower: they had been paid more than four thousand euros for the event (Francàs, 2004: 5). Jesús Contreras Hernández remarks that

he is sure that before long the *castellers* will have sponsors' names on
their shirts (Hernández, 1998: 829)!

Castells can still be said have deep local roots, because *colles*
represent particular towns and villages and the competitive element remains strong. However, this element may be undermined if
the competitive element is progressively downplayed in favour of
paid displays, or if the *colles* become professionalized to such an
extent that a 'transfer market' develops for the best *castellers* regardless of their place of residence. In this sense, they might turn out to
be vulnerable to the same pressures as local festivities such as the
festes majors, where the increasing professionalization of the spectacle has included a need to provide ever bigger and better attractions in order to woo visitors even if this conflicts with the desires of
local residents. In other words, the pressure to keep up with the
times may eventually erode even the apparently firm local basis of
the *castells*.

Hybrid Traditions

The progressive deterritorialization of Catalan traditions has been
accompanied by another phenomenon that has grown in importance since 1980: the increasing visibility of traditional cultural
forms that have been imported from outside Catalonia. Many of
these have Andalusian origins, as might be expected given the mass
immigration from the south of Spain that took place during the
Franco dictatorship. However, it was only after the transition to
democracy that these 'new Catalans' began to demand a public
space for these traditions in their new home. Indeed, Jordi Soler i
Amigó tentatively suggests that the fact that these kinds of
imported traditions have only become important since the granting of autonomy might indicate that they represent 'a reaction in
the face of politico-cultural manoeuvres which are felt to be assimi-
lationist' (Soler i Amigó, 2001: 79).[36]

One example of such a tradition is the so-called '15+1' Holy
Week parade in L'Hospitalet de Llobregat that first took place
spontaneously in 1978 and is now a fixed event in the local
calendar. While there is a Catalan tradition of processions on the
Thursday and Friday of Holy Week these are small-scale events and
do not have the exuberance of the week-long Andalusian festival.
The first procession in L'Hospitalet was initiated by fifteen men of

Andalusian origin who, while in a bar watching television coverage of the processions in Seville, bemoaned the lack of proper celebrations in their new home and decided to improvise an image of the Virgin which they then took out into the street. The response of their neighbours, which has already passed into the realms of myth, took the participants by surprise: many joined in, greeted them by singing *saetas* or even cried. As a result, the men named their group '15+1', representing the fifteen direct participants and the one united *pueblo* (people/town) that demonstrated solidarity with them. The procession became not only an annual fixture but an increasingly large-scale and professional affair: the *cofradía* (brotherhood) now boasts more than a thousand members. Jesús Contreras Hernández (1998: 831) points out the significance of the lack of direct involvement by the Church in the first years of the '15+1': the event was not so much a manifestation of respect for a particular holy day as an acknowledgement of the nostalgia felt by the participants for part of their native culture, and therefore a recognition of its importance to their identity.

Perhaps the most important manifestation of Andalusian culture in Catalonia, however, is the annual celebration of an April Fair modelled on the famous Seville event. The fair has become larger and more formalized over the years, although it has moved from venue to venue and has only recently taken root in a symbolically central location in Barcelona. Although the flavour of the fair is most definitely Andalusian, there have of course been some necessary modifications as the result of the translocation of the tradition to Catalonia. On a practical level, for example, the organizers have to take into account that there is no local holiday at this time and the timetable must reflect the fact that people can only attend in the evenings and at weekends. Perhaps more significantly, the *casetas* – the marquees belonging to particular groups – that form the heart of the fair and that in Seville have restricted access, in the Catalan version are free to enter and open to all (Soler i Amigó, 2001: 169). Although the event now has the support of the *Ajuntament de Barcelona*, it is organized by a private body, the *Federación de Entidades Culturales Andaluzas en Cataluña* (FECAC). The *Generalitat* was slow to give any form of recognition to the fair, and although it provided funding for the event this was done through the social welfare department (*Departament de Benestar Social*) and not the *Departament de Cultura*. Even as late as 2004 CiU (no longer in power by this stage) and ERC (part of the new tripartite government) were concerned to learn that the fair would overlap with the start of the Universal Forum of Cultures: it seems that Andalusian folklore was not considered a suitable prelude to this prestigious international event (Sabaté, 2004).

However, this has not been the only controversy surrounding the fair. In the last years of the CiU government, suspicions were raised that FECAC had been artificially inflating the number of visitors to the fair in order to increase its visibility and justify the large amount of funding that it receives from public bodies. While a report commissioned by the *Ajuntament* in 2001 suggested that only 100,000 people visited the fair, FECAC was claiming 2.5 million (Camprubí, 2005: 47–8). Calculations by other groups in other years also suggest that the maximum attendance was unlikely to exceed 500,000 (Camprubí, 2005: 47, 49). The report itself had not been made public by the *Ajuntament* and came into the public domain via an organization called *Els altres andalusos* ('the other Andalusians' – a play on the term 'the other Catalans' that has come to be used to describe people who are resident in Catalonia but have their origins outside the area). This pressure group was set up to try to end the kind of stereotypical portrayal of Andalusian Catalans that they say is perpetuated by the fair (see *www. altresandalusos.org/wordpress/*). They argue that the dominant political parties (CiU and PSC) have refused to allow barriers between incomers and native Catalans to be broken down because they insist on referring to the origins of 'the other Catalans' despite the fact that the main wave of immigration was forty years ago and many of them now consider themselves fully Catalan. The FECAC, they say, contributes to this by adopting a segregationist attitude and promoting the fair as the 'genuine' heritage of Catalans of Andalusian origin, when for many of them (especially in the second, third and even fourth generations) the fair has no real relevance (Camprubí, 2005: 48). As a result, social divisions are artificially heightened and maintained.

There is most certainly a complex relationship between the different cultural identities that are invoked by this kind of event. This can be illustrated using the poster for the 2003 fair, the thirty-second, which showed a doll wearing a typically Andalusian yellow frilly dress with shawl, hat and fan – the kind of doll that tourists would buy as a souvenir of their visit to Andalusia. The poster's designer was Claret Serrahima, and it is enlightening to read his explanation of his choice of subject for the poster, which he says is open to two different interpretations. 'The first reading is for people who experience the fiesta directly, most of them Barcelonans of Andalusian origin, and the second is more linked to contemporary graphic design, closer to Barcelona design and distanced from folkloric forms, to draw in, and assure the complicity of, a wide sector of Barcelonans'. (Ajuntament de Barcelona, 2003: 11) [37] He does not feel the need to explain the first, 'obvious' reading of the stereotypical image. Nor, evidently, does he see those Barcelonans of Andalusian origin as having the capacity to read the poster as a postmodern pastiche which invests traditional culture with new meanings – a capacity he nevertheless assigns to 'other kinds' of Barcelonans. The implication here is that while all Catalans, whatever their origin, can enjoy the fair, their ethnic background will determine their emotional and intellectual responses to its cultural messages. In other words, some participants will still be more 'Catalan' than others.

It is equally clear that some forms of traditional culture are also regarded as more 'Catalan' than others, although of course there are no agreed criteria for placing specific cultural manifestations within this hierarchy that is nevertheless firmly held to exist. Lovers of flamenco or of the April Fair complain that their forms of culture are undervalued and ghettoized, while *sardanista* associations and others accuse the *Generalitat* of funding these 'foreign' forms of culture to the detriment of 'indigenous' traditions. When in power, CiU were clearly more on the side of the *sardanistes*, although there was some limited broadening of support for hybrid or imported activities towards the end of their time in office, even if only under the 'social welfare' banner. The PSC saw this attitude as a substantial failing:

> Certainly, the government of CiU, which, in word if not in deed, made its own the phrase that came from the left at the time of the transition to democracy 'anyone who lives and works in Catalonia is Catalan', has not made its own, either in theory or in practice, a second vital idea: 'any culture that is created and produced in Catalonia is part of Catalan culture.[38] (Mascarell, 1999: 44)

In contrast, they insisted in their *Llibre blanc de la cultura a Catalunya* that a more fluid conception of culture should prevail – one in which the nation is not seen as the ultimate 'giver' of cultural forms (Mascarell, 1999: 19). In an increasingly plural society, this may seem like the only practical way forward to ensure social harmony.

However, many Catalans are convinced that a strong, distinctive culture is the only answer to a growing threat: the destruction of local specificities by the seemingly unstoppable tide of globalization. This was clearly one of the strongest fears behind CiU's desire to create versions of Catalonia's history, heritage and traditions that could be used even in the context of the twenty-first century to produce a unifying and homogenizing effect on an increasingly plural society, as will be discussed in the next chapter.

NOTES

1 See Lamikiz (2002) for an exploration of how this was attempted with respect to the Basque Country.
2 See also Balcells, 1994.
3 Llei 9/1993, de 30 de setembre, del Patrimoni Cultural Català (DOGC núm. 1807, d'11.10.1993).
4 DOGC núm. 1719, de 12 de març de 1993. All the relevant legislation has been collected in a volume entitled *Legislació sobre patrimoni cultural*, 2nd edn. (Barcelona: Departament de Cultura de la Generalitat de Catalunya, 2004a).
5 'La cultura tradicional i popular, com a conjunt de les manifestacions, els coneixements, les activitats i les creences passats i presents de la memòria col·lectiva, és el punt de referencia a partir del qual les iniciatives de la societat s'emmarquen en un context configurador de Catalunya amb una identitat nacional pròpia arrelada en una pluralitat de formes d'expressió popular i, alhora, en una ferma voluntat de projectar-se cap al futur.'
6 Llei 9/1993.
7 'El patrimoni cultural és un dels testimonis fonamentals de la trajectòria històrica i d'identitat d'una col·lectivitat nacional'.
8 *http://cultura.gencat.cat*
9 'Potenciarem l'espai del Born com a símbol històric de la nostra identitat nacional.'
10 This discussion of the MHC relates only to the period up to the end of 2003 and does not take account of changes that have been made since then.
11 Llei 17/1990, de 2 de novembre, de Museus (DOGC núm. 1367, de 14.11.1990).
12 Decret 47/1996, de 6 de febrer, de creació i d'estructuració del Museu d'Història de Catalunya (DOGC núm. 2171, de 21.02.1996).
13 'conservar, exposar i difondre la història de Catalunya com a patrimoni col·lectiu, i enfortir la identificació dels ciutadans amb la història nacional'.
14 'Aquest museu és molt singular, ja que no s'origina perquè existeixi una col·lecció de peces d'un valor històric que es vol conservar i

exposar i potser explicar la història del país a través d'ella. Aquí hi ha un programa polític del partit que governa Catalunya, la coalició Convergència i Unió, i en el seu programa de cultura de legislatura inclou la creació d'un Museu d'Història de Catalunya, i aquest és el mandat que se m'encarrega: que gestioni aquest projecte.'

15   'el museu i el coneixement d'una història comuna ajuda a la cohesió social, sobretot perquè la Història de Catalunya mai no ha estat una història excloent'.

16   'no obeïa a cap necessitat museística ni a cap demanda social'.

17   'consolidar els mecanismes de consens nacional de centredreta'.

18   This phrase is taken from a quotation from Alma S. Wittlin, *Museums in Search of a Usable Future* (1970), pp. 203–4, which Hudson uses to back up his point.

19   See also Morgan, 2000: 89 in which he comments that the museum 'presents Catalan history as a cameo of nationhood and victimization'.

20   'intuïció del mot nació en el seu sentit modern'.

21   The museum now intends to extend its coverage beyond 1980.

22   'Viu de la tradició, del que té de permanent, de la memòria, del patrimoni dels avis [. . .] però posant tot això constantment al servei de noves adaptacions'.

23   'formes i continguts de la vida de cada dia, de pràcticament tothom.'

24   'La capacitat, heretada i ampliada, de recrear i d'inventar, sobre sòlides bases documentals, noves formes culturals i fins i tot noves tradicions i noves festes.'

25   'La celebració moderna – costa de dir-ne festa – ja no és la d'un lloc o la d'un temps, sinó la d'una oferta comercial que es pot celebrar a tot arreu i a tota hora.'

26   'la festa com a mostra del nostre patrimoni viu no pot viure allunyada de les expressions culturals més polides i, definitivament, ha de desterrar aquells tics que massa sovint encara l'emparenten amb una certa idea de descurança i provisionalitat'.

27   'la cohesió social i la participació ciutadana'.

28   'una major paleta de colors que reforça les identitats compartides, l'expressivitat col·lectiva, la creativitat transferible i una vocació d'autonomia i autoabastiment'.

29   'perquè es considerava que no responien al tarannà català'.

30   See Llobera 1996 (201–3) for an exploration of the celebration of the centenary of the Bases de Manresa.

31   'el naixement polític de Catalunya i no simplement els origens de Catalunya. És com si la preocupació de la classe política per la distribució de poders en l'Estat de les Autonomies hagués influït (conscientment o inconscientment) en l'elecció'.

32   'Ara, en reprendre Catalunya el seu camí de llibertat, els representants del Poble creuen que la Cambra Legislativa ha de sancionar allò que la Nació unànimement ja ha assumit'. *www10.gencat.net/gencat/ AppJava/cat/catalunya/simbols/onze.jsp*, accessed 12 January 2005.

33   'Missatge del president de la Generalitat amb motiu de la Diada Nacional de Catalunya11–09–04', *gencat.accesoresearch.com/wai/ 1002.17516.html*, accessed 12 January 2005.

34   'la sardana havia estat de sempre, des de la més remota antigüitat, *el*
     ball nacional, el de *tots* els catalans, l'expressió mateixa de la pura
     catalanitat'.
35   'estendre-la [the sardana] a poc a poc per tot el món convertint-la en
     una dansa de tots, en una dansa universal que uneixi tots els pobles en
     l'alegria i la pau'.
36   'una reacció enfront de maniobres politicoculturals sentides com a
     assimilacionistes'.
37   'La primera lectura, per a les persones que viuen directament la festa,
     la majoria barcelonins d'origen andalús, i la segona, més vinculada a la
     gràfica contemporània, més propera al disseny de Barcelona i
     allunyada de les formes folklòriques, per així implicar i aconseguir la
     complicitat d'un ampli sector de barcelonins.'
38   'Certament, el Govern de CiU, que de paraula va fer seva aquella frase
     sorgida de l'esquerra en l'època de la transició democràtica «és català
     qui viu i treballa a Catalunya», no ha fet seva, ni en teoria ni de fet, una
     segona idea essencial: «forma part de la cultura catalana tota cultura
     que es crea i es produeix a Catalunya»'.

Chapter Six

Challenges for the Twenty-first Century

The year 2003 saw the last in the series of advertisements marking St George's Day placed by the Pujol-led *Generalitat* in the foreign press. As usual, the text of the 2003 advertisement explained the connection between Catalonia, St George, and the book:

The word: a bridge between cultures

In Catalonia we have a very long-standing tradition: every 23 April we celebrate the festival of Saint George, the patron saint of our country, by giving one another books and roses. It is our simple and affectionate way of promoting tolerance and mutual respect, inviting us to culture, words and love.

This year we are celebrating the festival in memory of Ramon Llull (1235–1315). For two reasons. Firstly, because he engaged in dialogue between the Christian, Jewish and Muslim cultures. That is, because he was a universal man, open to peace and understanding.

Secondly, because he was the author of the first books of philosophy that were not written in Latin, Greek or Arabic. They were written in Catalan. A language that was persecuted for centuries, but which today is Catalonia's own language and is spoken by 7 million people. It is good to remember this and celebrate it at a time when there is a need to compensate for the effects of globalization by fully preserving our identities. And remember it with words and roses. (*The Times*, 23 April 2003, Catalonia supplement, p. 11.)

The tone and main message of the text (and the rather unnatural English) are very similar to those of previous years. It is clearly intended that British readers should gain a sense of Catalonia's cultural and linguistic identity that will enable them to distinguish Catalonia from Spain, possibly for the first time. However, this particular advertisement contains two distinctive features: a reference to racial and religious tolerance, and a statement on the need to protect cultural identities from the effects of globalization. What lay behind the decision to highlight these factors in this particular year?

While it is logical to suppose that the reference to religious tolerance was included partly as a result of recent – post-September 11 – world events, the *Generalitat* was probably also thinking of something much closer to home: the growing numbers of non-Hispanic immigrants who were making their home in Catalonia, whether legally or illegally, and who were bringing with them cultural, religious and linguistic differences of a type that the region had not previously experienced in any significant way. Dialogue between different peoples had therefore become more than an abstract ideal and was part of the fabric of Catalonia's new society. Also shaping that fabric were the economic, social and cultural changes associated with globalization, which seemed to have gathered momentum in the previous decade. We can infer from the use of the word 'compensate' that these effects were viewed as a threat to Catalan identity, which is why it needed to be 'preserved'.

This statement of the *Generalitat*'s fears and ambitions towards the end of Pujol's presidency provides a window into some of the broader preoccupations that lay behind CiU's cultural policy and informed its plans for taking Catalonia into the twent-first century. This chapter will therefore examine CiU's views and actions on globalization and immigration, and the links between them, before concluding with a general discussion of the problem of maintaining a sense of local specificity in an increasingly connected world. We are not now concerned with the specific deeds of the *Departament de Cultura* but with issues that reached into all areas of CiU's activities and shaped its sociopolitical programme. Despite this, cultural and linguistic elements once more hold the key to understanding both CiU's worries and its proposed plan of action.

Globalization: Fighting Homogenization

Pujol made his fears about globalization clear in a speech given in May 2001 that was subsequently published as the pamphlet *Globalització i identitat.* He points out that questions of globalization have become central to his political discourse over the last few years because he sees it as an important challenge to Catalonia's future survival: 'globalization might threaten our continuity as the Catalan people. We might end up diluted in a great global magma. But we might equally succumb if we try to defend ourselves by shutting ourselves inside ourselves'. (Pujol, 2001: 5–6)[1]. For this reason, he advocates a form of self-belief that would allow Catalans to feel they had something to say to the rest of the world: 'to elaborate and spread a message with universal validity and a universal target audience' (7).[2] In order to achieve this global protagonism, they will need a strong and well-defined identity, which must be based on Catalonia's cultural heritage and the continuity of its traditionally cohesive society. This speech, along with others that were given in different settings at around the same time, clearly lays out Pujol's worries about globalization but also his recipe for fighting it. The main fear is that minority cultures will be the first to disappear under a tide of Americanized 'global' culture, losing their distinctiveness and personality. This seems to be conceived as an extension of the cultural threat represented by the Spanish state through its refusal to acknowledge and protect the multinational nature of Spain. In both cases, though, Pujol's answer is not to cut Catalonia off from these influences, and therefore condemn it to irrelevance, but to make sure it is strong enough to accept them only on its own terms and, crucially, to be in a position to project Catalan influences back into the wider sphere.

It is clear that Pujol's 'plan of attack' depends on a specific reading of the relationship between global and local cultures, in which the global cannot be constructed without reference to the local, thus giving the local power over the global. It is true that most theorists now recognize the fundamental interdependence of the global and the local, although there is less agreement regarding the extent to which a specific locality can influence the shape of the globalized culture that its inhabitants consume or to which they contribute. As Tony Schirato and Jen Webb explain (2003: 155–9), there are two major ways of conceptualizing this relationship, either as one of homogenization or hybridization. In the homogenization thesis, the formation of a global culture involves the rejection of local specificities and the eventual production of one dominant Westernized culture. (As Zygmunt Bauman has pointed out, societies or groups within societies that are not able or willing to access this culture will find themselves even further disadvantaged (Bauman, 1998: 86)). On the other hand, advocates of the hybridization thesis suggest that local elements can retain a degree of recognizability and enjoy some importance, although they will inevitably have to change as a result of the globalizing processes that they will be caught up in whether they like it or not. This will mean a redefinition of the concept of authenticity as it applies to local cultural forms, since any global culture is likely to be 'relatively indifferent to the maintenance of sharp discriminations of cultural origin and belonging' (Tomlinson, 1999: 147). Clearly, the threat of homogenization is what Pujol is referring to with the phrase 'great global magma', so we can infer that he hopes that the 'homogenizationists' will be proved wrong. However, as will be explored in more depth later, the idea of hybridization seems to hold little appeal for him either, since he advocates resistance to globalization through the maintenance of a strong identity, based on continuity, and changed only on the Catalans' own terms. He does not seem to be advocating that Catalan culture be permitted to be moulded into radically new shapes by outside forces.

Pujol often cited in his speeches theorists who believe that globalization increases the need for strong local identities (e.g. Pujol, 2001: 9–10). In a speech given in Harvard in 2000 he spoke approvingly of Manuel Castells's idea that identity provides an anchor in the choppy seas of globalization, and John Naisbitt's prediction that the development of a global lifestyle would also involve the rise of cultural nationalisms.[3] Pujol was not alone in preferring this particular theoretical approach, and this way of conceptualizing globalization became generalized not just within CiU but within Catalan political debate as a whole. The PSC-led *Ajuntament de Barcelona* was a key influence in this because of the way it used its cultural and urban planning policies in order to achieve global protagonism for the city of Barcelona (Degen, 2004). The strategy therefore owes as much to Pasqual Maragall and his successor Joan Clos as it does to Pujol. Given this context, it was inevitable that the Universal Forum of Cultures held in Barcelona in 2004 would include a debate on 'Globalization,

Identity, Diversity' chaired by Castells and closed, among others, by Pujol and Clos, all of whom stressed the potentially positive role of globalization in facilitating rather than weakening the preservation of individual differences at the local level.

However idealistic this may sound, CiU's version of 'glocalization' is more than the rather wishy-washy exhortation to 'think globally, act locally' articulated by *Conseller de Cultura* Joan Maria Pujals (1998: 10; see chapter 4 of this volume). Although the preservation of Catalan culture was at the heart of their public rhetoric on the issue, from the 1990s onwards Pujol and his team were clear that it was certain features of economic globalization that would be key to cultural salvation, and that Catalan cultural policy would have to adapt accordingly. In other words, by helping creators, producers and distributors to package Catalan products for sale in the global marketplace, the *Generalitat* could also help to ensure that Catalan culture was not as vulnerable to dilution in the 'great global magma'. We have already seen elements of this in the stress on the cultural industries that arose in the late 1990s, and we need to return to this subject now in order to illustrate Catalan strategies for fighting worldwide cultural homogenization by taking advantage of some of the mechanisms associated with economic globalization. Catalonia's cultural industries are not just fighting for market share within Spain, although this is difficult enough in its own right, but within the global marketplace as a whole. As was discussed in chapter 4, this does not just mean achieving business success but also preserving wherever possible a distinctive element of Catalanness that contributes to an awareness of where any particular cultural product has come from.

The *Llibre blanc* of the ICIC carries a specific section on the threats and opportunities presented by globalization (ICIC, 2002: 468–70). Among the opportunities, they see the increasing diversity of Catalan society as a stimulus for creativity that will enhance Catalonia's competitiveness in the global market. Among the threats, they list the standardization of cultural products resulting from the homogenizing forces related to globalization, and the tendency for multinationals to concentrate their production and distribution in the major cultural/linguistic markets, ignoring smaller cultures. These problems require a clear effort on the part of policymakers to enhance the international profile of Catalan cultural products, especially through better distribution networks (479, 514). The authors recommend that Europe and Latin

America be the initial targets for this, followed by the non-European Mediterranean and then the rest of the world. They accept that the presence of the Catalan language and specifically Catalan contents will be possible only in more locally based 'traditional' cultural forms, and that any product dependent on mass production and distribution will be unlikely to have a recognizably Catalan provenance (540). This means that, on their own, the benefits of these types of products can only really be evaluated in terms of economic success or failure, and other ways will need to be found of projecting a strong image of a Catalan identity onto them.

Catalonia®

The promotion of Catalonia and Barcelona as 'brand names' signifying creativity, quality and innovation was supposed to go some way towards achieving this. As Mari Paz Balibrea points out, the transformation of Barcelona since the Transition has led to it being seen as a model for successful urban regeneration, an idea which has more recently been developed into a 'Barcelona brand', mainly at the hands of the *Ajuntament* (Balibrea, 2004; see also Balibrea, 2001, and Degen, 2004). This has meant a form of cultural and social standardization of the city in order to offer the tourist or potential investor a coherent package to buy into; the visual trademark for the package is the work of Antoni Gaudí. The importance of creativity in this branding process ensures that 'Culture and urban redevelopment, culture and spatial restructuring continue to go hand in hand in Barcelona, continuing to justify each other' (Balibrea, 2001: 200). As a result, Barcelona has been refashioned according to the tastes and assumptions of its ruling elite, who have used their own cultural capital as the basis upon which to construct Barcelona as a European capital of culture (Balibrea, 2004). This is of course essential to the development of a brand image for Catalonia as a whole, although the *Generalitat* could not allow Barcelona to become the sole icon of the Catalan brand, partly because of the danger that the *Ajuntament* would use this to push Barcelona further down the road to becoming a city state (Balibrea, 2001: 196–7; see also Muñoz, 2002). It was therefore important to CiU that Catalan creativity in all its guises and from all areas – traditional culture, literature, audio-visual products, theatre, design, crafts, local cuisine etc. – could be symbolically tagged with a general *denomenació d'origen* as if they were bottles of *cava*.

In fact, Catalonia is a particularly good example of what John Urry calls 'brand nationalism' (Urry, 2003: 107), especially when we take into account its situation as a nation without a state. Developing Michael Billig's ideas on banal nationalism, Urry points to the role of 'mega events' – events staged in a single location for a global audience with the help of the international media (Roche, 2000) – in creating a brand image for a particular nation: 'Mega events increasingly occur when the nation and its "banal" characteristics are placed upon the world's stage for display and consumption [. . .] Each such banal nationalism is increasingly consumed by others, compared and evaluated, and turned into a brand' (Urry, 2003: 107; Billig, 1995). The Barcelona Olympics are a good example of this, as the Universal Forum of Cultures would have been if it had received the international media attention the Catalans had been hoping for. In any case, Catalonia's willingness to 'package itself' illustrates both the 'move from banal nationalism to brand nationalism in the new global order' postulated by Urry (2003: 107), and the possibility that stateless nations might have a part to play in this process, even if the messages they are able to give out are subject to confusion with those of their state.

The Catalan brand is being sold to international buyers not just through the direct or televised consumption of Barcelona and its cultural offerings, but also through agencies that operate in other countries, whose job is specifically to take Catalan culture out of its homeland. One of these is the *Institut Ramon Llull*, which was created in 2002 as a collaboration with the Balearic Islands, although tensions between the two parties led the Balearics to withdraw from the agreement in 2004. The main objective of the Institute is the promotion of the Catalan language and culture throughout the world. Its creation was in many ways a response to the failure of Spain's *Instituto Cervantes* to provide adequate representation for Catalan culture, although it was also a way of bringing existing activities under a single umbrella. The IRL took charge of the administration of Catalan language examinations for non-residents, the distribution of funds for translations from Catalan into other languages, and the organization of international promotional activities. However, the IRL is concerned very much with language and 'high culture' and its remit is therefore quite limited. Another institution, COPEC (translated on their London office website as the Catalan Consortium for the External Promotion of Culture) has a broader base and a mission to 'increase awareness of Catalonia's creativity in other countries while building positive cultural relations between Catalonia and other nations'.[4] Created in 1992, COPEC has built up a network of offices in Europe and has particularly capitalized on Catalonia's interregional links (such as the Four Motors and a bilateral agreement with Quebec).[5] It provides advice and liaison services for anyone wanting to take Catalan culture abroad, as well as administering grants and looking for new opportunities for Catalan culture to be represented in festivals and so on. As such, it is especially concerned with the performing and visual arts, music, and traditional culture.

A good illustration of the work of COPEC is the festival of traditional Catalan culture that took place in Britain in August 2003. COPEC was one of the organizations that supported the not-for-profit group *Adifolk* (a Catalan association for the promotion of traditional culture) in taking its annual international festival of the *sardana* and traditional culture to the centre of Manchester. For two days, shoppers tired of the delights of Selfridges were able to watch dancing, *castellers*, and *gegants* (giant figures), and enjoy Catalan music. If they were curious enough to pick up a programme, it would have informed them that 'Catalonia is a country of six million people in the Mediterranean Europe' that 'has enjoyed 700 years of sovereignty and, in spite of having invariably failed, it has always had the will to regain it' (Adifolk, 2003: 1). Six hundred Catalan performers participated in the event, along with some invited British 'giants'. The event was lively, colourful and well received and would certainly have raised awareness of Catalan culture among the spectators. However, it is doubtful that the implications of the description of Catalonia given in the programme would have been fully realized by those reading it, and it is hard to judge what impression of Catalonia itself they would take away with them.

The rationale for having organizations such as these corresponds to the general attempt by CiU to project Catalan culture outwards in such a way that it was defined by a clear provenance and not seen as part of an undifferentiated Spanish stereotype. In other words, it was hoped that this was how local specificities could be maintained, inviting the global market to accept Catalan cultural products as ready-made commodities. Kevin Robins reveals one of the problems with this approach when he discusses what 'local' actually means in the context of the relationship between global markets and local identities (Robins, 1991: 35). He warns that it would be misguided to equate the terms 'local' and 'national' in this context.

> We should not invest our hopes for the future in the redemptive qualities of local economies, local cultures, local identities. It is important to see the local as a relational, and relative, concept. If once it was significant in relation to the national sphere, now its meaning is being recast in the context of globalization.

> [. . .] globalization entails a corporate presence in, and understanding of, the 'local' arena. But the 'local' in this sense does not correspond to any specific territorial configuration. The global-local nexus is about the relation between globalizing and particularizing dynamics in the strategy of the global corporation, and the 'local' should be seen as a fluid and relational space, constituted only in and through its relation to the global.

In other words, the definition of a particular 'local' space for a specific sector, such as the cultural industries, might be carried out solely with reference to the characteristics of the market with no regard for regional or national identities. If this is the case, then the Catalans' attempts to 'act locally' may come into conflict with globalization processes that need to impose their own definitions of 'localness' within, or over the top of, Catalan territory. On the other hand, it is possible that a Catalan market which has already been individualized in terms that are specifically relevant to that sector might influence these definitions so that a limited territorial aspect is retained.

More importantly, if John Urry is correct, then the very complexity and unpredictability of globalization might work in Catalonia's favour. In *Global Complexity* Urry uses descriptions of complexity drawn from the natural sciences to argue that globalization involves such a large number of processes and elements that it can only be analysed in terms of 'non-linear relationships' and 'mobile connections', which produce 'non-equilibrium conditions of global ordering' (Urry, 2003: 123). It is therefore an error to look for linear relationships of cause and effect, or to believe that globalization presupposes a particular outcome in the long term, whether that outcome be viewed as positive (e.g. the spread of democracy) or negative (e.g. increased socio-economic inequality). Instead, Urry highlights the fact that the dynamic interactions between the global and the local can produce unexpected outcomes, in the same way that events in the physical world are now understood to be much less ordered and predictable than was once thought: 'minor changes in the past are able to produce potentially massive effects in the present or future' (23). In this model, then, the actions of one small stateless nation to preserve its cultural distinctiveness are not automatically doomed to be merely 'symbolic', as Mark Schuster suggests (Schuster, 2002: 14–15). However, neither is there any guarantee of the outcomes it might achieve. To use a crude analogy, just as attempts by humans to save endangered species have regularly produced unexpected side effects that have weakened the species in question (Urry, 2003: 32–3), so any cultural policy intervention, no matter how sensible it seems, might actually produce negative effects because of the impossibility of controlling or even understanding the complex variables involved.

Immigration: Fighting Hybridization

The discussion so far has mainly concentrated on CiU's attempts to avoid being swept up in a tide of cultural homogenization by strengthening Catalan identity and securing a differentiated niche within global culture. We now need to turn to the other face of globalization: hybridization. CiU's stress on 'singularity' as a positive feature of Catalonia's future potential (Pujals, 1999: 17) actually highlights the absence of any discussion of hybridity in their internal debates on globalization. Certain key questions remained unarticulated, or were kept separate from the globalization debate, largely because of their controversial nature. Does the preservation of singularity in the face of global homogenization presuppose the need to limit internal cultural diversity? If so, does this also entail the avoidance of any form of internal cultural hybridization? CiU's policy on immigration provides a logical starting point from which to begin to answer these questions.

Until very recently, overall numbers of immigrants living in Spain were small in comparison with figures for other western European countries. However, since the beginning of the 1990s there has been a significant year-on-year increase in immigration, especially in the *Països Catalans*. In 1993 only 1.8 per cent of the population of Catalonia was composed of foreign residents, but by 2004 this had risen to 9.4 per cent (Alonso Calderón, 2001: 15; INE, 2005: 10). This rapid upward trend meant that CiU saw immigration as 'one of the main challenges for Catalonia in the next decades' (Convergència i Unió, 2003: 79).[6] There are several reasons for this: Catalonia has a higher proportion of immigrants than the rest of Spain, whose average in 2004 was 7 per cent (INE, 2005: 10), and it also attracts greater numbers of north Africans than other areas of Spain where the main immigrant groups are European and Latin American (Alonso Calderón, 2001: 39). The *Generalitat* was also frustrated by its inability to regulate the flow of immigrants to the area, as this was the sole responsibility of the Spanish state.

In a speech given in Madrid in 2000, Pujol warned of the need for a clear 'doctrine' to inform Spanish immigration policy (Pujol, 2001b). At the time, the legal basis of that policy was undergoing a process of revision which generated much debate and resulted in the controversial immigration laws of 2000.[7] Under the terms of the Spanish constitution of 1978 (article 149), powers to regulate the admission and legal status of immigrants are reserved by the state. However, the *Generalitat*, like the other governments of Spain's autonomous communities, is responsible for the welfare, education, and cultural and social integration of immigrants once they arrive in their region (article 148).[8] Catalonia can therefore devise a 'doctrine' of its own to guide its handling of these new residents. CiU decided that its policies should be based on the goal of socio-cultural integration and the requirement that new residents learn Catalan as well as Castilian. The bottom line for Catalonia as far as Pujol was concerned was that 'we can't just throw away our identity' (*El Mundo*, 2002).[9] Immigrants were therefore told that they must see their presence in the region as dependent on entering into a pact: the *Generalitat* would provide the necessary help and advice to allow immigrants to settle in Catalonia, but in return they had to be willing to respect Catalonia's 'fundamental values' and 'learn Catalan, the country's language' (Generalitat de Catalunya, 2003b). The immigrant's mastery of Catalan therefore became a litmus test of his or her acceptance of this pact.

This position is entirely consistent with the development of Catalan attitudes to immigrants over the last century. Ever since the days of the medieval Catalan-Aragonese Empire (at its most glorious during the lifetime of Ramon Llull), the Catalans have welcomed traders, visitors and settlers, and have regarded Catalonia as a space open to intercultural encounters. However, the influx of workers from other parts of Spain that began in earnest in the 1950s and peaked in the 1960s proved a significant challenge for Catalan society (McRoberts, 2001: 130–6; Conversi, 1997: 187–221; Woolard, 1989). Catalonia experienced a population explosion that was entirely due to immigration (native birth rates were falling), and the demographic profile of the region changed dramatically in just two decades. The complicating factor was the timing of this phenomenon, at the heart of the Franco dictatorship when Catalan culture and language had been forced into private and unofficial spaces by the repressive policies of the regime.

The main strategy that was eventually adopted to deal with this problem, partly thanks to Jordi Pujol's interventions on the issue both before and after he became president of the *Generalitat*, was based on finding an answer to the question 'who is Catalan?' which provided both a route to integration and a reinforcement of Catalan difference from the rest of Spain. It was felt that an openly inclusive strategy was the best way to win the loyalty of the 'new Catalans' and to encourage solidarity among all residents – this was crucial if Catalonia was to make its voice heard by the Spanish state. The policy therefore involved, first and foremost, a stress on residence as opposed to birthplace or descent: it is enough to live and work in Catalonia to call yourself a Catalan if you wish to (McRoberts, 2001: 131). Secondly, a general invitation was issued to all residents, wherever they came from, to demonstrate acceptance of this identity and to facilitate their integration by learning the Catalan language. Daniele Conversi has shown that this approach has been comparatively successful and 'implies a remarkable capacity to absorb external cultural elements' (Conversi, 1997: 220). Writing in the mid 1990s, he also comments that 'Should this integrative trend still persist, Catalonia could constitute a model for those who fear immigratory waves from the Third World as a threat to European cultural "integrity"' (Conversi, 1997: 221, note 50). Of course, a decade later Catalonia itself is now perceived by some of its residents as facing such a 'threat' because of the greater cultural diversity of the people now making their way to the area.

Another advertisement, placed this time in the Catalan-language magazine *El Temps* (15–21 May 2001: 36) among others, could be seen as a warning from the *Generalitat* to the people of Catalonia to prepare themselves for this challenge. 'Ara ja som més de sis milions' ('Now there are more than six million of us') provided a new spin on a campaign entitled 'Som sis milions' ('There are six million of us') which was used in 1987 as a way of persuading Catalans to take pride in their identity. The 2001 campaign talks about the need for new Catalans, of whatever origin, to be involved in the project to construct tomorrow's Catalonia. The image used is a series of hands of all shapes, sizes and colours, each of which is drawing with its fingers four red stripes, the 'quatre barres' which appear on the Catalan flag and are one of the symbols of Catalan nationhood. Part of the accompanying text reads: 'To make the Catalonia of the future, of generations to come, we will need everyone who wants to love our country, wherever they come from, whatever they are called, and whatever they look like'.[10] This idea of a 'common project' to construct a better Catalonia, to which all can – or must – contribute, has become the key theme in the *Generalitat*'s plans for the integration of immigrants.

In theory, then, this new twenty-first-century immigrant was to be treated no differently from those who had arrived throughout the twentieth century from the rest of Spain. The prevailing rhetoric continued to be one of inclusion and integration in which language was key, both to the acceptance of the immigrant by Catalans and to the acceptance of a Catalan identity by the immigrant. However, the much greater cultural differences between the new immigrants and their host society complicated the issue considerably. Reports of racially motivated violence, controversies over such things as the building of mosques, and the increasing stereotyping of immigrants as perpetrators of crime, revealed tensions which could not be solved by inclusionary rhetoric alone. However, it is not my intention here to examine the social aspects of immigration and the practical responses of the *Generalitat* to the needs of immigrants, but to look more specifically at the implications of immigration for Catalan cultural policy – and indeed of Catalan cultural policy for the immigrants. If the *Generalitat* was indeed trying to create 'a bridge between cultures' as their advertisement suggests, was this a bridge that could be crossed and recrossed at will, by both native and non-native Catalans, or a one-way bridge to integration in the hegemonic culture endorsed by CiU? I would argue that, to all intents and purposes, the bridge being constructed by CiU was indeed 'one way', and largely dependent on 'the word', i.e. the Catalan language.

Looking at key aspects of the background to CiU's stance on immigration, and specifically their emphasis on language and culture as means of integration, it becomes clear that the prevailing discourse which constructs Catalonia as a place of inclusiveness and tolerance is as important in its own way as any practical policy or effort to integrate new immigrants. As usual, there is an invisible party here which is implicated in the discourse although it is never explicitly named: the Spanish state. Resentment at the Spanish government's refusal to allow the *Generalitat* to control the number and skill-profiles of immigrants who settle in Catalonia is only one limited manifestation of the role of the Spanish state in generating the discourse of inclusivity which forms part of mainstream Catalan nationalism. Attempts to create a hegemonic Catalan culture are predicated on the existence of a hegemonic Spanish culture which crosses unopposed into Catalan territory and is accepted to varying degrees by all Catalans. We should therefore bear in mind Michel Foucault's reminder that power is not just located at the level of state institutions but runs through networks involving all social groupings and individuals, and furthermore 'it needs to be considered as a *productive* network' (Foucault, 1980: 122, 119; my italics). The Catalan discourse of inclusion is sustained through government and educational institutions, non-governmental organizations that have a role in ensuring the welfare of immigrants, and the Catalonia-based media, among others, but it is also sustained through individual acceptance of the idea of Catalan openness to outside influences, whether this individual is a native of Catalonia or a recent arrival. The discourse is therefore actively productive in the sense that it gives rise to an atmosphere of inclusiveness within which obvious acts of exclusion are seen as 'out of character'. The other side of the coin is the extent to which more subtle forms of exclusion and coercion are generated by the same discourse.

Routes to Integration

It was mentioned in chapter 1 that one of the keys to understanding contemporary Catalanism is the distinction between ethnic and civic types of nationalism. It is clear that the dominant ideology in

Catalonia regarding the integration of immigrants corresponds quite closely to the definition of the civic nation given by John Hargreaves (2000: 16–17): 'the civic nation's criteria of membership are primarily universalistic – allegiance to and equality before the laws governing a given territory. Cultural criteria are secondary'. Moreover, crude questions of race have only very occasionally surfaced in regard to Catalanism and have normally been rejected by the majority of Catalans (Conversi, 1997: 192–6). However, Hargreaves warns that the distinction between the two types of nationalism is not clear cut, since elements of one can be present even when the other is predominant (see also Llobera, 2004: 83–4). Indeed, differing ideas on how the linguistic and cultural elements of Catalanism should be viewed are central to disagreements over the extent to which Catalan nationalism can be described as 'purely' civic. On one hand, it could simply be the case that since the Catalan language is open to all, and learning Catalan gives full access to Catalan culture, this element is universalistic and therefore civic (McRoberts, 2001: 162). On the other hand, it could be argued that learning the language implies a necessary recognition of, and engagement with, cultural, historical and political elements of Catalan identity which are based on 'presumed cultural characteristics' and are therefore ethnic factors (Woolard, 1989; Llobera, 1996). Furthermore, some individuals 'feel Catalan' but, for whatever reason, prefer to speak Spanish: does their linguistic choice exclude them from full recognition as Catalans even though they are fully committed in other ways to Catalonia's 'common project'? Whichever interpretation we opt for, we should bear in mind Nicholas Stargardt's observation that 'It may be easier to join the *citoyens* than the *Volk*, but both have historically required that recruits assimilate to the dominant culture' (1998: 34).

Chapter 3 examined the ideas of Albert Branchadell, who has suggested that if Catalan nationalism is to be wholly civic and divest itself of its last remnants of ethnic nationalism, the primacy of the Catalan language should no longer be regarded as 'axiomatic' but should follow only from a fully democratic projection of the desires of Catalan civil society (Branchadell, 1999: 50–64). In this scenario, the role of Catalan in constructing the identity of the Catalan people would be important only in so far as it described the current consensus, and not because of its historical importance or the ideological legacy of Catalonia's nationalist thinkers. This attitude might be seen as the most likely to provide a situation in which new

immigrants could be integrated into Catalan civil society whatever
their linguistic preferences or abilities, but it might also remove the
factor that Daniele Conversi has identified as basic in making
Catalonia a 'model' of social integration: the possibility of becoming Catalan by learning the language. Adoption of Branchadell's
policy could therefore complicate the situation still further.

At any event, there is much more to consider than simply
linguistic factors. As McRoberts (2001: 184) says, 'current immigration trends mean that the basic nationalist premise of openness to
newcomers will be tested as never before. [. . .] Moreover, this
trend may pose issues of religion and race.' The main difficulty for
the *Generalitat* in dealing with the new social reality was that
political liberalism, on which Catalan concepts of civil society are
based, demands some form of recognition of an immigrant's right
to maintain pre-existing cultural, religious and linguistic allegiances if s/he so desires. In other words, for Catalanism to be truly
inclusive it must be open to some form of multiculturalism or
cultural pluralism. However, cultural pluralism is an obvious threat
to Catalan identity and unity, if it is considered that the best (or
only) way to maintain these is the reinforcement of core cultural
aspects of Catalan identity.

We have already noted that the approach the *Generalitat* decided
to use to the integration of new immigrants was the same in essence
as has historically been used for migrants from the rest of Spain.
However, there is an obvious complicating factor affecting an
immigrant from, say, Eastern Europe or the Maghreb: they are not
native speakers of Spanish, and may not in fact have any knowledge
of the language at all when they first arrive. This means that when
they settle in Catalonia they are faced with a choice of which
language to learn first, or indeed whether to attempt to learn both
simultaneously. Sarah Gore's study has shown that most immigrants decide to start with Spanish as this is perceived as the more
necessary of the two languages for daily communication (Gore,
2002: 98–100). The desire to learn Catalan in many cases comes
later, once the fundamental issues of subsistence, legality and some
kind of employment are sorted out and they can start to think
about improving their lot rather than simply existing. Gore men-
tions two key incentives for learning Catalan: it increases the
chances of finding a good job (as opposed to just any job), and
allows immigrants to feel more culturally and socially integrated
into their new community. Patrícia Gabancho agrees that these are

the main motivations for learning Catalan, but points out that, depending on the individual, this point may not be reached until many years after they first set foot in Catalonia (Gabancho, 2001: 75, 115–16). She says that one of the key reasons for this is the concentration of Catalan speakers in the middle classes, which is itself a product of the migrations of the Franco period when Spanish speakers escaping rural poverty came to occupy the lowest rung on the Catalan social ladder. Now, Gabancho argues, immigrants will not tend to consider learning Catalan until they are in a position to consider social advancement a real possibility.

Another complicating factor is the attitude of Catalans themselves towards people who are attempting to use the language for the first time. Catalans are used to making fairly instinctive judgements about which language to use with a particular person based on such things as appearance, profession or the place in which the encounter occurs, and this will often lead to anyone who looks 'foreign' being addressed in Spanish. When some degree of competence in Catalan is demonstrated this attitude changes to one of acceptance and even admiration, although as Kathryn Woolard shows, conflicting signals about the stranger's 'suitability' to speak Catalan can still lead to confusion (Woolard, 1989: 74–5). So far, the only solution to this problem seems to be a renewed call for Catalan-speakers to take pride in their language and use it whenever possible, especially with learners who are keen to have the chance to practice their new skills. It is felt that only by setting a good example to immigrants will Catalan-speakers convince them of the need to learn the language as a priority.

It is clear that learning Catalan is a viable route to integration but requires a considerable effort on the part of the immigrant, who may not actually be in a position to make this effort. This means that in practice language can function as a form of exclusion even though it is meant to promote inclusion (Gore, 2002: 102). In effect, it is second-generation immigrants who have been through the Catalan education system who are most easily integrated through language. We should therefore ask whether there are any easier ways for a recent immigrant to participate in Catalan culture. Daniele Conversi suggests one alternative:

> Language is thus the hallmark of integration, but not its only avenue. Immigrants often find an easier way into Catalan identity by participating in folksy events of popular culture, such as popular

dances, *colles de castellers* (human towers), choral singing, trekking etc. In the crucial years of resistance and transition these activities provided a relatively painless means of integration [. . .] (Conversi, 1997: 216)

Conversi is right to point to these forms of popular culture as ways in which the Andalusian or Murcian immigrant could integrate into Catalan society in the past, and in theory there is no reason why a Moroccan or Polish immigrant should not do the same today. Indeed, the discourse of inclusivity that surrounds forms of popular culture such as the *sardana* and *castells* is as strong as ever. For example, 'the *sardanista* manifesto makes it clear that anyone who knows how to dance the sardana will be admitted without any distinction regarding sex, age, race, nationality, education, way of thinking, social class or economic position' (Mas i Solench, 1993: 180).[11] However, admission to the dance carries with it certain responsibilities, and it is made clear that each dancer must know the rules and obey them: 'if the right of admission is open to all, anyone wanting to dance is under an obligation not to disrupt proceedings'.[12] This implies that the traditions themselves are expected to remain 'pure' – there is no sign of openness to change or enrichment through the incorporation of new elements which might be brought by different participants. In other words, the immigrant is still assimilated into a pre-existing cultural order even if s/he chooses to integrate through traditions rather than (or as well as) language.

What, then, of the immigrants' right to integration through citizenship while maintaining strong links with their culture of origin? While there are many individuals who champion this right, CiU's own stance on the matter is contradictory. This is illustrated by the rhetoric used in the 'Welcoming Guides' produced by the *Generalitat* to give to new residents (Generalitat de Catalunya, 2003b). These were bilingual guides, each one in Catalan and a language commonly spoken by immigrants, which explained some of the cultural and social aspects of Catalonia as well as giving practical information. The introduction stated that 'Catalonia recognizes its diversity as enrichment. For this reason, it protects and respects everyone's private life [. . .]' (Generalitat de Catalunya, 2003b: Introduction).[13] However, the guides also stressed that learning Catalan was key for fitting in, making friends, being able to help children with their school work, finding a job and dealing with bureaucracy. Furthermore, the new immigrant was told that 'If you have chosen to reside on a permanent basis in Catalonia, this means that you must have the desire to become integrated into the Catalan society, and form a part of its common project'. The stress is therefore firmly on both civic and cultural/linguistic integration.

However, another sentence in the guide raises the spectre of more worrying ethnic criteria: 'It is important to be able to choose the number of desired children and when to have them. In Catalonia, contraceptives are used on a regular basis' (Generalitat de Catalunya, 2003b: 8). Even as little as twenty-five years ago it would have been quite shocking to suggest that the use of contraceptives was a fundamental part of Catalan society, because it was the teachings of the Roman Catholic Church that were seen as the essence of Catalan moral behaviour. As a party heavily influenced by Catholicism, the statement surely went against the personal beliefs of some members of CiU at the time it was drafted. Not only is this a good example of how seemingly 'essential' characteristics of a society actually change over time – quite rapidly in this case – it is also an example of an area in which Catalonia as the host nation is trying to impose its own values not on the public behaviour of immigrants but on their private morality. There is no good reason to suggest that a 'new Catalan' should see the use of family planning as part of their commitment to their new society. This is surely unacceptable within liberal concepts of the rights of individuals in a democracy, and might suggest a more sinister explanation for its inclusion: the worry that the low birth rate of the Catalans compared with the higher birth rate among immigrants will quickly alter the ethnic make-up of Catalonia. The stress on contraception could actually be an underhanded effort to prevent this from happening. Indeed, Artur Mas and Josep Antoni Duran i Lleida made a commitment in October 2003 to triple the amount of money available to families for child support payments if CiU won the upcoming elections. *El País* reported that 'Only in this way, according to the leaders of CiU, will population increase not "depend on immigration" and will we be able to guarantee an organic growth that will not "denature what we are" (Garriga, 2003).[14] Pujol backed up their stance in the storm of criticism that followed.

This kind of rhetoric seems to suggest an ethnic vision of culture and language rather than the civic vision outlined earlier. It is certainly the case that the potentially 'ethnic' component of CiU's discourse on identity has become more visible in recent years as a result of widespread concerns about the effects of immigration. (This is not to suggest that such responses to immigration are exclusive to Catalan nationalists, since on the contrary they have been seen in many parts of Spain since immigration became an issue.) There does not seem to be room for the creation of 'hyphenated identities' in which 'Catalan' would be the 'civic' component (e.g. Moroccan-Catalan, Polish-Catalan). Instead, the overriding impression is of a very French, and therefore paradoxically Jacobin, definition of citizenship such that once you are Catalan, you are Catalan, full stop (see Pujol, 2001b). This paradox suggests that the political scientist Miquel Caminal was right to define Pujol's policy on immigration as 'confused and borrowed': he even goes as far as to suggest that the mixed messages Pujol gave out are partly responsible for the degree of success his policies enjoyed (Noguer, 2003).

Cosmopolitanism, or the Preservation of Identity?

No matter how blurred Pujol's discourse on immigration might have been, it was fundamentally an attempt to avoid the hybridization of Catalan culture. This is the subtext behind the call to 'fully preserv[e] our identities' in the 2003 St George's Day advertisement. It is also related to the idea of using Catalonia's 'singularity' to avoid the homogenization that many people associate with the processes of globalization. While what might be described as 'racial' hybridization was accepted as a historical fact and a continuing inevitability, and not seen as a major issue, cultural hybridization which might result in the weakening of the Catalan language or of identifiably Catalan cultural forms was to be resisted. This meant that an increase in cultural diversity within Catalonia was problematic as it could create the conditions within which hybridization might occur. Moral panics about the influence of the Castilian language on the development of Catalan testify to this fear. Of course, increased cultural diversity brought by immigration is not the only source of influences that might lead to cultural hybridization. The physical and virtual mobility of the resident Catalan population is another major factor, but this is much more difficult to control. Immigration was a more visible, and therefore potentially more controllable, influence.

As far as cultural policy is concerned, there is a clear tension between seeing cultural diversity within Catalonia as an asset or a threat. The writers of the ICIC handbook were clear that it represented an opportunity because it enhanced the possibilities for creativity and innovation and also made Barcelona an attractive destination for cultural practitioners from around the world (ICIC, 2002: 468). This means that Catalonia conforms to Tony Bennett's observation that 'cultural diversity policies [. . .] are seen as having a significant role to play in developing the varied cultural skills and resources required by a vibrant cultural economy' (Bennett, 2001: 51). He goes on to explain that:

> From this perspective, diversity enriches the cultural capital of national or regional economies. It results – in the case of the connections of cultural diversity to cultural tourism, for example – in niche products for marketing in the global marketplace. Or, and more commonly, diversity is seen as necessary for the processes of 'product innovation' as new artistic and cultural forms are seen to depend on the syncretism and cross-cultural fertilisation that is possible only in culturally diverse societies.

However, different nations see cultural diversity in very specific terms that are related to their own circumstances (23). Even where diversity is welcomed, there is a limit to this since certain kinds of diversity are regarded as more manageable, in terms of being more easily integrated into the nationalizing project, than others (27; see also Hutchinson, 2005: 112). In the case of CiU's conception of cultural diversity, it seems to fit best into Bennett's definition of a particular set of approaches to sub or multinational diversity, 'which dispute the homogenising tendencies of national cultures, but do so on the basis of essentially similar strategies by articulating a competing set of associations between a territory, its people and their culture' (29). Cultural diversity is seen as positive when it refers to the diversity of the historic nations within Spain, but problematic when it refers to a degree of internal diversity within Catalonia that threatens to alter that 'set of associations'.

There is of course a difference between simply having cultural diversity within a community, which might involve a surprisingly limited degree of actual contact between cultures, and cultural hybridization. According to Bauman, hybridization is more likely to take place at the 'globalized top' of the cultural spectrum – the area which is accessed and created by those who have the mobility that is associated with wealth, education, neo-liberal economies and democratic societies (Bauman, 1998: 3, 86). Catalan society as a whole fits into this top end although there are of course stratifications within the region that mean that some individuals have less mobility, choice, and access to information flows than others. The paradox as far as nationalist movements in wealthy stateless nations are concerned is that it is those with the least mobility who retain their territorial and cultural loyalties with fewest difficulties (Szerszynski and Urry, 2006), but they are not the best asset when it comes to economic and industrial competitiveness or the creation of a 'brand nationalism'. On the contrary, the economic future and brand image of the nation depend on its most mobile, and so potentially most fickle, members. It is therefore necessary to convince these particular people to apply some kind of prioritization of local elements not just in their consumption of culture but, in some cases, in their professional or amateur role in producing and distributing it.

One of the ways in which this can be achieved is by presenting cultural change as a crisis that threatens the well-being of the nation and, by extension, of its citizens. As Giner et al. (1996: 70) have said, 'the debate about Catalan culture forms part of Catalan culture itself'.[15] Issues such as immigration – reflected in political debates, the media or discussions between friends – help to keep the question of Catalan identity (and by extension, the problem of resisting both Spanish cultural domination and indiscriminate globalization) at the forefront of as many people's minds as possible. We can apply Eva Mackey's comments on Canada to Catalonia: 'national identity is not so much in a constant state of crisis, but [. . .] the production of 'crisis' allows the nation to be a site of a constantly regulated politics of identity' (1999: 13). Even more illuminating is this suggestion from John Hutchinson: 'one might propose that economic success and stability make national ossification the norm, and that mass nationalist mobilisation depends on a sense of crisis' (Hutchinson, 2005: 136). This does not mean either that the sense of crisis has to revolve around threats to economic stability, or that it necessarily has to be imposed from the top by a nationalist elite (148–53). Since Catalonia's cultural distinctiveness is the core element of its national identity, and that distinctiveness is felt throughout Catalan society in different ways, this is the most fertile ground for the production of crises that seek to perpetuate a state of 'hot nationalism' (Billig, 1995). Such crises can just as well be articulated by nationalist groups within civil society as by any political party. It is the congruence between the worries of ordinary Catalans and the messages from the *Generalitat* that account for the general acceptance of Pujol's discourse on immigration and cultural change.

Of course, other political parties in Catalonia have also been addressing these worries, although from different perspectives. CiU's stress on the preservation of Catalonia's existing cultural make-up is not directly reproduced in the approach to immigration of the other major parties, although elements of it can still be seen even where the party in question is supposedly taking an opposing line.[16] We have already seen that the PSC's official stance is that Catalan culture is culture produced by Catalan citizens, whatever language it uses and whatever cultural tradition it draws on. CiU's insistence on 'authenticity' is regarded by the PSC as exclusionary and counterproductive (Mascarell, 1999: 87). However, even for the PSC, hybridity is not something to be actively encouraged, although it is not to be irrationally feared either:

> It is not so much a question of encouraging *métissages*, mixtures, syntheses, fusions or multicultural cocktails that might lead to a 'new' culture or a hybrid culture, as of dynamically adding together the manifestations of culture that are created in Catalonia. (Mascarell, 1999: 89)[17]

In a speech given in 2001, Pasqual Maragall stressed the fact that any culture is dynamic, not static, and appealed for a diverse and cosmopolitan future for Catalonia (Maragall, 2001). However, he was also clear that a universal culture and civilization has to be based on local specificities and 'a diversity of languages and cultures that must be preserved and enriched'.[18] The construction of the sentence seems to indicate that he meant that diversity itself must be preserved, suggesting a disapproval of homogenization, but this also implies the need to preserve particular languages and cultures, which once again indicates worries about hybridization.

It is clear that as Catalanist politicians faced the uncertainties of the twenty-first century they were having to tread a very careful line between acceptance of internal diversity, external cultural influences, and the opportunities associated with the global trade in cultural commodities, on one hand, and keeping control of the ways in which these would shape Catalan culture and society on the other. CiU's reaction to these circumstances was to opt for the preservation of core elements of Catalan culture. This was its way of ensuring that Catalonia retained its distinctiveness, which could only be conceived of as being based squarely on the region's history and cultural heritage. This also had the advantage that this distinctiveness could be used in the creation of a brand nationalism that would enhance Catalonia's competitiveness in the global cultural marketplace. Such an approach indicates a rather contradictory mixture of economic neo-liberalism and cultural neo-tribalism in CiU's thinking (Bauman, 1998: 3). The difficulty was how to make this tactic compatible with a genuinely inclusive form of Catalanism that would be perceived as such by the immigrants themselves. Pride in Catalonia's historic openness to diversity and its traditionally cohesive society may turn out to have less relevance in tackling the challenges ahead than many Catalans assume. Although this positive attitude – that the integration of newcomers has been achieved before and can be done again – is clearly better than many other conceivable starting points, it also carries with it the danger of complacency. As Josep Llobera has said, 'The reality of the country is multidimensional, and the implication of this fact is often ignored by the locals' (Llobera, 2004: 113). Salvador Cardús goes even further, by declaring that the conventional Catalan discourse on immigration is constructed upon a fundamental contradiction in terms, since the concept of a present-day identity based on particular cultural roots is quite simply 'not compatible with the idea of having been a country of immigrants' (Cardús, 2005: 41).

Montserrat Guibernau proposes that the future for Catalan nationalism might lie in helping to create the conditions within which a global cosmopolitanism might develop, and it is the idea of a 'cosmopolitan Catalanism' with which I will end the current discussion. Guibernau defines cosmopolitanism as 'world citizenship free from national prejudices' (Guibernau, 2004: 163), but says that the starting point for this must be that all nations need first to be 'free' to join in this world citizenship as sovereign equals. Only by valuing one's homeland can one become a citizen of the world, and this is why in her view 'Democratic nationalism is legitimate' (164). Since Catalans have been prevented from fully realizing the potential of their nation up to now, she feels that it would not be legitimate to ask them to miss a step in the process and become cosmopolitan before attaining equal status as a world nation. This vision relies on acknowledgement of Catalonia as a nation and an enhancement of its self-determination largely through the actions of outside agencies: the Spanish state – to provide greater autonomy and a more satisfactory financial arrangement – and wider organizations such as the EU or UN – to accord real recognition to stateless nations rather than dealing solely with states or lumping stateless nations together with regions. In other words, this is a 'classic' cosmopolitanism that would be achieved by taking the right political (not cultural) steps, rather than a postmodern cosmopolitanism involving cultural mixing (Llobera, 2004: 111; Szerszynski and Urry, 2006: 114).

A different conception of cosmopolitanism developed by John Urry helps us to extend Guibernau's analysis of the Catalan situation. Urry sees cosmopolitanism as a 'global fluid' – a set of global dispositions that are increasingly conditioning the actions of nation states so that they risk isolation or even military intervention if they fail to conform to certain standards of behaviour (Urry, 2003: 133–4). As this 'global fluid' increases its influence, people are becoming more open to cultural and ethnic diversity, but also feel increasingly insecure because of the presence of potential 'enemies' within their own borders rather than having them confined within traditional enemy states (see also Guibernau, 2004: 157–8). In whatever way cosmopolitanism might operate on a global level, then, it is also relevant to the local level because it affects the way we treat the representatives of diversity within our own neighbourhood. For this reason, 'Cosmopolitanism should be seen as produced by, and further elaborating, the glocalization attractor through transforming relations *between* the global and the local' (136–7).[19] This is why Urry too concludes that there is a need for people to value the specificity of their homeland as well as to develop a cosmopolitan outlook.

> Cosmopolitan fluidity thus involves the capacity to live simultaneously in *both* the global and the local, in the distant and proximate, in the universal and the particular. Such cosmopolitanism involves comprehending the specificity of one's local context, to connect to other locally specific contexts and to be responsive to the complex threats and opportunities of a globalizing world. (Urry, 2003: 137)

If cosmopolitanism and glocalization continue to function in this way, then they could at least provide the conditions within which the recognition of Catalonia's specificity by higher political entities could be achieved. The Catalans' willingness to think of themselves as cosmopolitan should also put them in a good position to be able to value both the global and the local. However, cultural specificity is not the same as the 'preservation' of a culture that is defined in terms favoured by the dominant ethnonational group, and therefore Urry's argument cannot be used to back up CiU's desire to resist either homogenization or hybridization. Rather, it invites them to recognize their specificity as contingent – but no less specific for all that.

It is therefore helpful to acknowledge the changing face of cultural specificity in the terms set out in John Hutchinson's *longue durée* analysis of the relationship between nations and ethnic groups (Hutchinson, 2005). For Hutchinson, neither nationalism nor globalization are recent phenomena but new iterations of processes that can be traced back through the history of inter and intraethnic relations over many centuries. Looked at in this way, it becomes clear that the more recent intensification of globalization is indeed responsible for a rise in nationalism. As a result, it has tended to produce differentiation rather than homogenization. However, the key element in Hutchinson's argument is that this points to the need to accept 'a non-essentialist concept of ethnicity', since 'ethnic formations even when strongly institutionalised are subject to recurring external challenges of different kinds, which may result in internally generated innovation, imposed syncretisation through conquest, or possibly dissolution through voluntary or coerced assimilation and ethnocidal programmes' (166). These changes give rise to an overlaying of old myths with new conceptions which can themselves become myths, and elites can use different symbols to mobilize the population as required, since members of the ethnic group still recognize them even if they have not had to think about them for a while (74). Modernizing initiatives by nationalist elites always correspond in some way with the deep roots of the ethnic past and so continue to produce difference rather than homogenization (193).

Extrapolating from this, and bearing in mind Urry's assertion that the recognition of local specificities is a precondition of cosmopolitanism, it can be suggested that no matter how much identities might alter over time, it is highly unusual for there to be a radical break with the ethnic past. (The most obvious circumstance that might create such a rupture is genocide.) The present is always conditioned by the past – the survival of Catalan culture during the

Franco regime testifies to this strongly enough. Even if forces such as the increased mobility of populations, information and culture change the shape of the cultural specificity that is Catalonia, it will still produce another Catalan specificity that will include ethnic elements from the past, even if these have become overlaid with new elements. In fact, Margaret Moore goes as far as to argue that national identities can survive quite dramatic cultural changes:

> All that is required for a national identity to persist is some marker to tell the groups apart [. . .] To achieve the complete eradication of all signs of a distinct identity is extremely difficult, especially for a group that is living on its own territory and has the demographic strength to survive as a distinct community. Globalization may make the groups appear, to the outsider, more alike; but it will probably not have any bearing on the group identities that people have. (Moore, 2001: 53)

Nevertheless, CiU's fear of homogenization and hybridization led them to try to manage the influences to which Catalan culture was exposed. As Hutchinson points out, different nations have specific ideas about their own strengths and the elements they therefore hold sacred (Hutchinson, 2005: 147). If one of these elements is threatened, they will react more quickly than if the threat is to an element with only a secondary priority. The stress on culture and language that derived from Catalonia's ethnic past and CiU's own ideological heritage meant that this was one of the primary threats that they responded to when they came to power in 1980, with the general approval of the people they represented. However, the rise in popularity of other political options and other ways of viewing Catalan culture over the last twenty-five years suggests that it is no longer considered disloyal to question some of the fundamental tenets of cultural nationalism. As Hutchinson points out 'such battles seem to have the character of a family quarrel, one that is intensely felt but one that marks off the disputants from those outside this cultural tradition' (Hutchinson, 2005: 104). These kinds of disputes are healthy when they produce positive innovation, and unhealthy when they are not resolved. CiU's insistence on the symbolic value of language, coupled with its failure to back up its rhetoric with radical legislation or enough hard cash, was in danger of drawing attention away from the real challenges Catalonia would face in the twenty-first century.

NOTES

1. 'la globalització podria amenaçar la nostra continuïtat com a poble català. Podríem quedar diluïts en un gran magma global. Però igualment podríem sucumbir si provéssim de defensar-nos tancant-nos en nosaltres mateixos.'

2. 'elaborar i expandir un missatge de validesa universal i amb destinataris universals'.

3. 'Europa: globalització i identitats'. Speech given 18 April 2000, reproduced on *www.jordipujol.com.*

4. *http://www.copec.es/* (follow links to London office website).

5. Since 2005 it has been part of the ICIC.

6. 'Un dels principals reptes de Catalunya en els propers decennis'.

7. Ley Orgánica 8/2000, de 22 de diciembre, de reforma de la Ley Orgánica 4/2000, de 11 de enero, sobre derechos y libertades de los extranjeros en España y su integración social.

8. The statute of autonomy of 2006 extends Catalonia's powers in matters of immigration so that the *Generalitat* now deals with the bureaucracy related to the official regularization of immigrants, rather than the state authorities in Catalonia. The *Generalitat* also has the right to be consulted on state immigration policy and settlement plans, although the state retains overall control of these matters.

9. 'No podemos tirar a la basura nuestra identidad.'

10. 'Per fer la Catalunya del futur, la de les properes generacions, necessitarem tots aquells que vulguin estimar el nostre país. Vinguin d'on vinguin. Es diguin com es diguin. I siguin com siguin.'

11. 'El Manifest sardanista concreta que, a la sardana, s'hi admet tothom qui sàpiga ballar-la sense distinció de sexe, edat, raça, nacionalitat, instrucció, manera de pensar, classe social o posició económica'.

12. 'Si el dret d'admissió està obert, qui vulgui dansar té el deure de no destorbar.'

13. All quotations are taken from the English version of the guide.

14. 'Sólo así, opinan los dirigentes de CiU, el incremento demográfico no "dependerá de la inmigración" y se podrá garantizar un crecimiento vegetativo que no "desnaturalice lo que somos".'

15. 'El debat sobre la cultura catalana forma part de la mateixa cultura catalana.'

16. See Guibernau, 2004: 169, for a summary of the attitudes and objectives of the main parties re immigration.

17. 'No es tracta tant d'impulsar mestissatges, barreges, síntesis, fusions o còctels multiculturals que desemboquin en una «nova» cultura o en una cultura híbrida, com de sumar dinàmicament les manifestacions culturals que es fan a Catalunya.'

18. 'una diversitat de llengües i cultures que cal preservar i enriquir'.

19. If a dynamic system eventually ends up in one restricted place (a 'basin'), this is said to be as the result of an attractor. Urry regards

glocalization as a 'strange' attractor: this results in a system that never returns to the same place. Strange attractors are sensitive to the conditions from which they develop. (See Urry, 2003: 26–7.)

Conclusion

Whatever the limitations of CiU's particular stance on globalization and cultural diversity, one thing is clear from the Catalan case: one of the ongoing outcomes of globalization, in Europe at least, is likely to be further increases in demands for political power from many regions and stateless nations. The logical result of the Catalans' attempts to tackle globalization head on was to increase demands for greater political autonomy in order to have more control over resources and more flexibility for the *Generalitat* to tailor its policies to Catalonia's situation. Indeed, the calls for a rewriting of the Catalan statute of autonomy that began in the late 1990s (and led to a new statute being approved in 2006) were directly influenced by the simultaneous debates on the potential effects of globalization and the need to be in a better position to deal with immigration. These debates reveal that for regions and stateless nations in the West, cultural autonomy now has no real meaning unless it is combined with a high degree of political and financial autonomy. Cultural autonomy as it was conceived for the purposes of the Spanish constitution does have a role to play in safeguarding threatened traditional or folkloric elements. It also allows for the implementation of regional arts policies that can contribute to the maintenance or success of specific sectors such as literature or museums. However, it is too limited to allow Spain's 'historic nations' to tackle, on their own terms, challenges such as cultural globalization, the increasing physical and virtual mobility of populations and ideas, and regional competitiveness within the global cultural industries. If even established nation states 'face a declining capacity to regulate global media and communications flows, and engage in "cultural boundary maintenance" in the face of economic and cultural globalization' (Flew, 2005: 356), then such a task might seem Herculean for stateless nations and they will want every possible weapon at their disposal.

CiU's approach to cultural policy demonstrates their growing realization of this problem over the period that they were in power. As cultural diversity within Catalonia became more of an issue, so did the worry that Catalan culture might still be as vulnerable as it had been during the dictatorship, although for different reasons which were now (paradoxically) to do with the effects of democracy and liberalization. It was perfectly legitimate for CiU to seek to influence the way these forces affected Catalan culture, in accordance with the democratically expressed wishes of the electorate, even though the amount of control it had was limited and undermined by the Spanish state. However, in doing so, CiU went against contemporary trends by addressing Catalans as cultural citizens rather than as consumers. To those who were not direct supporters of CiU's form of cultural nationalism, the *Generalitat* therefore appeared to be restricting cultural freedoms (by imposing ideological factors on consumer choices) at a time when the global market in cultural commodities would (however misleadingly) appear to be enhancing them.

One of the most important effects of this approach was that those who were involved in producing and disseminating culture were supposed to fit into this institutionalized and nationalizing model. Acceptance of this requirement was pragmatically necessary if practitioners were going to receive financial support for their work from the *Generalitat*, but many also felt it was patriotically necessary if Catalonia was to recover from the damage done by Francoism. This meant that some of those working in the cultural field followed these 'rules' even if they had no particular sympathy for CiU's politics. It also made it difficult for artists to adopt anti-establishment positions, since an attack on Catalonia's institutions could automatically be perceived as a form of support for Spanish institutions. Any form of critical artistic engagement with questions of cultural politics or national identity rendered the individual concerned susceptible to being placed in one camp or the other. This meant that the autonomy of cultural producers in Catalonia was severely compromised. Even if they tried to avoid the system of patronage and operate on the margins of the establishment (rejecting or rendering themselves ineligible for subsidies, prizes and institutional posts), they could not avoid being caught up in the struggle to create a legitimate space for Catalan culture.

It appears that the political elites of other stateless nations have also become seduced by the idea that an arm's length cultural policy is not the best way to approach the problems of minority cultures. In 2004, the Welsh Assembly proposed taking direct control of the funding of some key organizations in Wales, including the Welsh National Opera and the National Theatre of Wales. The proposed legislation was narrowly defeated in 2006 after opposition parties and independents united to pass an amendment that led instead to a full review of arts funding in Wales, as they were worried that such a close association would give rise to political interference in culture. It would not have escaped their notice that Catalonia did not have an arm's length policy, as was also highlighted in a consultation document prepared for the Scottish Parliament in 2000 as part of the development of a National Cultural Strategy for Scotland (Keenlyside, 2000: section 5.9). Moves to boost the role of the Scottish Executive in the management of culture over the last few years have prompted some people to protest that the arm's length principle is being damaged there too, although this is attributed to a misguided anti-elitism rather than to a sense of cultural nationalism. The Culture (Scotland) Bill that will implement major changes in the sector is still at the consultation stage at the time of writing. It includes a proposal that the Scottish Arts Council be scrapped and replaced by a body with a broader remit (especially in the creative industries) called Creative Scotland. Its board will be appointed by the Scottish ministers, who may also issue 'guidance' or 'directions' on its activities.

While those who create culture necessarily have to engage with political and financial institutions in order to secure public recognition and public/private funding, this does not mean that these institutions have to be allowed to assume the controlling position. Bourdieu's work reminds us that the degree of autonomy or 'lawlessness' of any particular cultural field can be an important determinant of the capacity for innovation and creativity of the artists that operate within it (Bourdieu, 1993: 238–53; Ahearne, 2004: 71–6). Jeremy Ahearne points out that one possible interpretation of Bourdieu's simultaneous rejection and recognition of the state's role in culture is that the producers of culture might have to use different strategies at different times:

> At one moment, or in one historical conjuncture, cultural producers will have to use what symbolic leverage they might have to impose their independence with regard to governmental agendas. At another, they will have to cultivate an alliance with the apparatus of

government in order to overcome a structural subordination to national or transnational market forces. (Ahearne, 2004: 75)

However, Ahearne's suggestion seems too simplistic to describe the Catalan situation, even if we are only looking at relationships with the *Generalitat* without introducing the complicating factor of the Spanish state. Those who produce culture in Catalonia cannot be lumped together into a group with broadly similar interests that might be best served by adopting one strategy or another. Instead, analysis of the reactions to CiU's cultural policy reveals disparate groups with a broad range of concerns that cannot be reduced to the question of whether or not they should sacrifice some autonomy in return for protection from market forces. It is not only the 'historical conjuncture' that determines their strategies, but also the diachronic pull of the different political and cultural influences that act simultaneously on Catalans. These not only have different degrees of institutionally derived legitimacy, but also give rise to different feelings of belonging which might be more import-ant to a particular individual than the recognition s/he might be afforded by cultural or political institutions. This in turn might mean sacrificing cultural or economic capital in order to achieve a greater degree of '"comfort" in place' (Savage, Bagnall and Longhurst, 2005: 8). The dynamism of the Catalan cultural field is produced, to a large degree, by this diversity of influences and the positions they generate.

The left-wing tripartite government elected in 2003 made a commitment to recognize and support this diversity, but their room for manoeuvre was of course limited by the degree to which Catalans would tolerate departures from the directions that were so firmly established before and during CiU's long period in power. This would especially be the case if such departures challenged 'common sense' notions such as the association of language with identity, or Catalonia's openness to global cultural influences. These kinds of doxa have of course already been subject to chal-lenge, but, as Salvador Cardús points out (referring specifically to popular misunderstanding of the contribution of immigration to Catalan society) the critical contributions of academics and polit-icians 'have not come to form part of a generalized common knowledge' (Cardús, 2005: 39). This seems to be attributable to the high level of congruence between CiU's discourse on culture and the established perceptions of the Catalan public, which made it more difficult for competing discourses to penetrate the national imaginary. This congruence was crucial to the success of CiU, since, as John Hutchinson argues, 'It is implausible [. . .] to conceive of modernising nationalists as outside their society mobilising it from above' because the public needs to feel that the nationalists' message is appealing and acceptable (Hutchinson, 2005: 33). The exercise of cultural policy as 'display' fed into this dynamic by generating a 'feel-good factor' that reinforced the appeal of the message and acted as a further barrier against competing discourses.

Nevertheless, as we have seen in the case of reactions to globalization and immigration, this 'feel-good factor' was also accompanied by constant warnings about impending crises. In the case of warnings from the *Generalitat*, the potential threats were largely external to the core Catalan reality and yet determined to impinge upon it: Spanish culture and media (legitimized by the more powerful institutions of the state), increasing European integration without adequate protection for minority languages and cultures, immigration, globalization. Catalans were urged to respond to these crises by making an effort to value and make use of their own cultural and linguistic heritage. In the case of many intellectuals and practitioners who were not aligned with CiU's concept of culture, the sense of crisis had both internal and external dimensions since CiU's approach was believed to exacerbate the problems.

As early as 1984, Raymond Williams had concluded that the very idea of a national cultural policy was becoming outdated, since the nation state was too small to cope with developments in areas such as the media, and too big to ensure the proper recognition of the cultural diversity that exists within any community (Williams, 1984: 5). His proposed solution was to move cultural policy out of the domain of the nation state and locate it within a European context of support for the arts, on one hand, and a city-based local cultural framework, on the other. The problem with this suggestion as far as stateless nations and regions are concerned is that it does not give scope for the construction of a specific cultural space at these levels. As John Tomlinson says, 'there is the simple but important fact that we are all, as human beings, *embodied and physically located*. In this fundamental material sense the ties of culture to location can never be completely severed and the locality continues to exercise its claims upon us as the physical situation of our lifeworld. So, deterritorialization cannot ultimately mean the end of locality but its transformation into a more complex cultural space.' (Tomlinson, 1999: 149). A national or regional community with a strong sense of identity that is not permitted to manage the complexities of its own cultural space is more likely to become antagonistic towards the nation state, and so it seems counterproductive to prevent it from doing so. However, the precise means of construction of that space need to be carefully devised, and it should not be assumed that models derived from city, nation state or European contexts will also work at these levels.

Apart from reminding government bodies at all levels of their obligation to give a voice to the diverse cultural communities they represent, one of the ways that cultural policy studies might contribute to this debate is to help articulate new ways of making policy at an intermediate stage between the city and the state. This level of policy should not just be concerned with capitalizing on culture for regional economic growth, but should also look at other areas where cultural policy might enhance the well-being of any self-defined community. It might, for example, aim to combat any sense of marginalization within the nation state by working in partnership with state institutions to provide opportunities for dialogue that would broaden the state's own definition of its cultural identity. It might improve opportunities for access to culture by supporting initiatives from clusters of smaller towns and villages that do not have the kinds of resources enjoyed by cities. It might also contain elements of cultural policy 'proper' – 'for the development of the arts themselves' (Williams, 2004: 5) – while finding ways of responding to the specificity of the group from which particular forms of cultural expression have arisen without converting that context into the *raison d'être* of the arts themselves. In short, cultural policy studies needs to be prepared to engage both critically and productively with the desire of regions and stateless nations to create their own recognized cultural spaces. It clearly has a role to play in the development of forms of policy-making that are appropriate to the very significant challenges of the kind of cultural context exemplified by Catalonia.

Bibliography

Adifolk (2003). *16è aplec internacional de la sardana i mostra de grups folklòrics* (event programme), Barcelona.

Aguilera, G. (2005). 'La descatalanització de les ones', *El Temps*, 29 November, 70–3.

Ahearne, J. (2004). 'Between cultural theory and policy: the cultural policy thinking of Pierre Bourdieu, Michel de Certeau and Régis Debray', Centre for Cultural Policy Studies, University of Warwick, (Research Papers, no. 7).

Alay, A. (ed.) (2003). *Antologia política de Jordi Pujol*, Barcelona, Pòrtic.

Alonso Calderón, J. (2001). *Pla interdepartamental d'immigració 2001–4*, Barcelona, Generalitat de Catalunya.

Andreu, M. (1999). 'Tradicions: moviment associatiu i cultura popular', *L'Avenç*, 236, 22–6.

Antich, J. (1994). *El Virrey: ¿Es Jordi Pujol un fiel aliado de la Corona o un caballo de Troya dentro de la Zarzuela?*, Barcelona, Planeta.

Aragay, I. (2004). Interview with Jaume Sobrequés, Director of the Museu d'Història de Catalunya, *Quadern d'Història del Centre d'història Contemporània de Catalunya*, in *Avui: Suplement Especial*, 29 May, 26.

Artigas, J. (1989). 'Una ocasió desaprofitada: la "Història de Catalunya" en dibuixos animats', *L'Avenç*, 127–8, 105.

Avui, (1977). 'Cal votar', *Avui*, 14 June, 1.

—— (2000). 'Un informe de Cultura revela que la gent vol més català on n'hi ha dèficit', *Avui*, 7 June, *www.avui.com*, accessed 7 June 2000.

Ayén, X. (2001). 'Aluvió de traducciones del catalán', *La Vanguardia Digital*, 8 March, *www.vanguardia.es*, accessed 30 May 2001.

Balcells, A. (1994). *La història de Catalunya a debat: Els textos d'una polèmica*, Barcelona, Curial.

—— (1996). *Catalan Nationalism: Past and Present*, ed. G. J. Walker, London, Macmillan.

Balibrea, M. P. (2001). 'Urbanism, culture and the post-industrial city: challenging the "Barcelona model"', *Journal of Spanish Cultural Studies*, 2/2, 187–210.

—— (2004). 'Barcelona: del modelo a la marca', *Desacuerdos*, *www.desacuerdos.org* ('Casos de estudio'), 9 November, accessed 4 August 2005.

Barker, C. (2000; repr. 2002). *Cultural Studies: Theory and Practice*, London, Sage.

Baulenas, Ll-A. (2004). *El català no morirà: un moment decisiu per al futur de la llengua*, Barcelona, Edicions 62.

Bauman, Z. (1998). *Globalization: The Human Consequences*, Cambridge, Polity.

Bell, I. A. (ed.) (1995). *Peripheral Visions: Images of Nationhood in Contemporary British Fiction*, Cardiff, University of Wales Press.

Bennett, T. (1992). 'Putting policy into cultural studies', in L. Grossberg, C. Nelson, and P. A. Treichler (eds), *Cultural Studies*, London, Routledge, pp. 23–37.

—— (1995). *The Birth of the Museum: History, Theory, Politics*, London, Routledge.

—— (1998). *Culture: A Reformer's Science*, London, Sage.

—— (ed.) (2001). *Differing Diversities: Cultural Policy and Cultural Diversity*, Strasbourg, Council of Europe Publishing.

Berger, V. (2005). 'Presencia y ausencia del teatro castellano en Barcelona', in S. King (ed.), *La cultura catalana de expresión castellana. Estudios de literatura, teatro y cine*, Kassel, Reichenberger, pp. 123–42.

Berrio, J. (1998). 'Els intel·lectuals a Catalunya', in S. Giner (ed.), *La societat catalana*, Barcelona, Institut d'Estadística de Catalunya, 951–64.

Bertran, J. and Nadal, E. (2000). *Manual de producció tècnica: Contribució a l'organització d'espectacles i festes populars*, Barcelona, Generalitat de Catalunya.

Billig, M. (1995). *Banal Nationalism*, London, Sage.

Bloom, H. (1996). *The Western Canon*, London, Macmillan.

Boadella, A. (1993). *El Nacional* (programme notes), reproduced on *www.elsjoglars.com/català/Espectacles/elnacional.htm*, accessed 8 March 2005.

Bonada, Ll. (2005). Interview with Baltasar Porcel, *El Temps*, 19–25 April, 77–9.

Bonet, Ll. (2001). 'Les polítiques culturals a Catalunya: un espai d'acords bàsics en un context d'alt dinamisme', in R. Gomà and J. Subirats (eds), *Govern i polítiques públiques a Catalunya (1980–2000)*, vol 1: 'Autonomia i benestar', Barcelona, Universitat de Barcelona, pp. 303–25.

Bonet Mojica, Ll. (2000[?]). 'Un fracàs per decret', *Barcelona. Metròpolis Mediterrània*, 53, *www.bcn.es/publicacions/bmm/53/ct_cronica.htm*, accessed 14 April 2005.

Bou, Ll. (2000). 'Pujol admet que s'ha abandonat massa la defensa de la identitat', *Avui*, 2 June, *www.avui.com*, accessed 2 June 2000.

Bourdieu, P. (1984; repr. 2005). *Distinction: A Social Critique of the Judgement of Taste*, trans. R. Nice, London, Routledge.

—— (1991). *Language and Symbolic Power*, ed. and introduction J. B. Thomson, Cambridge, Polity.

—— (1993). *The Field of Cultural Production*, ed. and introduction R. Johnson, Cambridge, Polity.

—— (1998). *On Television and Journalism*, trans. P. Parkhurst Fergusson, London, Pluto Press.

—— (2000). *Pascalian Meditations*, trans. R. Nice, Oxford, Polity.

Branchadell, A. (1996). *La normalitat improbable*, Barcelona, Empúries.

—— (1999). 'La política lingüística a Catalunya: liberals vs nacionalistes', in M. À. Pradilla (ed.), *La llengua catalana al tombant del mil·leni*, Barcelona, Empúries, 35–66.

Bru de Sala, X. (1987). *Barcelona: proposta cultural*, Barcelona, Edicions del Mall.

—— (1999). *El descrèdit de la literatura*, Barcelona, Quaderns Crema.

—— (2003). 'Traumatisme cultural', *Avui*, 18 December, 'Pujol en 24 imatges' (special supplement), S15.

Bru de Sala, X. et al. (1997). *El modelo catalán: un talante político*, Barcelona, Flor del Viento.

Buffery, H. (2006). 'Theater space and cultural identity in Catalonia', *Romance Quarterly*, 53/3, 195–209.

Buil i Feliu, A. (2003). Interview with Josep Maria Flotats, *Canarias 7: Cultura*, 3 July, *www.canarias7.es/20030703/p.cultura.shtml*, accessed March 2005.

Busquet, J. (1998). 'Les indústries culturals a Catalunya: nous reptes i velles solucions', in S. Giner (ed.), *La societat catalana*, Barcelona, Institut d'Estadística de Catalunya, 881–95.

Camprubí, X. (2005). 'Els misteriosos números de la Feria de Abril', *El Temps*, 10 May, 47–9.

Canals, E. (1987). 'Televisió i cultura de masses', in *Segones reflexions crítiques sobre la cultura catalana: una perspectiva de futur* by J. Gifreu et al., Barcelona, Departament de Cultura de la Generalitat de Catalunya, 191–204.

Cardús i Ros, S. (1988). 'Les polítiques culturals de les administracions públiques a Catalunya', vol. D of the *Llibre blanc de la cultura* produced for the Fundació Jaume Bofill Barcelona, unpublished.

—— (1992). *Algú sap cap a on anem?*, Barcelona, Edicions de la Revista de Catalunya.

—— (1999). 'Paradoxes de la festa actual. Una perspectiva sociològica', in Ll. Puig i Gordi (ed.), *Les festes a Catalunya*, Barcelona, Generalitat de Catalunya, 27–31.

—— (2005). 'The memory of immigration in Catalan nationalism', *International Journal of Iberian Studies*, 18/1, 37–44.

Casals, X. (1994). 'Carme-Laura Gil: el Museu d'Història de Catalunya' (interview), *L'Avenç*, 182, 58–61.

Casassas, J. and J. Termes (1997). *El futur del catalanisme*, Barcelona, Proa.

Cendrós, T. (2003). 'TV-3 y Catalunya Ràdio, líderes con deudas', *El País*, 8 October, Cataluña, 6.

—— (2004). 'La consejera de Cultura promete apoyar el cine catalán "porque es un sector estratégico"', *El País*, 28 January, Cataluña, 8.

Cester, X. (2002). 'Harry Potter parla poc en català', *Avui*, 7 November, *www.avui.com*, accessed 7 November 2002.

Contreras Hernández, J. (1998). 'La cultura tradicional a la Catalunya d'avui', in S. Giner (ed.), *La societat catalana*, Barcelona, Institut d'Estadística de Catalunya, 821–37.

Convergència i Unió (2003). *Bases per a un nou Estatut nacional de Catalunya*, *www.ciu.info/img/site/documents/estatut.pdf*, accessed 7 May 2003.

—— (2005). *Propostes sobre cultura i llengua*, *www.ciu.info/media/311.pdf*, accessed 23 September 2005.

Conversi, D. (1997). *The Basques, the Catalans and Spain: Alternative Routes to Nationalist Mobilisation*, London, Hurst.

Corner, J. and Harvey S. (1991). 'Mediating tradition and modernity: the heritage/enterprise couplet', in Corner and Harvey (eds) *Enterprise and Heritage: Crosscurrents of National Culture*, London, Routledge, 45–75.

Corporació Catalana de Ràdio i Televisió (CCRTV) (2003). *Comptes anuals: 2003*, *www.ccrtv.com/informe/2003/ccrtv_comptes.pdf*, accessed 12 April 2005.

Cortacans, O. (2003). 'La joia de la corona', *El Temps*, 1003, 2–8 September, 20–4.

Crameri, K. (2000). 'The role of translation in contemporary Catalan culture', *Hispanic Research Journal*, 1/2, 171–83.

—— (2005). 'La política cultural catalana (1980–2003) y los escritores catalanes de expresión castellana', in S. King (ed.), *La cultura catalana de expresión castellana. Estudios de literatura, teatro y cine*, Kassel, Reichenberger, 15–30.

Crystal, D. (2000). *Language Death*, Cambridge, Cambridge University Press.

Cubeles, X. and X. Fina (1999). *La cultura en Cataluña*, Barcelona, Fundació Jaume Bofill.

Cunningham, S. (1991). 'Cultural studies from the viewpoint of cultural policy', *Meanjin*, 50/2–3; reproduced in Lewis and Miller (2003), 13–22.

—— (2005). 'Creative enterprises', in J. Hartley (ed.), *Creative Industries*, Oxford, Blackwell, 282–98.

Degen, M. (2004). 'Barcelona's games: the Olympics, urban design, and global tourism', in M. Sheller and J. Urry (eds), *Tourism Mobilities: Places to Play, Places in Play*, London, Routledge.

Delclós, T. (2003). 'El vaivén lingüístico', *El País*, 12 October, Cataluña, 4.

Delgado, E. (1999). '30 anys de cultura i participació', *L'Avenç*, 236, 60–5.

Delgado, M. M. (2003). *'Other' Spanish Theatres: Erasure and Inscription on the Twentieth-Century Spanish Stage*, Manchester, MUP.

Deltell, B. (2002). 'Malestar a les llibreries', *Avui*, 22 April, 32–3.

Departament de Cultura (1990). 'Cultura a Catalunya anys noranta'/'Un nou impuls a la política lingüística', text of speeches given by J. Guitart i Agell and M. Reniu i Tresserras, Barcelona, Generalitat de Catalunya.

—— (2000). *Memòria del Departament de Cultura 2000*, Barcelona, Generalitat de Catalunya.

—— (2002). *Memòria del Departament de Cultura 2002*, Barcelona, Generalitat de Catalunya.

—— (2003a). *Els premis literaris*, Barcelona, Generalitat de Catalunya.

—— (2003b). *Estadístiques culturals de Catalunya*, Barcelona, Generalitat de Catalunya.

—— (2003c). *Memòria del Departament de Cultura 2003*, Barcelona, Generalitat de Catalunya.

—— (2003d). *Informe sobre política lingüística 2002*, Barcelona, Generalitat de Catalunya.

—— (2005). 'Museus de Catalunya', *http://cultura.gencat.es/museus/flash/CAT.htm*, accessed 9 February 2005.

Department for Culture, Media and Sport (DCMS) (2001). 'The creative industries mapping document 2001', *www.culture.gov.uk/global/publications/archive_2001/ci_mapping_doc_2001.htm*, accessed October 2005.

Diputació de Barcelona (2000). *Networked Culture: The Cultural Policy of the Diputació de Barcelona*, Barcelona, Diputació de Barcelona.

Du Gay, P. (1996; repr. 1997). 'Organizing identity: entrepreneurial governance and public management', in S. Hall and P. du Gay (eds), *Questions of Cultural Identity*, London, Sage, 151–69.

Eagleton, T. (2000). *The Idea of Culture*, Oxford, Blackwell.

The Economist (1997). 'Devolution can be salvation', *The Economist*, 344, 20 September, 51–5.

Edensor, T. (2002). *National Identity, Popular Culture and Everyday Life*, Oxford, Berg.

Ellingham, M. and Fisher, J. (2001). *The Rough Guide to Spain*, 9th edn, London, Rough Guides.

El Mundo (2002). 'Pujol aboga por que los inmigrantes se integren y no actúen como topos', 12 March, *www.elmundo.es/2002/03/12/espana/1117144.html*, accessed 12 April 2002.

Escande, S. and Delvainquière, J-C. (eds) (2005). 'France', in the *Compendium of Cultural Policies and Trends in Europe*, 6th edn (Council of Europe/ERICarts), *www.culturalpolicies.net/*, accessed 7 February 2007.

Etherington, J. and Fernández, A-M. (2006). 'Political parties in Catalonia', in D. Hanley and J. Loughlin (eds), *Spanish Political Parties*, Cardiff, University of Wales Press, 74–107.

Fancelli, A. (2003). 'La desconfianza de la cultura', *El País*, 13 October, Cataluña, 4.

Faura, N., Paloma, D. and Torrent, A. (eds) (1998), *La llengua de Televisió de Catalunya: materials per l'anàlisi*, Bellaterra, UAB.

Feldman, S. (1998), 'National theater/national identity: Els Joglars and the question of cultural politics in Catalonia', *Gestos*, 25, 35–50.

Fernàndez, J-A. (1997). 'La cultura està trista, què tindrà la cultura? La normalització i el malestar en la cultura catalana', *1991. Literatura*, 5, *www.vilaweb.cat/media/imatges/AREES/biblioteca/1991/5/5_4.html*, accessed 5 February 2007.

Fernández, M. (1999). 'Un llarg camí per a la llengua', *Avui*, 13 October, 18.

Flaquer, Ll. (1996). *El català, ¿llengua pública o privada?*, Barcelona, Empúries.

Flew, T. (2005). 'Creative economy', in J. Hartley (ed.), *Creative Industries*, Oxford, Blackwell, 344–60.

Font i Cardona, J. (1991). *Papers de política cultural*, Barcelona, Edicions 62.

Forcadell Lluís, C. (2001). 'La millor nota per al català', *Avui*, 26 January, *www.avui.com*, accessed 26 January 2001.

Foucault, M. (1980). *Power/Knowledge*, Hemel Hempstead, Harvester Press.

Francàs, R. (2004). 'Vilanova se queda sin "castells" de nueve pisos', *La Vanguardia*, 2 August, 'Vivir' section, 5.

Gabancho, P. (2001). *Carta a la societat catalana: Sobre la immigració*, Barcelona, Columna.

Gallén, E. (1996). 'Catalan theatrical life: 1939–1993', in D. George and J. London (eds), *Contemporary Catalan Theatre: An Introduction*, Sheffield, Anglo-Catalan Society Occasional Publications, 19–42.

Garcia, A. A. (1999). 'Els museus d'una ciutat que era «un poc nostra» i d'un país que anàvem fent', *L'Avenç*, 236, 47–52.

Garnham, N. (1993). 'Concepts of culture – public policy and the cultural industries', in A. Gray and J. McGuigan (eds), *Studying Culture, An Introductory Reader*, London, Arnold 54–61; originally published as a discussion paper by the Greater London Council in 1983.

—— (2005). 'From cultural to creative industries. An analysis of the implications of the "creative industries" approach to arts and media policy making in the United Kingdom', *International Journal of Cultural Policy*, 11/1, 15–29.

Garriga, J. (2003). 'CiU ofrece ayudas a la natalidad para que Cataluña no se "desnaturalice"', *El País*, 14 October, Cataluña, 4.

Gellner, E. (1994). *Encounters with Nationalism*, Oxford, Blackwell.

Generalitat de Catalunya (1999). *Acció del Govern de Catalunya 1997*, Barcelona, Generalitat de Catalunya.

—— (2001). *Acció del Govern de Catalunya 1999*, Barcelona, Generalitat de Catalunya.

—— (2003a). *1% cultural: Fem reviure el nostre patrimoni*, Barcelona, Generalitat de Catalunya.

—— (2003b). *Guia d'acollida (Welcoming Guide)*, www.gencat.net/benestar/immigracio/web_ac/Angles/MENU/menu.html, accessed 16 February 2007.

—— (2004a). *Legislació sobre patrimoni cultural*, 2nd edn, Barcelona, Departament de Cultura de la Generalitat de Catalunya.

—— (2004b). *Annual Financial Report 2003*, Barcelona, Departament d'Economia i Finances.

George, D. and London, J. (eds) (1996). 'Introduction', *Contemporary Catalan Theatre: An Introduction*, Sheffield, Anglo-Catalan Society Occasional Publications, 11–18.

Gifreu, J. (2003). *La potenciació de l'espai cultural i audiovisual català*, Barcelona, Generalitat de Catalunya.

Gifreu, J. et al. (1987). *Segones reflexions crítiques sobre la cultura catalana: una perspectiva de futur*, Barcelona, Generalitat de Catalunya.

Giner, S. (1984). *The Social Structure of Catalonia*, Sheffield, The Anglo-Catalan Society.

Giner, S., Flaquer, Ll., Busquet, J. and Bultà, N. (1996). *La cultura catalana: el sagrat i el profà*, Barcelona, Edicions 62.

Gore, S. (2002). 'The Catalan language and immigrants from outside the European Union', *International Journal of Iberian Studies*, 15/2, 91–102.

Graham, B., Ashworth, G. J. and Tunbridge, J. E. (2000). *A Geography of Heritage: Power, Culture and Economy*, London, Arnold.

Grau, A. (2001). 'Prop d'un 60% d'espanyols creuen que es parla català només per "diferenciar-se", *Avui*, 23 March, 13.

Graves, L. (2000). *A Woman Unknown: Voices from a Spanish Life*, London, Virago.

Guibernau, M. (2004). *Catalan Nationalism: Francoism, Transition and Democracy*, London, Routledge.

Guss, D. M. (2000). *The Festive State: Race, Ethnicity, and Nationalism as Cultural Performance*, Berkeley, University of California Press.

Hargreaves, J. (2000). *Freedom for Catalonia? Catalan Nationalism, Spanish Identity and the Barcelona Olympic Games*, Cambridge, CUP.

Hesmondhalgh, D. (2002). *The Cultural Industries*, London, Sage.

Hernández, F. X. (1997). 'Criteris didàctics i museològics en el Museu d'Història de Catalunya', *L'Avenç*, 212, 30–3.

Heumann Gurian, E. (1991). 'Noodling around with exhibition opportunities', in I. Karp and S. D. Lavine (eds), *Exhibiting Cultures: The Poetics and Politics of Museum Display*, London, Smithsonian Institution Press, 176–90.

Hobsbawm, E. (1983; repr. 2000). 'Inventing Traditions', in E. Hobsbawm and T. Ranger (eds), *The Invention of Tradition*, Cambridge, CUP, 1–14.

Holo, S. R. (2000). *Beyond the Prado: Museums and Identity in Democratic Spain*, Liverpool, Liverpool University Press.

Hudson, K. (1999). 'Attempts to define "museum"', reproduced in D. Boswell and J. Evans (eds), *Representing the Nation: A Reader*, London, Routledge, 371–9; taken from *Museums for the 1980s: A Survey of World Trends*, London, Macmillan/UNESCO, 1977, 1–7.

Hutchinson, J. (2005). *Nations as Zones of Conflict*, London, Sage.

Iniesta, M. (1995). 'Els referents internacionals del patrimoni etnològic', in Ll. Calvo and J. Mañà (eds) *De l'ahir i de l'avui: el patrimoni etnològic de Catalunya*, Barcelona, Generalitat de Catalunya, 30–5.

Institut Català de les Indústries Culturals (ICIC) (2002). *Llibre blanc de les indústries culturals*, Barcelona, Generalitat de Catalunya, *cultura.gencat.net/publicacions/llibreblanc.htm*, accessed 13 December 2002. (Page numbers refer to the web version downloadable in pdf format, not to the published version.)

Institut de Cultura (1999). *Pla estratègic del sector cultural de Barcelona*, Barcelona, Ajuntament de Barcelona, *www.bcn.es/accentcultura/f_dia.htm*, accessed April 2005.

Institut d'Estadística de Catalunya (2003a). *Enquesta de consum i pràctiques culturals de Catalunya, 2001*, Barcelona, Generalitat de Catalunya.

—— (2003b). *Estadística d'usos lingüístics a Catalunya, 2003. Dossier de premsa*, Barcelona, Generalitat de Catalunya.

Instituto Nacional de Estadística (INE), (2005). *España en cifras 2005: Población*, *www.ine.es/prodyser/pubweb/espcif/espcif05.htm*, accessed 16 February 2007.

Johnson, R. (1993). 'Editor's introduction' to P. Bourdieu, *The Field of Cultural Production*, Cambridge, Polity, 1–25.

Jordon, G. and Weedon, C. (1995). *Cultural Politics: Class, Gender, Race and the Postmodern World*, Oxford, Blackwell.

Keating, M. (1998). *The New Regionalism in Western Europe*, Cheltenham, Edward Elgar.

Keating, M., Loughlin, J. and Deschouwer, K. (2003). *Culture, Institutions and Economic Development: A Study of Eight European Regions*, Cheltenham, Edward Elgar.

Keenlyside, B. (2000). 'A national cultural strategy for Scotland: report of consultation', 1 February, *www.scotland.gov.uk/nationalculturalstrategy/ docs/keenlyside-00.asp*, accessed 2 February 2007.

King, S. (2005). *Escribir la catalanidad: Lengua e identidades culturales en la narrativa contemporánea de Cataluña*, Woodbridge, Tamesis.

—— (ed.) (2005b). *La cultura catalana de expresión castellana. Estudios de literatura, teatro y cine*, Kassel, Reichenberger.

Kymlicka, W. (2001). 'Immigrant integration and minority nationalism', in M. Keating and J. McGarry (eds), *Minority Nationalism and the Changing International Order*, Oxford, OUP, 61–83.

Lamikiz, A. (2002). 'Ambiguous "culture": contrasting interpretations of the Basque film *Ama Lur* and the relationship between centre and periphery in Franco's Spain', *National Identities*, 4/3, 291–306.

La Vanguardia (1998). 'El 31,5% no apoya la ley del catalán aunque la mayoría no juzga la lengua un problema', *La Vanguardia*, 22 March, *www2.vanguardia.es*, accessed 14 May 1998.

Lewis, J. and Miller, T. (eds) (2003). *Critical Cultural Policy Studies: A Reader*, Oxford, Blackwell.

Llobera, J. (1996). 'The role of commemorations in (ethno)nation-building. The case of Catalonia', in C. Mar-Molinero and A. Smith (eds), *Nationalism and the nation in the Iberian Peninsula: competing and conflicting identities*, Oxford, Berg, pp. 191–206.

—— (2004). *Foundations of National Identity: From Catalonia to Europe*, Oxford, Berghahn.

Lodares, J. R. (2005), 'La comunidad lingüística en la España de hoy. (Temas y problemas de diferenciación cultural)', *Bulletin of Hispanic Studies*, 82, 1–15.

Lorés, J. (1985). *La transició a Catalunya (1977–1984): El pujolisme i els altres*, Barcelona, Empúries.

MacDonald, S. and Silverstone, R. (1999). 'Rewriting the museums: fictions, taxonomies, stories and readers' reproduced in D. Boswell and J. Evans (eds), *Representing the Nation: A Reader*, London, Routledge, 421–34; taken from *Cultural Studies*, 4/2, 1990, 176–91.

MacInness, J. (1999). 'Consensus and controversy in language normalisation in Catalunya: the 1998 law', *Journal of Catalan Studies*, 2, *www.uoc.es/jocs/2/index.html*, accessed 9 February 2007.

Mackey, E. (1999). *The House of Difference: Cultural Politics and National Identity in Canada*, London, Routledge.

Maragall, P. (2001). 'Immigració: Oportunitat i repte per a Catalunya', speech given on 4 April, reproduced on the website of Ciutadans pel Canvi, *www.pelcanvi.com/arxiu/intervencions/040401.htm*, accessed 22 August 2005.

Marfany, J-Ll. (1995). *La cultura del catalanisme*, Barcelona, Empúries.

Bibliography 217

Mar-Molinero, C. (2000). *The Politics of Language in the Spanish-Speaking World*, London, Routledge.

Martí Font, J. M. (2000). 'Pujol: "Un lenguaje de otros tiempos"', *El País*, 29 June, *www.elpais.com*, accessed 15 February 2007.

Martínez, F. and Oliveres, J. (2005). *Jordi Pujol: En nombre de Catalunya*, Barcelona, Random House Mondadori.

Mascarell, F. (ed.) (1999). *El llibre blanc de la cultura a Catalunya*, Barcelona, Edicions 62.

Mas i Solench, J. M. (1993; repr. 1999). *La sardana: dansa nacional de Catalunya*, Barcelona, Editorial 92/Generalitat de Catalunya.

McGuigan, J. (2003). 'Cultural policy studies', updated version of the first chapter of *Culture and the Public Sphere*, London, Routledge, 1996, in J. Lewis and T. Miller (eds), *Critical Cultural Policy Studies: A Reader*, Oxford, Blackwell, 23–42.

—— (2004). *Rethinking Cultural Policy*, Maidenhead, Open University Press.

McRoberts, Kenneth (2001). *Catalonia: Nation Building without a State*, Oxford, OUP.

Menéndez i Pablo, F. X. and Pastor i Batalla, I. (2002). 'El futur del Born. Una polèmica ciutadana a l'entorn del patrimoni', *L'Avenç*, 273, 66–77.

Miller, T. and Yúdice, G. (2002). *Cultural Policy*, London, Sage.

Moix, Ll. and Massot, J. (2004). 'Entrevista: Caterina Mieras, consellera de Cultura', *La Vanguardia*, 9 January, reproduced on *http://intersincidcal. info/n.php?n=106*, accessed 17 October 2005.

Moix, T. (1998). 'Don Babelio Manent', *La Vanguardia*, 13 September, reproduced on the website of the Foro Babel, *www.forobabel.org/textos/ art98–09–13.html*, accessed 24 August 2000.

Molas, J. (1990). 'La cultura catalana i la seva estratificació', in P. Vilar et al. *Reflexions crítiques sobre la cultura catalana*, 3rd edn, Barcelona, Generalitat de Catalunya, pp. 133–55.

Monzó, Q. (1998). *Del tot indefens davant dels hostils imperis alienígenes*, Barcelona, Quaderns Crema.

Moore, M. (2001). 'Globalization, cosmopolitanism and minority nationalism', in M. Keating and J. McGarry (eds), *Minority Nationalism and the Changing International Order*, Oxford, OUP, 44–60.

Morgan, T. (2000). 'Heritage: devolution and the recovery of diversity', in B. Jordan and R. Morgan-Tamosunas (eds), *Contemporary Spanish Cultural Studies*, London, Arnold, 83–91.

Muñoz, Josep M. (1997). *Jaume Vicens i Vives: Una biografía intel·lectual*, Barcelona, Edicions 62.

—— (2002). 'Pasqual Maragall «La diversitat té sentit com a suma d'identitats»', *L'Avenç*, 271, 78–87.

Museu d'Història de Catalunya (2003). 'Un itinerari per la història de Catalunya' (guide leaflet).

Noguer, M. (2003). 'El doble filo de la inmigración', *El País*, 15 October, Cataluña, 5.

Olivares, J. C. (2004). 'L'ocàs d'un model de teatre públic', *Avui*, 12 April, 33.

Orozco, L. (2004). 'Els Joglars: quaranta anys de vida', *Journal of Catalan Studies*, 7, *www.uoc.edu/jocs/7/articles/orozco/index.html*, accessed 11 February 2005.

—— (2006). 'National identity in the construction of the theater policy of the Generalitat de Catalunya', *Romance Quarterly*, 53/3, 211–22.

Osborne, P. (2006). 'Whoever speaks of culture speaks of administration as well: disputing pragmatism in cultural studies', *Cultural Studies*, 20/1, 33–47.

Payne, J. (2004). *Catalonia: History and Culture*, Nottingham, Five Leaves.

Pla Nualart, A. (2003). 'La normalització lingüística, una ficció que ens volem creure', *Avui*, 27 February, 18.

Prat de la Riba, E. (1993). *La nacionalitat catalana*, ed. J. Casassas i Ymbert, Barcelona, Magrana.

Preston, P. (1999). 'Now we see how serious the Scots are. (Not very)', *The Guardian*, 26 April, *www.guardian.co.uk/Scotland/Story/0,,205613,00.htm*, accessed 5 February 2007.

Puigjaner, J. M. (2000). *Conèixer Catalunya*, 7th edn, Barcelona, Generalitat de Catalunya.

Pujals, Joan M. (1998). *Les noves fronteres de Catalunya*, Barcelona, Columna.

—— (1999). *Economia, llengua i cultura*, Barcelona, Generalitat de Catalunya.

Pujol, J. (1995). *Què representa la llengua a Catalunya?*, Barcelona, Generalitat de Catalunya.

—— (2001a). *Globalització i identitat*, Barcelona, Generalitat de Catalunya.

—— (2001b). 'Ante el gran reto de la inmigración', speech of 4 April reproduced in *La factoría*, 13, *www.lafactoriaweb.com*, accessed 16 February 2007.

Quintana, À. (1999). 'Cinema català: entre la recerca de la identitat i la crisi industrial', in *Història, Política, Societat i Cultura dels Països Catalans*, dir. B. de Riquer i Permanyer, vol 12, Barcelona, Enciclopedia Catalana, pp. 332–3.

Ramos, M. (2001). 'El negocio de la cultura en Cataluña crece menos que en el resto de España' and ' La Administración vasca invierte en ocio 20.000 pesetas más por habitante que la catalana', *El País*, 31 October, 14. The survey quoted in these articles is *La evolución de la industria de la cultura y el ocio en España por comunidades autónomas (1993–7)*, Sociedad General de Autores y Editores, 2001.

Real Instituto Elcano de Estudios Internacionales y Estratégicos (2004). *La política cultural en España*, *www.realinstitutoelcano.org/documentos/109/040428-JaimeEsp.pdf*, accessed 11 January 2007.

Reicher, S. and Hopkins, N. (2001). *Self and Nation*, London, Sage.

Robertson, R. (1992; repr. 1993). *Globalization: Social Theory and Global Culture*, London, Sage.

Robins, K. (1991). 'Tradition and translation: national culture in its global context', in J. Corner and S. Harvey (eds), *Enterprise and Heritage: Crosscurrents of National Culture*, London, Routledge, pp. 21–44.

Roca, F. (2000). *Teories de Catalunya: Guia de la societat catalana contemporània*, Barcelona, Pòrtic.

Roche, M. (2000). *Mega-Events and Modernity: Olympics and Expos in the Growth of Global Culture*, London, Routledge.

Roller, E. (2002). 'When does language become exclusivist? Linguistic politics in Catalonia', *National Identities*, 4/3, 273–89.

Roma i Riu, J.(1999). 'La festa com a patrimoni', in Ll. Puig i Gordi (ed.), *Les festes a Catalunya*, Barcelona, Generalitat de Catalunya, 15–26.

Roma, M. (2003). 'TV3 ha de prioritzar l'imaginari propi' (interview with Mònica Terribas), *El Temps*, 1003, 2–8 September, 34–7.

Ruiz Ramón, F. (1988). 'Del teatro español de la transición a la transición del teatro (1975–1985)', in S. Amell and S. García Castañeda (eds), *La cultura española en el posfranquismo*, Madrid, Playor, 103–13.

Sabaté, C. (2004). 'ERC i CiU lamenten que la Fira d'Abril coincideixi amb el Fòrum', *Avui*, 26 March, 27.

Salrach, J. M. (1988). 'El Mil·lenari com a pretext per a un debat entre historiadors', *L'Avenç*, 177, 42–3.

Salvat, R. (2005). 'Teatre de dues nits i gràcies i teatre d'un quart d'hora per un euro', *Avui*, 14 March, 15.

Santamaría, A. (1999). *Foro Babel: El nacionalismo y las lenguas de Cataluña*, Barcelona, Áltera.

Saumell, M. (1996). 'Performance groups in Catalonia', in D. George and J. London (eds), *Contemporary Catalan Theatre: An Introduction*, Sheffield, Anglo-Catalan Society Occasional Publications, 103–28.

Savage, M., Bagnall, G. and Longhurst, B. (2005). *Globalization and Belonging*, London, Sage.

Sayer, A. (1999). 'Valuing culture and economy', in L. Ray and A. Sayer (eds), *Culture and Economy After the Cultural Turn*, London, Sage, 53–75.

Schirato, T. and Webb, J. (2003). *Understanding Globalization*, London, Sage.

Schuster, J. M. (2002). 'Catalunya and its cultural industries: policy pitfalls and policy opportunities', The Cultural Policy Center at the University of Chicago, Working Paper 13, March 2002.

Scott, A. J. (2000). *The Cultural Economy of Cities: Essays on the Geography of Image-Producing Industries*, London, Sage.

Scullion, A. and García, B. (2005). 'What is cultural policy research?', *International Journal of Cultural Policy*, 11/2, 113–27.

Segura, A. (2001). 'Llibres de text i ensenyament de la història', *L'Avenç*, 261, 33–41.

Serra, M. (2004). 'El MNAC s'hauria pogut acabar abans', *El Temps*, 7–13 December, 54–6.

Siguan, M. (1992; repr. 1994). *España plurilingüe*, Madrid, Alianza.

Smith, A. D. (1991). *National Identity*, London, Penguin.

Smith, P. J. (2003). *Contemporary Spanish Culture: TV, Fashion, Art and Film*, Cambridge, Polity.

Soler i Amigó, J. (2000). *Sant Jordi: la diada, la tradició, l'actualitat*, Barcelona, Generalitat de Catalunya.

—— (2001). *Cultura popular i tradicional*, Barcelona, Pòrtic.

Sotorra, A. (1999). 'Núria Espert, actriu i directora' (interview), *Avui*, 7 February, reproduced on *www.andreusotorra.com/teatre/entrevista25. html*, accessed 12 February 2007.

Stanton, E. (1999). *Handbook of Spanish Popular Culture*, Westport CT, Greenwood Press.

Stargardt, N. (1998). 'Beyond the liberal idea of the nation', in Geoffrey Cubitt (ed.), *Imagining Nations*, Manchester, M.U.P., 22–36.

Strubell i Trueta, T.(1997). *El cansament del catalanisme*, Barcelona, La Campana.

Surroca i Tallaferro, R. (2004). 'L'origen de la Diada, la història que s'ha volgut diluir', *El Temps*, 7–13 September, 37–41.

Szerszynski, B. and Urry, J. (2006). 'Visuality, mobility and the cosmopolitan: inhabiting the world from afar', *British Journal of Sociology* 57/1, 113–31.

Terry, A. (2003). *A Companion to Catalan Literature*, Woodbridge, Tamesis.

Tobeña, A. (1998). *El nacionalisme diví: vectors psicològics del catalanisme*, Barcelona, UAB.

Todd, J. (2003). 'Europe's old states and the new world order', in J. Ruane, J. Todd and A. Mandeville (eds), *Europe's Old States in the New World Order: The Politics of Transition in Britain, France and Spain*, Dublin, University College Dublin Press, pp. 227–45.

Tomlinson, J. (1999). *Globalization and Culture*, Oxford, Polity.

Toury, G. (1995). *Descriptive Translation Studies and Beyond*, Amsterdam, John Benjamins.

Tree, M. (2002). 'Mort de dama?: una visió personal de l'estat actual de la literatura catalana', *Journal of Catalan Studies*, 5, *http://www.uoc.edu/ jocs/5/articles/tree2/*, accessed 20 February 2007.

Triadú, J. (1978). *Una cultura sense llibertat*, Barcelona, Aymà.

Urry, J. (1999). 'Gazing on history', reproduced in D. Boswell and J. Evans (eds) *Representing the Nation: A Reader*, London, Routledge, 208–32; taken from J. Urry, *The Tourist Gaze: Leisure and Travel in Contemporary Society*, London, Sage, 1990, 104–34.

—— (2003). *Global Complexity*, Cambridge, Polity.

Vicens i Vives, J. (1982). *Notícia de Catalunya*, Barcelona, Destino.

Vilar, P. et al. (1990). *Reflexions crítiques sobre la cultura catalana*, 3rd edn, Barcelona, Generalitat de Catalunya.

Vinyes, R. (2000). 'Un conflicte de memòries: el Museu d'Història de Catalunya', *L'Avenç*, 247, 34–7.

Wardhaugh, R. (2002). *An Introduction to Sociolinguistics*, 4th edn, Oxford, Blackwell.

Williams, R. (1984). 'State culture and beyond', in L. Appignanesi (ed.), *Culture and the State*, London, Institute of Contemporary Arts, 3–5.

Woolard K. A. (1989). *Double Talk: Bilingualism and the Politics of Ethnicity in Catalonia*, Stanford, Stanford U.P.

(Where *El País* is cited, this refers to the internet edition *www.elpais.com* in pdf format in which the Catalonia section appears as a separate supplement with its own page numbers.)

Index